101 Tax Saving Ideas

SIXTH EDITION

Randy Gardner, LLM, CPA, CFP™
Julie Welch, CPA, CFP™

Wealth Builders Press, LLC
800 West 47th Street, Suite 430
Kansas City, MO 64112

Publisher's Cataloging-in-Publication
(Prepared by Quality Books, Inc.)

Gardner, Randy.
101 tax saving ideas / Randy Gardner, Julie Welch.
-- 6th ed.
p. cm.
One hundred one tax saving ideas
One hundred and one tax saving ideas
Includes index.
Library of Congress Control Number: 2002101116
ISBN 0-9639734-5-2

1. Tax planning--United States. I. Welch, Julie (Julie Runtz) II. Title. III. Title: One hundred one tax saving ideas IV. Title: One hundred and one tax saving ideas

KF6297.Z9G37 2002 343.7305'23
QBI02-200075

In the preparation of this book, every effort has been made to offer the most current and correct information possible. Nonetheless, inadvertent errors can occur, and tax rules and regulations often change.

Further, the information in the text is intended to afford general guidance to taxpayers. The impact of tax laws can vary greatly based upon the unique facts of the individual. Accordingly, the information in this book is not intended to serve as legal, accounting, investment, or tax advice. If legal, accounting, tax, investment, or other expert advice is required, readers are encouraged to consult with professional advisers. The authors and publishers disclaim any responsibility for positions taken by taxpayers in their individual cases or for any misunderstanding on the part of readers.

This publication is designed to provide accurate and authoritative information in regard to the subject matter covered. It is sold with the understanding that the publisher is not engaged in rendering legal, accounting, or other professional service and that the authors are not offering such advice in this publication. If legal advice or other expert assistance is required, the services of a competent professional person should be sought.

Printed in the United States of America.

Cover design by Ted Stone

Preface

We are tax advisers. We make our livings explaining the tax law to people and developing strategies for them to use. We have been consulting with people like you about tax planning for more than 40 years.

We wrote this book with three goals in mind:

- First, to help you reduce your taxes. Many people pay too much tax because they do not know how to reduce their tax. This book shows you how to plan. It is not designed to tell you everything about tax. Rather, it is a collection of the advice we give that saves the most money and helps the most people.
- Second, to write a book on tax you can understand. This book explains in easy-to-read language 101 ideas for reducing your taxes. The ideas are short and straightforward. Numerous examples explain the ideas. We have found that when you understand an idea, it is easier to implement.
- Third, to alert you to current tax planning opportunities. The tax laws are constantly changing. We include in this book some of the best tax saving ideas under the current law to help you increase your awareness of the newest strategies.

In this sixth edition, we have changed and revised many of the 101 ideas to reflect current strategies as a result of the recent changes in the tax law. We included information on the new rules for minimum distributions from IRAs and retirement plans. We expanded the section on education planning since this is one of the prime areas benefiting from the recent tax law changes. We have again added chapters on recent tax law changes and proposed legislation to give you an idea of what Congress has done and plans to do. We have also included Appendix C, which explains how to look up answers for yourself; Appendix D, which lists useful Web sites; Appendix E, which provides a summary of education incentives; Appendix F, which provides a summary of retirement plan alternatives; and Appendix G, which provides a capital gains chart.

By using this book, you will be more aware of tax planning opportunities. If you find that an idea might work for you, you can research it further using the references in Appendix B. If you use an adviser, you will be a better participant in the planning process. You can mention the strategy and references to your adviser and implement the idea together.

The provisions in the Economic Growth and Recovery Tax Act of 2001 expire on December 31, 2010 unless Congress makes additional changes. Many of the new provisions, such as catch-up IRA contributions and education expense deductions, are included in this sixth edition.

How to use this book

This book includes a Tax Action Plan. It summarizes the 101 Tax Saving Ideas and leaves room for you to make notes. You can complete the plan as you read the book. You can also record your progress in implementing the plan.

There are three ways to read this book. One way is to scan the 101 Tax Saving Ideas that are in bold. Use the Tax Action Plan to remind yourself which ideas to consider further.

The second way is to read the text of the book, but not the examples. The examples are highlighted in gray so they stand out. You will probably reduce your reading time by half following this approach. For ideas that apply to you, read the entire planning idea. Use the Tax Action Plan to mark which apply.

The third way is to read the book cover to cover. The ideas are short and each idea will probably apply to you or someone you know at some point in your life. Use the Tax Action Plan to record your notes.

Use the final two chapters to review recent and proposed tax developments that might affect you.

Appendix B provides references for each idea. The references are the legal authority for the idea. They will save you or your adviser time researching whether the idea will work for you.

Appendix C explains how to look up answers for yourself if you are so inclined.

Appendix D lists some useful Web sites. They can help you find tax forms or additional information on various topics.

Appendices E and F provide a summary of education incentives and retirement plan alternatives.

Appendix G provides a capital gains chart to help you determine your tax rate on capital gains.

Acknowledgements

This book is the product of many people's efforts.

We would especially like to thank:

- Doug Welch;
- Laura Gardner;
- Bryn, Kara, Creyton, and Hope Gardner;
- the Heusted family;
- Louise, Doug, Alex, and Joseph Reeves;
- Joseph, Naomi, and Bryan Runtz; and
- Homer and Pat Welch

for their love, support, and patience.

We would also like to thank Alison Courtney; Pola Firestone; Sidney Kess; John Meara; Meara, King & Co.'s clients; Meara, King & Co.'s employees; Gene Meyer; Peter Newman; Ted Stone; UMKC faculty and students, and all of the other people who helped us. Without their help this book would not have been possible.

Randy
Randy Gardner

Julie
Julie Welch

TABLE OF CONTENTS

Exemptions and Filing Status

Tax Credits and Payments

Education Planning

Investments

Tax Planning

The goal of tax planning is to minimize your tax liability without sacrificing your other personal and financial goals. Your tax liability is the result of the application of the tax laws to your personal situation. Because most of us cannot alter the tax laws, we must work with what we can control — our personal situation.

Described below are principles and strategies to help you plan. Principles are guidelines to follow as you think about tax problems. Strategies are methods you can use to reduce your taxes.

Tax planning principles

Tax planning is a process. It is similar to the process of planning a vacation. First, you think about what you want to do. One week of relaxation. Then you think about different ways you can do it. Beaches or mountains? Fly or drive? Take the children? Camp or hotels? Finally, you choose among the alternatives.

Tax planning is similar to planning that vacation. Perhaps you want a new car. Will you use the car for business? Will your employer provide it? Should you buy or lease it? Can you use home equity financing to buy the car so your interest will be deductible? After considering all the alternatives including the tax ramifications, you choose a course of action.

Consider all types of taxes, not just the income tax. You may have heard of "Tax Freedom Day." It is the first day of the year that you earn a dollar that is not paid to some government in taxes. In other words, it is the first day of the year you get to keep your earnings for your own purposes. For most taxpayers, Tax Freedom Day is in the first week of May. In other words, over a third of your earnings goes to pay taxes of some type to some government.

When you plan to reduce taxes, do not think only of the income tax. The income tax represents only about 40% of all the taxes you pay. Although this book focuses on the income tax, you should also consider how to reduce sales tax, property tax, FICA, gift tax, estate tax, and the other taxes you pay.

Do not let the tax tail wag the dog. Most major decisions in your life are made because of nontax considerations such as family, business, and pleasure. Although you should take advantage of opportunities to reduce your taxes, you should not let tax motivations outweigh good business and personal judgment. Selling the stock you own may increase your tax this year, but you should still sell it if you think the stock's price is going to drop. Moving to Florida, or another state without state income tax, may reduce your state income tax. However, it is not a good idea if your family does not want to move.

Avoid tax, but do not evade it. Tax avoidance through legal techniques is the proper objective of tax planning. The Supreme Court Justice Learned Hand said: *"Over and over again courts have said that there is nothing sinister in so arranging one's affairs as to keep taxes as low as possible. Everybody does so, rich or poor; and all do right, for nobody owes any public duty to pay more than the law demands: taxes are enforced extractions, not voluntary contributions."*

While tax avoidance is acceptable, tax evasion is not. It is wrong to fabricate transactions, claim deductions for expenditures that were never made, or conceal income. Such efforts to reduce your tax liability can result in monetary or criminal penalties.

Use checklists. Tax planning checklists, like all checklists, are helpful for triggering ideas and making sure you do not forget something. Such checklists are available from a number of sources: the end of the year planners and organizers provided by many accountants and attorneys; tax preparation software packages; and tax publishers. The Tax Action Plan included in this book is an example of a checklist.

Know when to consult a tax adviser. This book explains and gives examples of numerous tax planning strategies. There are times, however, when you should pursue an idea further with a tax adviser. The tax law is complex. Even the major accounting firms designate specialists for their tax consultants to call for advice. If you have questions about the tax consequences of a transaction, especially if the transaction involves a large amount of cash or property, you should review your plan with your tax adviser.

Tax saving strategies

Tax saving strategies are helpful because they give you rules of thumb to follow. However, tax advice is situation sensitive. Do not fall into the trap of using general rules.

Time your income and deductions. You are probably familiar with the investment timing gem: "A dollar today is worth more than a dollar tomorrow." Timing strategies apply to tax planning as well.

The most frequently mentioned tax strategies are "defer income to future years" and "accelerate deductions to the current year." In other words, postpone paying tax on income as long as you can, but reap the tax savings from deductions as early as you can. Because a dollar today is worth more than a dollar tomorrow, you want to keep your money as long as possible. Also, the recent tax changes lower the tax rates over the next few years generally making it more beneficial to defer income and accelerate deductions.

There are numerous examples of these strategies. Selling stock at a gain next January rather than this December defers income. Asking your employer to pay your year-end bonus in January rather than December also defers income. Paying your real estate taxes, charitable contributions, and medical expenses in December rather than January accelerates deductions. These strategies are effective when your tax rates are approximately the same from year to year.

When you anticipate a change in your tax rates, however, it is better to recognize income in the low tax rate year and better to claim deductions in the high tax rate year. Your marginal tax rate may change up or down as a result of a job change, your spouse quitting work, retirement, inheritance, or, as we have recently experienced, a change in the law.

Bunch your expenses. Several deductions are subject to limitations that are based on your adjusted gross income (AGI). For example, you can only deduct medical expenses over 7.5% of your AGI. If your AGI is $50,000, only your medical expenses over $3,750 ($50,000 x 7.5%) are deductible. You can bunch your medical expenses in one year so you exceed the 7.5% floor by controlling when you pay for medical services.

Convert ordinary income to another type of income. The tax rate on ordinary income is potentially 38.6% (39.1% for 2001). You can reduce the tax you pay by converting ordinary income to long-term capital gain income. You have a capital gain if you sell an investment, such as stock, for more than you paid for it. The capital gain is long-term if you own the investment for more than one year. Long-term capital gains are good because they are generally taxed at a maximum tax rate of 20%, a potential savings of 18.6% (38.6% - 20%).

You are in the 30% tax rate bracket. You plan to sell stock with $10,000 of gain. You have owned the stock for 360 days. If you sell it now, the gain will be taxed as ordinary income and you will pay $3,000 ($10,000 x 30%) of tax. If you wait a week, the gain will be taxed as long-term capital gain and you will pay $2,000 ($10,000 x 20%) of tax. Converting this gain to long-term capital gain saves you $1,000 ($3,000 - 2,000).

Take advantage of what the law gives you. The tax law is full of breaks just waiting to be taken. One such example is if you sell your home, you can exclude up to $250,000 ($500,000 if you are married filing a joint return) of gain from your taxable income. This break turns your home into a nontaxable nest egg.

Another example is starting your own business. Business expenses are deductible while personal expenses are not deductible. By converting personal expenses into business deductions, you reduce your taxes. Examples of personal expenses you can convert include car, home, and computer expenses. You should not change your life to save tax, but take advantage of the breaks that apply to your situation.

Shift income to taxpayers with lower marginal rates. Usually, these taxpayers are children or entities, such as trusts or corporations. The goal is to save the extra tax that you would pay and still achieve your objectives.

You plan to sell stock worth $10,000 so you can pay the school expenses for your daughter. The stock will produce $6,000 of taxable gain. If you sell the stock, you will pay Federal income tax of 20% and state income tax of 5% (for a total of 25%) on the gain. After tax, you can give your daughter $8,500 ($10,000 - (6,000 x 25%)).

You could instead give the stock to your daughter, who is in the lowest tax rate bracket. Then when she sells it, she will be subject to a 10% Federal income tax rate and a 3% state income tax rate (for a total of 13%) on the gain. After paying tax, your daughter will have $9,220 ($10,000 - (6,000 x 13%)) to spend. If the stock was owned at least 5 years by you or your daughter, she will be subject to an 8% Federal income tax rate and a 3% state income tax rate (for a total of 11%) on the gain. After paying tax, your daughter will have $9,340 ($10,000 - (6,000 x 11%)) to spend.

Because the gift is not more than $11,000 ($10,000 for 2001), you are not subject to gift tax. Shifting income to your daughter saves $720 ($6,000 x (25% - 13%)) and still achieves your goal of paying your daughter's school expenses.

Keep organized tax records. The most common reason for missing deductions or losing them during an IRS audit is poor documentation. It is easy to forget all the deductible payments you make during the year if you do not have the records you need to support the deduction. Some people use folders to save tax-related receipts, cancelled checks, records of business mileage and entertainment expenses, and other tax-related information. Some people use computer programs to track their expenses. Not only will these systems help you remember your deductions and provide you with documentation in the event you are audited, they save you time organizing your tax information at the end of the year.

Look to the past, present, and future. The tax law is constantly changing. Courts are deciding cases that affect income and deductions claimed on returns years ago. The IRS releases rulings and announcements weekly. Congressional committees are wrestling with the next round of legislative changes.

Perhaps you did not claim a deduction for the medical expenses the court now says are deductible. You may still be able to amend your return for a prior year and claim the deduction. Perhaps the IRS is announcing a change to the records required to take a business deduction. To qualify for the deduction, you need to be aware of this change. You should plan for the change or perhaps contact your Congressional representatives to oppose the change.

Tax planning requires a crystal ball that allows you to see the past and the future. You can track these developments yourself or your tax adviser can help you. However you do it, remember that tax law changes present opportunities to recover taxes you paid in the past, reduce taxes due this year, and avoid future taxes.

The last two chapters provide:

- highlights of recent tax law changes, and
- a list of some of the proposals that are being considered.

In conclusion, tax planning is accomplished by arranging your personal affairs in a tax-wise fashion. The principles and strategies just discussed will help you think about your life in this way. The tax saving ideas contained in this book are specific examples of strategies you can use to reduce your taxes.

The Tax Formula

This section goes through the tax formula in detail. It defines the main tax terms and explains how to calculate your tax.

The bad news is this section is complicated. The good news is this is the only difficult section in the book.

The key to reducing your taxes is understanding tax terminology and knowing how taxes are computed. The tax formula is outlined below. The outline follows the format of the Form 1040. Explanations of the terms in the formula follow.

	All income
–	Exclusions
=	Gross Income
–	Deductions for adjusted gross income
=	Adjusted Gross Income
–	The greater of itemized deductions or the standard deduction
–	Exemptions
=	Taxable income
	Tentative tax
–	Nonrefundable credits
+	Additional taxes
=	Total tax
–	Refundable credits
=	Balance due or refund

All income is the starting point in the tax formula. Congress has the power to tax virtually every dollar you receive except amounts that are borrowed or amounts that represent a return of your investment, such as the purchase price of stock. The most common income items are:

- wages,
- interest,
- dividends,
- alimony,
- business and rental income,
- gains from the sale of property, and
- retirement income from pensions and annuities.

Your income is reduced by **exclusions.** Exclusions are income items that Congress chooses not to tax. The most common examples include:

- gifts,
- life insurance proceeds,
- scholarships used to pay for tuition and fees, and
- fringe benefits such as employer-provided health and life insurance.

All income less exclusions produces the subtotal **gross income.**

Adjusted gross income (AGI), an important tax term, is arrived at by reducing your gross income by the **deductions for adjusted gross income**. Deductions for AGI are also called adjustments to income and above the line deductions (the line being adjusted gross income). The most common deductions for AGI are:

- student loan interest,
- alimony paid,
- individual retirement account (IRA) contributions,
- Keogh plan contributions,
- business expenses,
- rental expenses, and
- moving expenses.

AGI is important because it is the starting point for the calculation of tax on many state returns. On your Federal return, AGI is important because some itemized deductions, such as medical expenses, are not deductible unless they exceed a percentage of AGI . Furthermore, when your AGI is more than $137,300 ($132,950 in 2001), your itemized deductions and exemption deductions are "phased out." Phased out means your deductions are reduced — the higher your AGI, the lower your deductions.

From AGI, you can deduct the greater of your itemized deductions or the standard deduction. **Itemized deductions** are also called below the line deductions and personal deductions. They include the deductions that you are most familiar with:

- medical expenses to the extent they exceed 7.5% of AGI;
- state and local income taxes, and real estate and personal property taxes;
- home mortgage and investment interest expense;
- charitable contributions of cash and property;
- casualty and theft losses to the extent they exceed 10% of AGI;
- gambling losses to the extent of gambling winnings; and
- miscellaneous itemized deductions to the extent they exceed 2% of AGI.

The Average Itemized Deductions For 1999
(the latest figures available)
By Adjusted Gross Income Range:

AGI Range	Medical Expenses	Taxes	Interest	Contributions
0 under $15,000	$7,500	1,963	5,958	1,350
$15,000 under $30,000	5,137	2,200	5,866	1,619
$30,000 under $50,000	4,992	2,991	6,247	1,774
$50,000 under $100,000	5,950	4,918	7,544	2,282
$100,000 under $200,000	10,494	9,262	10,806	3,727
$200,000 and over	32,259	36,592	21,735	19,454

NOTE: The above figures are the averages for the people who itemize deductions, not all taxpayers. Use these figures for comparison purposes only.

If you have AGI over certain amounts, your itemized deductions are phased out (reduced). For 2002, the amount of the phase-out is generally 3% of your AGI in excess of $137,300 ($68,650 if you are married and file separately from your spouse). For 2001, the phase-out level is $132,950 ($66,475 if you are married and file separately from your spouse).

You have AGI of $160,000 and itemized deductions of $25,000 for 2002. You must decrease your itemized deductions by $681 (($160,000 - 137,300) x 3%). Thus, you can deduct $24,319 ($25,000 - 681) of itemized deductions.

The sum of your itemized deductions (after the phase-out if applicable) is compared to your standard deduction. The **standard deduction** is set by the Federal government and adjusted for inflation each year. The standard deduction is based on your filing status. The 2001 and 2002 standard deduction amounts are shown below.

	2001	2002
Single	$4,550	$4,700
Married filing jointly	7,600	7,850
Head of household	6,650	6,900
Married filing separately	3,800	3,925

If you are either over age 65 or blind, you can increase your standard deduction by $1,150 ($1,100 for 2001) if you are single and by $900 if you are married. If you are over 65 and blind, you double your additional standard deduction. In other words, if you are single, over 65, and blind, your standard deduction in 2002 is $7,000 ($4,700 + 1,150 + 1,150).

If you are claimed as a dependent on someone else's return, your standard deduction is reduced to the greater of $750 or your earned income, such as wages, plus $250 up to your regular standard deduction amount ($4,700 for 2002 if your dependent is single). Thus, a single child who earns $1,400 from a paper route and $50 of interest may claim a standard deduction of $1,650. If, instead, the child earns $350 from the paper route and $500 of interest, the child's standard deduction is $750.

To arrive at the amount of deductions from AGI, you compare your standard deduction with the sum of your itemized deductions. Your deduction from AGI is generally the larger of the two amounts.

If you are married filing jointly, have itemized deductions of $4,900, and have a standard deduction of $7,850, then you would want to claim the standard deduction of $7,850. If, instead, your itemized deductions total $9,000 and your standard deduction is $7,850, then you would want to itemize your deductions on Schedule A of your tax return and claim a deduction from AGI of $9,000.

You cannot claim both your itemized deductions and your standard deduction on the same return. You must choose one or the other. There is no restriction on claiming itemized deductions in one year and the standard deduction in another year. You make the choice each year.

The deduction allowed for **exemptions** is also a deduction from AGI. For 2002, this deduction is $3,000 per exemption. For 2001, the amount is $2,900. Usually you can claim an exemption deduction for yourself. If you are married and file jointly, you can claim two exemption deductions — one for yourself and one for your spouse. You can claim additional exemption deductions for individuals who are your dependents such as your children.

You cannot claim an exemption deduction for yourself if someone else claims you as a dependent. In other words, only one exemption deduction can be claimed for each person. If you claim your child as a dependent on your return, then your child cannot claim an exemption deduction on his or her own return.

Similar to itemized deductions, you must phase out (reduce) your exemption deduction if you have AGI over certain amounts. For exemptions, the phase-out level varies with your filing status. The 2001 and 2002 phase-out levels are shown below.

	2001	2002
Single	$132,950	$137,300
Married filing jointly	199,450	206,000
Head of household	166,200	171,650
Married filing separately	99,725	103,000

For every $2,500 of AGI you have over these amounts, you must reduce your exemption deduction by 2%.

You are single with $150,000 of AGI for 2002. Because your AGI of $150,000 exceeds the phase-out level of $137,300, you must reduce your $3,000 exemption deduction by 12% (($150,000 - 137,300)/2,500 = 5.1 (rounded up to 6) x 2%). After the phase-out, your exemption deduction is $2,640 ($3,000 - (3,000 x 12%)).

Adjusted gross income less deductions from AGI and your exemption deduction produces the end total, **taxable income.** Your **tentative tax** is calculated on this amount. The tax is tentative because it may be increased by additional taxes or decreased by credits . If your taxable income is less than $100,000, you must use the Tax Tables (found in the Form 1040 Instructions) to calculate your tax. If your taxable income is $100,000 or more, you must use the Tax Rate Schedules to calculate your tax. The Tax Rate Schedules for 2002 are shown in Exhibit 1. The Tax Rate Schedules for 2001 are shown in Appendix A. As you can see, the tax rate schedules differ by filing status. All of the filing statuses are subject to the progressive rates of tax — 10%, 15%, 27%, 30%, 35%, and 38.6%, but these rates apply to different levels of income.

EXHIBIT 1

Single Individuals

If Taxable Income Is:	*The Tax Is:*
Not over $6,000	10% of taxable income
Over $6,000, but not over $27,950	$600.00 plus 15% of the excess over $6,000
Over $27,950, but not over $67,700	$3,892.50 plus 27% of the excess over $27,950
Over $67,700, but not over $141,250	$14,625.00 plus 30% of the excess over $67,700
Over $141,250, but not over $307,050	$36,690.00 plus 35% of the excess over $141,250
Over $307,050	$94,720.00 plus 38.6% of the excess over $307,050

Married Filing Jointly or Qualifying Widow(er)

If Taxable Income Is:	*The Tax Is:*
Not Over $12,000	10% of taxable income
Over $12,000, but not over $46,700	$1,200.00 plus 15% of the excess over $12,000

Over $46,700, but not over $112,850	$6,405.00 plus 27% of the excess over $46,700
Over $112,850, but not over $171,950	$24,265.50 plus 30% of the excess over $112,850
Over $171,950, but not over $307,050	$41,995.50 plus 35% of the excess over $171,950
Over $307,050	$89,280.50 plus 38.6% of the excess over $307,050

Married Filing Separately

If Taxable Income Is:	*The Tax Is:*
Not Over $6,000	10% of taxable income
Over $6,000, but not over $23,350	$600.00 plus 15% of the excess over $6,000
Over $23,350, but not over $56,425	$3,202.50 plus 27% of the excess over $23,350
Over $56,425, but not over $85,975	$12,132.75 plus 30% of the excess over $56,425
Over $85,975, but not over $153,525	$20,997.75 plus 35% of the excess over $85,975
Over $153,525	$44,640.25 plus 38.6% of the excess over $153,525

Head of Household

If Taxable Income Is:	*The Tax Is:*
Not Over $10,000	10% of taxable income
Over $10,000, but not over $37,450	$1,000.00 plus 15% of the excess over $10,000
Over $37,450, but not over $96,700	$5,117.50 plus 27% of the excess over $37,450
Over $96,700, but not over $156,600	$21,115.00 plus 30% of the excess over $96,700

Over $156,600, but not over $307,050	$39,085.00 plus 35% of the excess over $156,600
Over $307,050	$91,742.50 plus 38.6% of the excess over $307,050

The Tax Tables are prepared from the Tax Rate Schedules. Thus, there is no advantage gained by using one or the other. The Tax Tables are merely a convenience provided by the government.

When your taxable income includes long-term capital gain income from mutual fund distributions or the sale of property, such as stock, you should use Schedule D to calculate your tax. You use Schedule D because the maximum rate of tax on gains from the sale of stock is 20% (as opposed to the maximum on ordinary income of 38.6%).

Dependent children under the age of 14 with investment income greater than $1,500 can use Form 8615 to calculate their tax. This form imposes the "kiddie tax." The kiddie tax discourages parents from shifting investment income to children. It taxes a child's investment income over $1,500 at the parent's marginal tax rate rather than the child's lower tax rate.

Your tentative tax can be reduced by **nonrefundable credits.** Credits are like deductions, only better, because credits reduce <u>tax</u> rather than taxable income. Thus, dollar for dollar, you would rather have a credit than a deduction.

The most common credits claimed by individuals are the child credit and the credit for child and dependent care expenses. Other credits include the HOPE Scholarship credit, the Lifetime Learning credit, the saver's credit, the elderly and disabled credit, the foreign tax credit, and the earned income credit.

Credits may be nonrefundable or refundable. With nonrefundable credits, the excess credit is lost if the amount exceeds your tax liability. It is not refunded. The child and dependent care credit is an example of a nonrefundable credit. Some nonrefundable credits, such as the foreign tax credit, can be carried over to other years if they exceed the current year's tax liability. If a refundable credit, such as the earned income credit, exceeds your tax liability, the excess is refunded to you.

You also may be subject to **additional taxes**, such as:

- the self-employment tax,
- the 10% penalty tax on early distributions from retirement plans, and
- the alternative minimum tax.

Your **total tax** is calculated by adjusting your tentative tax for credits and additional taxes. This total tax is compared to your **refundable credits** to determine whether you have a **balance due** or are entitled to a **refund**. Examples of refundable credits are:

- withholding,
- estimated taxes,
- the earned income credit, and
- excess social security tax withheld.

With the tax formula in mind, you can see there are five ways to reduce your tax.

1. Take advantage of exclusions, such as tax-free fringe benefits, excludable retirement plan contributions, and tax-free growth in your retirement plans.

2. Maximize your deductions by contributing to retirement plans, starting a business, or better tracking your deductions such as charitable contributions.

3. Reduce your tax rate by investing in assets that appreciate in value and generate capital gains.

4. Claim credits such as the child tax credit, dependent care credit, and education credits.

5. Improve your filing status if possible, such as qualifying for head of household rather than single filing status.

The ideas in this book give you specific ways to reduce your tax.

Tax Action Plan

Use this Tax Action Plan to note the ideas that will benefit you now. You can use this as a checklist when you do your tax planning either by yourself or with your tax adviser.

TAX SAVING IDEA	POSSIBLE SAVINGS	NOTES
Income		
1. You should take advantage of nontaxable income.		
2. Your state tax refund may not be taxable.		
3. You can deduct your gambling losses up to the amount of your gambling winnings.		
4. Do not assume that your Social Security benefits are taxable.		
Standard and Itemized Deductions		
5. You get something for nothing with the standard deduction.		
6. Identify all of your qualifying medical payments.		
7. Long-term care expenses qualify as medical expenses.		
8. Avoid splitting the medical care expenses for one person among several people.		
9. Include all your state and local tax payments in your itemized deductions.		
10. Pay your 4th quarter state estimated tax payment by December 31st.		
11. Deduct all of your real and personal property taxes.		
12. You can deduct the mortgage interest on your primary home and a second home.		

TAX SAVING IDEA	POSSIBLE SAVINGS	NOTES
13. Deduct the points in the year you buy your primary home.		
14. You can deduct the interest when you borrow money to buy investments.		
15. Keep records of your cash charitable contributions.		
16. Document your noncash charitable contributions to get the maximum deduction.		
17. Give appreciated property to charity.		
18. Know what qualifies as a casualty and take the maximum deduction for the loss.		
19. Bunch your miscellaneous deductions into one year.		
20. Deduct your moving expenses when you move because of a new job.		
Exemptions and Filing Status 21. Give the exemption deduction to the family member who will benefit most.		
22. Choose the best filing status each year.		
23. Marriage may not be the answer.		
24. If you are single, file as a head of household if you can.		
Tax Credits and Payments 25. Reduce your tax with the child tax credit.		
26. Reduce your tax with the dependent care credit.		
27. Increase your refund with the earned income credit.		

TAX SAVING IDEA	POSSIBLE SAVINGS	NOTES
28. Change your tax planning strategy when you are subject to the alternative minimum tax.		
29. When you adopt a child, be sure to claim the adoption credit.		
30. Stay on the IRS's good side by following the rules for your household help.		
31. Using a Form W-4, set your withholding to the amount of tax you expect to owe.		
32. Make estimated tax payments to avoid underpayment penalties.		
33. If you cannot pay the IRS, request a payment plan.		
Education Planning		
34. Use a qualified tuition savings plan to save even more for college.		
35. Your scholarships may be tax-free.		
36. You can use Coverdell Education Savings Accounts to save for college and let your money grow tax-free.		
37. You can deduct interest on higher education loans.		
38. You can claim Lifetime Learning credits for continuing education courses.		
39. Use the HOPE Scholarship credit to significantly reduce the cost of college.		
40. Allow your child to claim either the HOPE or Lifetime Learning credit.		
41. Deduct your education expenses when the HOPE credit is not available.		

TAX SAVING IDEA	POSSIBLE SAVINGS	NOTES
Investments		
42. You can deduct your capital losses against your capital gains.		
43. You do not pay tax on investments that appreciate until you sell them.		
44. Make sure you deduct all of your costs when you sell an investment.		
45. Make a special election on your 2001 tax return to obtain a more favorable capital gains rate in the future.		
46. You do not have to pay tax on nontaxable dividends.		
47. You can select one of several options for calculating gain or loss when you sell shares in a mutual fund.		
48. With taxable bonds, you can choose when to report your interest income.		
49. You can defer and possibly exclude interest income from U.S. Savings Bonds.		
50. You can buy municipal bonds and not pay tax on the interest income.		
51. You can use options to defer gains.		
52. You can deduct your losses from worthless stock.		
53. Investing in small business stock has its advantages whether you sell the stock at a gain or a loss.		
54. You can deduct your nonbusiness bad debts as short-term capital losses.		
55. You can reduce your tax by investing in rental real estate.		

TAX SAVING IDEA	POSSIBLE SAVINGS	NOTES
56. Avoid tax by trading your property for similar property.		
57. Defer your gains from the sale of property using the installment method.		
Homes		
58. Compare the pros and cons of renting versus owning a home.		
59. You can exclude up to $500,000 of gain from the sale of your home.		
60. If your home is declining in value, convert it to business or rental use.		
61. You can deduct your home office expenses.		
62. You can significantly reduce your costs of owning a vacation home by renting out the vacation home.		
63. Move to a low-tax or no-tax state before you receive a large gain.		
Fringe Benefits		
64. Save money by taking advantage of fringe benefits your employer provides.		
65. Participate in tax-free health insurance and medical reimbursement plans.		
66. You can increase your take-home pay by taking advantage of dependent care assistance plans.		
67. Go back to school, have your employer pay for it, and exclude your tuition costs from your income.		
68. Take advantage of other tax-free fringe benefits that your employer offers.		
69. Tailor your benefits with a cafeteria plan.		

TAX SAVING IDEA	POSSIBLE SAVINGS	NOTES
Start Your Own Business		
70. Reap the tax benefits of starting your own business.		
71. Use the 20 factors to show you are an independent contractor.		
72. Avoid having your business classified as a hobby.		
73. Deduct the full cost of your equipment and furniture purchases.		
74. Use your personal car for business and deduct your car expenses.		
75. Deduct the cost and other expenses of your home computer.		
76. Write off 70% of the health insurance premiums for you and your family.		
77. Deduct your tax return preparation fees against your business income.		
78. Hire your children in your business.		
79. Choose the right business entity for you.		
Retirement Plans		
80. You can use IRAs to save for your retirement and let your money grow tax-deferred.		
81. Make your IRA contributions to a Roth IRA so all future withdrawals are tax-free.		
82. Convert your IRA to a Roth IRA so all future distributions are tax-free.		
83. Even a nonworking spouse can contribute $3,000 to an IRA.		
84. Encourage your employer to set up a qualified retirement plan or 401(k) and take advantage of it.		

TAX SAVING IDEA	POSSIBLE SAVINGS	NOTES
85. If you are self-employed, you can set up your own retirement plan.		
86. Contribute the maximum to a SIMPLE plan.		
87. If you are 50+, contribute an extra $500 to your IRA and an extra $1,000 to your 401(k).		
88. Avoid 50% penalties on distributions from your retirement plan.		
89. You may be able to withdraw money penalty-free from your retirement plan or IRA before age 59 1/2.		
90. Consider the ways to get money out of your retirement plans.		
91. Borrow money from your IRA for less than 60 days without paying tax or penalties.		
Divorce		
92. Work with your spouse to reclassify child support as alimony.		
93. When dividing property in a divorce, look at the after-tax values of the property.		
94. Before you are divorced, you may be able to use the abandoned spouse rule to claim head of household filing status.		
95. By getting custody of your children in a divorce, you can claim the exemption deduction, file as head of household, and take the child care credit.		
96. You can deduct payments for tax-related legal advice.		

TAX SAVING IDEA	POSSIBLE SAVINGS	NOTES
Family Tax Planning		
97. You can avoid the Kiddie Tax by choosing investments that do not increase your child's taxable income.		
98. You can reduce your tax by making gifts to others.		
99. Keeping property until you die can reduce the income tax your heirs pay.		
Working With Your Tax Adviser		
100. Do not throw your tax returns away.		
101. Use the 5 Cs when selecting your tax adviser.		

Income

You Should Take Advantage Of Nontaxable Income

Generally, you must pay tax on the value of everything you receive. This includes your wages, alimony, gambling winnings, investment income, and pension income.

However, many items you receive are specifically excluded from tax. The most common nontaxable items are:

Personal

- Gifts
- Inheritances
- Life insurance proceeds
- Child support payments
- Disability insurance payments when you paid the premiums
- Workers' compensation
- Personal injury damage awards
- Scholarships and fellowship grants used to pay tuition and fees
- Car-pool receipts, a tax-free reimbursement of your expenses
- Garage sale proceeds as long as they are less than what you paid for the property

Benefits you receive from your employer

- Fringe benefits, such as health insurance premiums and employee discounts
- Meals and lodging provided by your employer
- Awards from your employer for length of service or safety
- Employer reimbursements for work-related expenses
- Meal money provided by your employer when you occasionally work overtime
- Outplacement services, such as counseling and resume writing
- Transit passes
- Qualified retirement planning services (beginning in 2002)
- Parsonage allowances for members of the clergy

Purchase discounts

- Rebates, such as car rebates from a manufacturer
- Grocery store coupons
- Frequent flyer mileage

Government payments

- Medicare benefits
- State benefit payments to blind persons
- Military allowances, such as combat pay
- V.A. disability payments
- Foster care provider payments
- Aid to families with dependent children (AFDC payments)
- Home relief and emergency relief payments
- Grants received under the Disaster Relief Act of 1974
- Payments to handicapped persons employed in community services under the Employment Opportunities for Handicapped Individuals Act
- Mortgage assistance payments under Section 235 of the National Housing Act
- Replacement housing payments received under the Uniform Relocation Assistance and Real Property Acquisitions Act of 1970

You become disabled and begin collecting disability insurance. You bought the disability policy several years ago and have personally been paying the premiums. The payments you receive are not taxable to you. However, if your employer paid the disability premiums for you, the payments you receive are taxable.

Your father gives you $10,000. You do not pay income tax on this gift.

Your employer gives you $6 for supper when you occasionally work overtime. You do not pay income tax on this meal allowance.

Your State Tax Refund May Not Be Taxable

In many cases, the tax refund you receive from your state is not taxable. Tax refunds are taxable only if you previously deducted the state tax on your Federal return, and the deduction reduced your Federal tax. In other words, state tax refunds are not taxable on your Federal return unless you received the benefit of a Federal tax deduction in an earlier year. By including the state tax refund in your Federal income, you are repaying the Federal tax you saved earlier when you took the deduction.

If you use the standard deduction

Any state tax refunds you receive from a year you used the standard deduction on your Federal return are not taxable on your Federal return. Because you did not itemize deductions, you did not lower your Federal tax with a deduction for state taxes.

> You did not itemize on your Federal return for 2002. You get a state tax refund of $500 in 2003. The $500 is not taxable.

If you itemize deductions

If you itemize deductions, then your state tax refund is generally taxable. However, a portion may be nontaxable if your Federal itemized deductions were close in amount to your Federal standard deduction for the year you deducted the state tax. Your refund is taxable only to the extent your itemized deductions exceed your standard deduction.

> You and your spouse had $8,050 of Federal itemized deductions for 2002. Your deductions included $3,000 of state and local income taxes. You only owed the state $2,400 for 2002. Thus, in 2003, you received a state income tax refund of $600 ($3,000 - 2,400). Since your Federal itemized deductions ($8,050) only exceeded your Federal standard deduction ($7,850) by $200, only $200 of your refund is taxable. The other $400 ($600 - 200) is nontaxable.

Several major cities including Baltimore, Cincinnati, Cleveland, Kansas City (Missouri), New York, Philadelphia, and St. Louis impose earnings taxes. The rules described above for state tax refunds also apply to refunds of city earnings taxes. City tax refunds are taxable only if you reduced your Federal tax in an earlier year with a deduction for the city taxes.

When you receive a Form 1099-G from your state or city showing the refund you received, do not automatically assume the refund is taxable.

NOTE: If you paid the alternative minimum tax in the prior year, you may not have received a tax benefit from your state or local tax refund. Because taxes are not deductible for the alternative minimum tax, you may not have to pay tax on your state or local tax refund.

You Can Deduct Your Gambling Losses Up To The Amount Of Your Gambling Winnings

Gambling winnings are includable in your adjusted gross income (AGI). Gambling winnings include money you receive from dog and horse racing, black jack, slot machines, lotteries, raffles, bingo, and any other wagering activities. Prizes you win for entering contests are also taxable. Thus, if you buy a raffle ticket and win a car, you are taxed on the value of the car.

If you have income from gambling, remember to add up your gambling losses. Your losses are deductible as itemized deductions up to the amount of your gambling winnings. If you are married, your combined losses are deductible up to the amount of your combined winnings. You cannot deduct your gambling losses if you claim the standard deduction.

> You bought $400 of lottery tickets and won $500. Your spouse bought $200 of lottery tickets and won $40. You and your spouse must include the $540 ($500 + 40) on your return as miscellaneous income. If you and your spouse itemize deductions, you can deduct $540, the amount of your winnings. You cannot deduct the remaining $60 (($400 + 200) - 540).

Gambling losses on one type of gambling can offset winnings from another type of gambling. In other words, you can offset the $400 you win on horse racing with the $300 you lose in slot machines. However, the limitation of deducting your gambling losses up to the amount of your gambling winnings is an annual limitation. For example, if you win $5,000 this year and your gambling losses are $3,000 last year and $200 this year, you can only deduct $200.

Even though gambling losses are a miscellaneous itemized deduction, they are not subject to the 2% of AGI limitation. In other words, your gambling losses are deductible up to the amount of your winnings even if they are not more than 2% of your AGI. Gambling losses are also not subject to the phase-out (reduction) of itemized deductions if your AGI is over $137,300 ($132,950 for 2001).

Generally, if your gambling winnings from one event, such as one horse race, exceed $600, the payer is required to withhold Federal income tax. Currently 27% of your gross winnings is withheld. So if you win $1,000, then $270 will be withheld and sent to the IRS. The payer will give you Form W-2G. This withholding is applied against your total Federal income tax liability, similar to withholding from your wages. If you are in a tax rate bracket lower than 27% or if you have gambling losses to offset your winnings, you may get a refund.

To support your gambling losses, you should keep records. The records should list the date, amount, type of bet, name and address of the gambling establishment, and the names of the other people who were with you. It is also a good idea to keep losing tickets and cancelled checks.

If you are a full-time gambler and your primary source of income is from gambling, you may be in the business of gambling. If you are, your losses are business expenses and are deductible against your gambling income. However, you cannot deduct losses in excess of your gambling income.

Do Not Assume That Your Social Security Benefits Are Taxable

Up to 85% of your Social Security benefits can be taxed. However, it is possible that none of your Social Security benefits is taxable.

To determine how much of your Social Security benefits is taxable, you must figure your modified adjusted gross income. Generally, your modified adjusted gross income is the sum of:

- your income,
- one half of your Social Security benefits, and
- your tax-exempt interest.

You compare this amount to a base amount. The base amounts are $25,000 for single people, $32,000 for married couples filing jointly, and $0 for married people filing separately. If your modified adjusted gross income is less than your base amount, then none of your Social Security benefits is taxed.

If your modified adjusted gross income is more than your base amount, then a portion of your benefits is taxable. Use the following worksheet to determine the amount that is taxable.

How much of your Social Security benefits is taxable?

Modified Adjusted Gross Income (MAGI)

Adjusted gross income (excluding taxable Social Security)	______
+ 1/2 of Social Security benefits	______
+ Tax-exempt interest	______
+ Excluded income from U.S. Savings Bonds used to pay higher education expenses	______
+ Excluded income from employer's adoption assistance program	______
+ Qualified education loan interest deduction	______
+ Foreign income excluded under IRC Section 911, 931, 933	______
TOTAL MAGI	☐

Is your MAGI more than the following:
- $44,000 if married filing joint?
- $34,000 if single, head of household, or married filing separately if you and your spouse lived apart the entire year?
- $0 if married filing separately and you and your spouse live together?

If NO, go to 50% Rule

If YES, go to 85% Rule

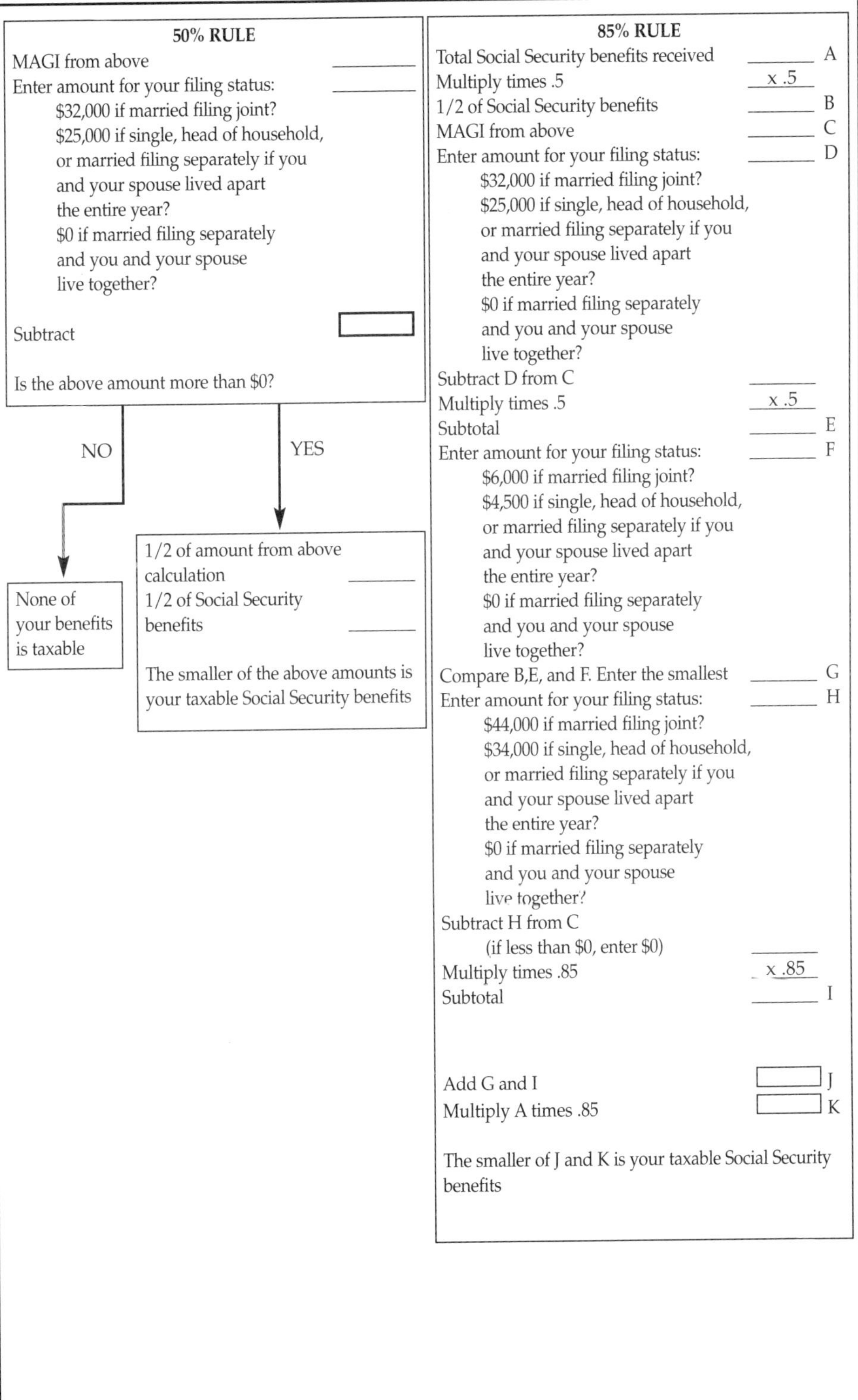

50% RULE

MAGI from above ______
Enter amount for your filing status: ______
$32,000 if married filing joint?
$25,000 if single, head of household, or married filing separately if you and your spouse lived apart the entire year?
$0 if married filing separately and you and your spouse live together?

Subtract [ ]

Is the above amount more than $0?

NO → None of your benefits is taxable

YES → 1/2 of amount from above calculation ______
1/2 of Social Security benefits ______

The smaller of the above amounts is your taxable Social Security benefits

85% RULE

Total Social Security benefits received ______ A
Multiply times .5 x .5
1/2 of Social Security benefits ______ B
MAGI from above ______ C
Enter amount for your filing status: ______ D
$32,000 if married filing joint?
$25,000 if single, head of household, or married filing separately if you and your spouse lived apart the entire year?
$0 if married filing separately and you and your spouse live together?
Subtract D from C ______
Multiply times .5 x .5
Subtotal ______ E
Enter amount for your filing status: ______ F
$6,000 if married filing joint?
$4,500 if single, head of household, or married filing separately if you and your spouse lived apart the entire year?
$0 if married filing separately and you and your spouse live together?
Compare B,E, and F. Enter the smallest ______ G
Enter amount for your filing status: ______ H
$44,000 if married filing joint?
$34,000 if single, head of household, or married filing separately if you and your spouse lived apart the entire year?
$0 if married filing separately and you and your spouse live together?
Subtract H from C
(if less than $0, enter $0) ______
Multiply times .85 x .85
Subtotal ______ I

Add G and I [ ] J
Multiply A times .85 [ ] K

The smaller of J and K is your taxable Social Security benefits

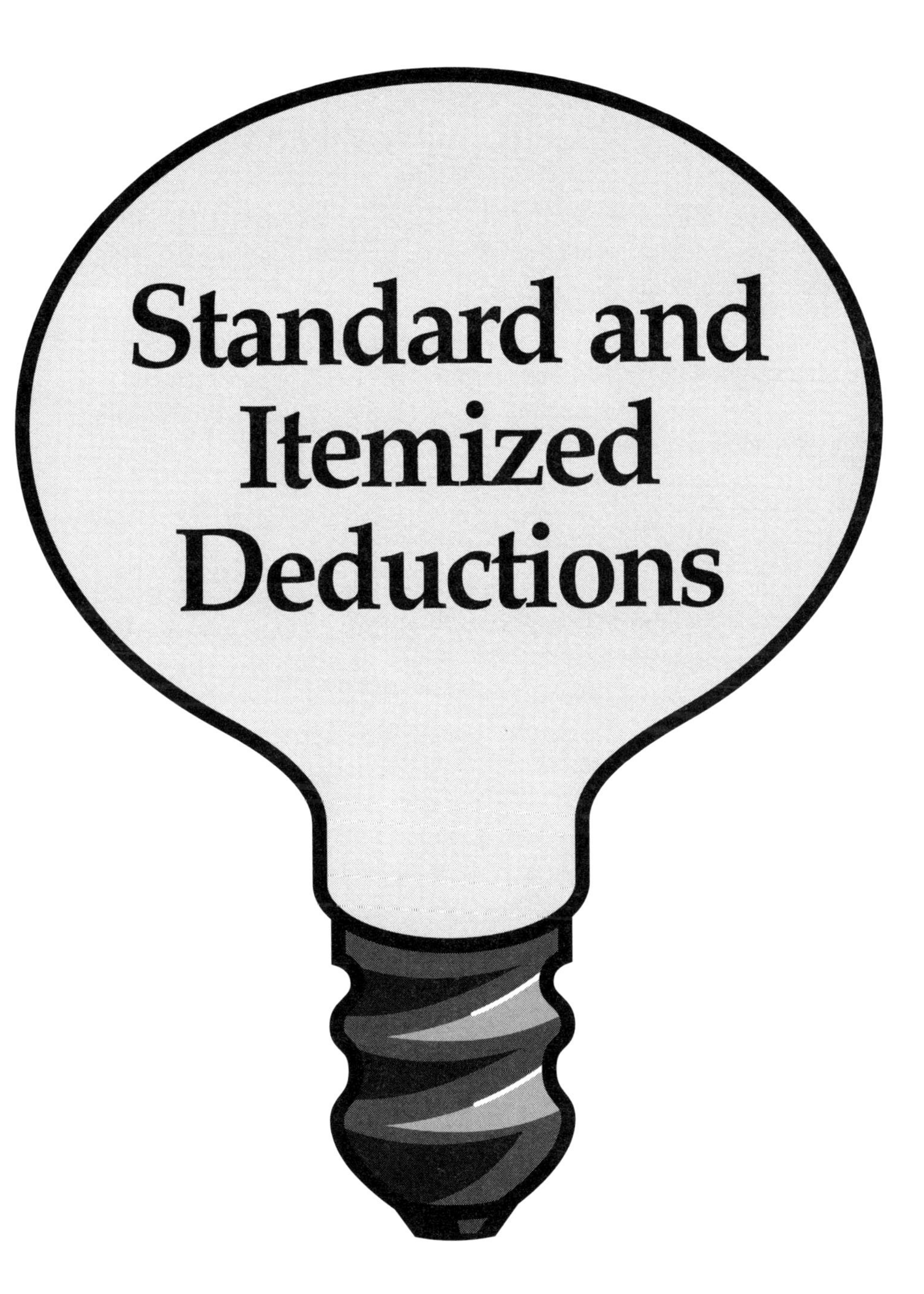
Standard and
Itemized
Deductions

You Get Something For Nothing With The Standard Deduction

You may think you are a "tax nobody" because you do not itemize deductions. Nothing could be farther from the truth. Claiming the standard deduction is great tax planning.

With the standard deduction, you are getting a tax deduction with no cash outlay. Itemized deductions, on the other hand, require cash outlays of at least the deductible amount. Because of the limitations on deducting medical and miscellaneous expenses, often the cash you pay for deductible items is significantly more than the amount you can deduct.

> You are single and pay $2,500 in state taxes and $1,200 in charitable contributions. You would claim the standard deduction. For 2002, your deduction is $4,700 even though you have payments of only $3,700. You receive $1,000 ($4,700 - 3,700) of deduction with no cash outlay. If you are in the 27% tax rate bracket, you save $270 ($1,000 x 27%) in Federal tax.
>
> If you contribute $2,300 to charity rather than $1,200, you would itemize deductions, because $4,800 ($2,500 + 2,300) exceeds $4,700. You receive a $4,800 deduction for $4,800 of cash outlay.

Do not spend money you would not otherwise spend just to itemize. You may actually be getting a better deal by using the standard deduction.

NOTE: You are not eligible for the standard deduction if you file separately from your spouse and your spouse itemizes deductions, or if you are a nonresident alien. Also, your standard deduction may be reduced if someone else claims you as a dependent.

When your itemized deductions are approximately equal to your standard deduction, you can save taxes by taking the standard deduction one year and itemizing the next year. In the year you take the standard deduction, keep your controllable deductions such as charitable contributions, medical expenses, and miscellaneous expenses to a minimum. In years you itemize, maximize your controllable deductions. By bunching your expenses in this way, you get a larger benefit over the two year period.

You are single with a standard deduction of $4,550 in 2001 and $4,700 in 2002. Your itemized deductions are as follows:

	2001	2002
Charitable contributions	$1,850	$1,800
Other itemized deductions	2,450	2,450
Total	$4,300	$4,250

In this situation, you would take the standard deduction in both years because $4,550 is higher than $4,300 in 2001 and $4,700 is higher than $4,250 in 2002. There is nothing wrong with this approach. Over the two years, you get $9,250 ($4,550 + 4,700) of deductions for $8,550 ($4,300 + 4,250) of payments.

However, if you shift your 2002 charitable contribution to 2001, your itemized deductions are as follows:

	2001	2001
Charitable contributions	$3,650	$ 0
Other itemized deductions	2,450	2,450
Total	$6,100	$2,450

Now you will itemize in 2001 because $6,100 is greater than $4,550. You will take the standard deduction in 2002 because $4,700 is greater than $2,450. Over the two years, you claim $10,800 ($6,100 + 4,700) of deductions for $8,550 of payments. At a 27% tax rate, shifting deductions in this way will reduce your taxes by $419 (($10,800 - 9,250) x 27%).

Identify All Of Your Qualifying Medical Payments

You can deduct medical and dental expenses that are over 7.5% of your adjusted gross income (AGI). Medical insurance reimbursements reduce your deductible amount.

> You pay $10,000 for medical and dental care for the year. Your AGI is $100,000. You can deduct $2,500 ($10,000 - (100,000 x 7.5%)) as an itemized deduction.
>
> If your medical insurance reimbursed $8,000 of your expenses, you cannot take a deduction. The $2,000 ($10,000 - 8,000) of unreimbursed expenses does not exceed $7,500 ($100,000 x 7.5%).

Because of these limitations, many individuals cannot take a deduction for medical and dental expenses. Nonetheless, you can increase the likelihood of getting a deduction by identifying all of your qualifying medical expenses.

Payments for the diagnosis, cure, mitigation, treatment, or prevention of disease qualify. These expenses can be for you, your spouse, or relatives you support. However, expenses that are merely beneficial to your general health such as vacation costs and health club dues do not qualify.

Checklist of deductible medical and dental expenses:

- Medical and dental insurance premiums including Medicare Part B premiums and limited amounts for long-term care insurance premiums
- Prescription medicines and insulin
- Fees for doctors, dentists, and other medical practitioners
- Fees for hospitals and medical centers providing psychiatric, drug, or alcohol treatment, including meals and lodging
- Fees for stop-smoking programs (including prescription drugs)
- Fees for physician-prescribed weight-loss programs to treat an existing disease

- Special equipment, such as wheelchairs, crutches, artificial limbs, eyeglasses (including contact lenses), and hearing aids
- Improvements to your home such as elevators, air filtration equipment, and swimming pools to the extent they exceed the increase in value of your home and are needed for medical purposes
- Transportation costs, including auto expenses at either 13¢ (12¢ for 2001) per mile or your actual costs
- Cosmetic surgery, if it corrects a deformity arising from a birth abnormality, a personal injury, or a disfiguring disease
- Special schools or homes for people with mental or physical disabilities
- Nursing homes and other costs for long-term care

This list includes some examples of the types of medical expenses that are deductible. If you have made a payment that might qualify, research it. The list of qualifying deductions is growing daily.

Do not forget to include medical and dental insurance premiums that are withheld from your wages. Check your pay records to see if you are sharing your health insurance costs with your employer.

NOTE: If you are self-employed, you may be able to deduct 70% (60% for 2001 and 100% for 2003) of your health insurance costs in arriving at your adjusted gross income. See Tax Saving Idea #76.

NOTE: Employees of small businesses and self-employed people may be able to take advantage of medical savings accounts (Archer MSAs) to pay health care costs. Archer MSAs are a test program for high-deductible health insurance plans. They are only available to the first 750,000 plans started before 2003.

Long-Term Care Expenses Qualify As Medical Expenses

Medical expenses include long-term care expenses for chronically ill people. Thus, unreimbursed long-term care expenses are deductible as medical expenses subject to the 7.5% of adjusted gross income limitation. See Tax Saving Idea #6.

Long-term care expenses are necessary diagnostic, preventive, therapeutic, curing, treating, mitigating, and rehabilitative services. They also include maintenance and personal care services. If your relative provides the services, you can only deduct the expenses if your relative is licensed to provide these services.

To qualify for the medical expense deduction, you, your spouse, or your dependent who is chronically ill must incur the expense. You are chronically ill if a licensed health care practitioner certifies you as unable to perform at least two activities of daily living, such as bathing, eating, toileting, or dressing, for at least 90 days due to a loss of functional capacity. You also qualify as chronically ill if you require substantial supervision because of severe cognitive impairment, such as Alzheimer's disease.

You can also deduct premiums paid for long-term care insurance as medical expenses. The deduction for the premiums is limited based on your age each December 31. The deductible premium amounts are:

	Maximum Deductible Premium	
Age on December 31	2001	2002
40 or younger	$ 230	$ 240
41-50	$ 430	$ 450
51-60	$ 860	$ 900
61-70	$ 2,290	$ 2,390
71 or older	$ 2,860	$ 2,990

These limits are increased for inflation annually.

John is 45 in 2002. He pays $500 annually for long-term care insurance. John can include $450 when he calculates his medical expense deduction.

If you are self-employed, you may be able to deduct 70% (60% for 2001 and 100% for 2003) of your long-term care insurance premiums in arriving at your adjusted gross income. See Tax Saving Idea #76.

If you are chronically ill and begin receiving benefits under your long-term care insurance policy, you can exclude these benefits from your income. Generally, your long-term care policy must have been issued after December 31, 1996. However, there is a grandfather rule available in some circumstances. The maximum you can exclude is $210 per day for 2002. However, if you receive more than this amount and you spend the full amount you receive on long-term care services, you can exclude the full amount from your income.

NOTE: Your state may allow a deduction for all or part of your long-term care insurance premiums if you do not itemize deductions or if your medical deductions are limited.

Avoid Splitting The Medical Care Expenses For One Person Among Several People

For purposes of the medical expense deduction, the definition of a dependent is expanded. The medical expenses of relatives you support, such as parents, grandparents, and children living away from home, are deductible even if you cannot claim the relatives as dependents because they received too much income or were married. Also, for these purposes, dependents include children from a previous marriage even if your former spouse claims them as dependents.

In many cases, children will share the medical care expenses, such as nursing home costs, of a parent. Sharing the expense decreases the likelihood that anyone can get a medical expense deduction. Instead, designate one family member who will benefit from the medical expense deduction as the person who pays. The other family members can give their share to the payer. From year to year, the family members can take turns paying the bills.

For the same reason, do not split the medical care costs of children with your former spouse. Continue to share the costs, but identify which of you is most likely to obtain a medical expense deduction. That parent should actually pay the children's medical bills for the year. Alternatively, one of you can pay the bills one year and the other pay the next year.

A child who pays taxes can often benefit from a medical expense deduction when a parent cannot. The parent can give the money to the child so the child can make the payment.

In short, have a person who can benefit from the medical expense deduction make the payments.

Include All Your State And Local Tax Payments In Your Itemized Deductions

You can deduct all state and local taxes you pay during a year as an itemized deduction. This includes state taxes you pay on interest that is tax-exempt for Federal tax purposes.

Many people forget to deduct some of the state and local taxes they pay. The most common state and local tax payments include:

- the state tax withheld from your wages,
- the state estimated tax payments you make, and
- the state tax you pay when you file your state tax return and owe money.

Use the following worksheet to make sure you deduct the full amount of state taxes you pay for 2002.

State tax withheld from your wages (Form W-2)	$ ________
Local (city) tax withheld from your wages	________
2002 state estimated tax payments you paid in 2002	________
2001 state estimated tax payments you paid in 2002	________
State tax you paid with a request to extend your 2001 state tax return that you paid in 2002	________
Balance due on your 2001 state tax return that you paid in 2002	________
Balance due on your 2001 local (city) tax return that you paid in 2002	________
Overpayment on your 2001 state tax return that you requested to be applied toward your 2002 state tax	________
State tax withheld during 2002 by a partnership to cover your portion of that state's tax	________
Other amounts paid during 2002 for prior years such as late payments or audit adjustments	________
Mandatory contributions to your state disability fund (California, New Jersey, New York, and Rhode Island)	________
Total state and local tax deduction on Schedule A	$ ________

Pay Your 4th Quarter State Estimated Tax Payment By December 31st

One of the tax planning strategies is to accelerate your deductions. Generally, your 4th quarter state estimated tax payment is due January 15. However, you can accelerate your state tax deduction by paying your 4th quarter state estimated tax payment by December 31. By making the payment a few weeks earlier than necessary, you can take the deduction one year sooner.

Maybe you do not make quarterly state estimated tax payments. If you think you will owe money to the state when you file your state return, you can ask your employer to withhold more state tax. Generally, your employer will have you fill out a new state withholding form. Remember, any state taxes withheld from your wages are deductible as an itemized deduction.

You can deduct a payment to your state for estimated taxes if you reasonably expect to owe the state tax. You cannot deduct a payment to your state for estimated taxes if you purposely overpay the state just to get the Federal tax deduction.

NOTE: When you are subject to the alternative minimum tax, your state and local tax payments are not deductible. If you are in this situation, consider the consequences before you make an early state estimated tax payment.

Deduct All Of Your Real And Personal Property Taxes

You can deduct state and local real property taxes and personal property taxes as described below.

Real property taxes

The most common source of real property tax deductions is your home. Other sources include vacation homes and investment acreage. If you borrowed to buy your home, your lender will usually inform you of the real property taxes paid from your escrow account.

Real estate taxes charged for improvements that specifically benefit you, such as special assessments for sidewalks, roads, and sewers, are not deductible. They do increase your basis in the property. Local benefit taxes paid by the community for maintenance, repairs, or interest charges are deductible.

In the year you buy or sell real estate, the real estate taxes are divided between the buyer and the seller. This allocation is based on the number of days in the year that each party owned the property. If either the buyer or seller agrees to pay the taxes, the sales price and cost of the property are adjusted to reflect the apportionment.

Be sure to thoroughly review your closing documents in the year you buy or sell real estate. There are numerous tax items that are often missed. For example, your share of interest expense and property tax is deductible in the year of closing. Other items, such as transfer fees, either increase your basis in the property or decrease your gain from the sale.

Personal property taxes

Personal property taxes are deductible if they are assessed annually and are based on the value (not weight) of your property.

The most common source of personal property tax deductions is your car. These taxes, which you usually pay annually, are frequently overlooked. Only the property tax portion of your annual registration fees is deductible.

Registration, licensing, and inspection fees charged by many states and localities are not deductible.

Other sources of personal property tax deductions are mobile homes, motorcycles, recreational vehicles, trailers, boats, and wave runners.

NOTE: Real and personal property taxes related to your business are deductible on Schedule C of your return. Property taxes related to rental property are deductible on Schedule E of your return. Deducting these taxes on Schedules C or E is preferable because they reduce your adjusted gross income.

If you deduct expenses for a home office, show the business portion of your real estate tax on Form 8829. See Tax Saving Idea #61.

You Can Deduct The Mortgage Interest On Your Primary Home And A Second Home

Whether interest expense is deductible depends on how you use the borrowed money. Personal interest expense from car loans and credit cards is not deductible. Interest paid on business loans is deductible. Interest paid on your home mortgage may be deductible.

You can deduct the interest on your home mortgage if the loan qualifies as either acquisition indebtedness or home equity indebtedness. Acquisition indebtedness is a loan that is used to acquire, build, or improve your primary home or second home. Home equity indebtedness is any loan on your primary home or second home other than acquisition indebtedness. Both types of loans must be secured by your primary home or second home for the interest to be deductible.

Acquisition loans

Most people know they can deduct the interest on their primary home. What many people do not know is that they can also deduct the interest on a pleasure home. What qualifies as a home may surprise you. A home must have sleeping accommodations, a toilet, and cooking facilities. Thus, vacation homes, condos, mobile homes, travel trailers, recreational vehicles, and some boats qualify as homes.

There are several special rules that apply. First, the total amount of the loans used to buy or improve the two homes cannot exceed $1,000,000 ($500,000 for married individuals filing separate returns). This limitation does not apply to amounts borrowed before October 14, 1987.

Second, be careful if you rent out your second home. If you rent out the second home for more than 14 days, you must personally use the second home for 14 days or 10% of the rental days, whichever is more, to deduct the interest as personal mortgage interest.

Third, home mortgage interest only includes the interest on the loans on your primary home and one other home even if the total amount of the loans on more than two homes is less than $1,000,000. If you own more homes, think about which homes you want to qualify as your primary and second homes. You may be able to deduct the interest from the loans on the other homes as business or rental interest. Each year you may choose a different residence as your second home.

Home equity loans

If you are paying interest on nondeductible personal loans and have equity in your home, it might make sense to consolidate your personal loans into a home equity loan. The interest you pay on a mortgage secured by your home is deductible if the loan is a home equity loan. Unlike acquisition loans which must be used to acquire, build, or improve your home, home equity loans can be used for any purpose. In other words, you can deduct the interest on home equity loans even if you use the money for personal purposes such as medical expenses, vacations, or a car purchase.

> You are in the 27% tax rate bracket. You have a $10,000 car loan, a $3,000 vacation loan, and $2,500 of credit card debt. At a 9% rate, you pay $1,395 ($15,500 x 9%) of nondeductible personal interest. If you take out a 9% home equity loan and pay off your $15,500 of personal debt, you will still pay $1,395 of interest expense. However, because the interest is deductible, you reduce your Federal taxes by $377 ($1,395 x 27%).

The interest deduction on home equity loans may be limited. The interest on home equity loans of up to $100,000 is potentially deductible. However, if the difference between the fair market value of your home and your acquisition loan balance is less than $100,000, you can only deduct the interest on the lower amount.

> You purchased your home for $120,000 three years ago by paying $12,000 cash and borrowing $108,000. Your home is now worth $140,000 and the balance on your acquisition loan is $104,000. You can deduct interest on a home equity loan of up to $36,000 ($140,000 (fair market value of your home) - 104,000 (acquisition loan balance)). Even if you can borrow more than $36,000, you can only deduct interest on a home equity loan of $36,000 (the lesser of $100,000 or $36,000).

NOTE: If you take out a home equity loan, remember that your home is the collateral. Thus, if you cannot make the payments, you could lose your home.

Deduct The Points In The Year You Buy Your Primary Home

Many home buyers pay points to get a more favorable mortgage rate. Points, including loan origination fees, are prepaid interest. You can deduct the points in the year you or the seller pay them (immediately) if:

- the loan is used to buy or improve your primary home and is secured by your home, and
- the points are calculated as a percentage of the loan amount.

If the loan does not meet these requirements, you cannot deduct all the points in the year you pay them. Instead, you deduct the points monthly over the life of your loan. Typically, points paid when you buy a second home, take out a home equity loan, or refinance your mortgage are deducted monthly over the life of the loan.

Points do not include lender charges for processing expenses, credit reports, settlement fees, or recording fees. These charges are not deductible. However, they are added to the basis of your home, which may reduce your gain when you sell your home.

> In March, you bought two homes. On your primary home, you paid two points, $2,000 (2% x $100,000 mortgage amount), to obtain a 7% rate for thirty years. On the vacation home, you paid one point, $720 (1% x $72,000), to obtain an 8% rate for thirty years.
>
> You can deduct the $2,000 in points you paid to acquire your primary home. Your vacation home, however, is not your primary home. Therefore, you must deduct the points on the vacation home monthly over the life of the loan. For this year, you can deduct $20 ($720/360 (the number of months in thirty years) x 10 months in this year) of the points you paid to buy the vacation home.

NOTE: In the year you buy your home, you may pay points but still not have enough deductions to itemize. You may elect on that year's tax return to deduct the points monthly over the life of the loan, thereby allowing you to take deductions in future years.

Refinancing your home mortgage

Many people are refinancing their homes to take advantage of low mortgage rates. There are several things to remember when you refinance.

First, the new loan on your first or second home continues to qualify as an acquisition loan if you refinance. As long as the refinanced amount is not more than the old loan balance, the new loan qualifies as acquisition indebtedness and you can deduct the interest. However, you can borrow more than the old loan balance if you plan to substantially improve your home.

Second, if you refinance your home, you must deduct any points you pay over the life of the loan. Points paid for refinancing are not deductible immediately because you did not pay the points in connection with the purchase or improvement of your primary home.

Many lenders offer "no cost refinancing." By paying an interest rate slightly higher than the market rate, you can reduce your mortgage payment below its current level with no points or other closing costs. In this way, you avoid a large payment of points, the deduction of which is spread over the term of your loan.

Third, if you pay points when you refinance your home, remember to deduct the points monthly over the life of the loan. More importantly, remember to deduct the undeducted points when you sell your home or refinance your home again.

> You refinanced your home in March 2002 and paid $1,080 (1% x $108,000) in points. You deducted points of $30 ($1,080/360 months in thirty years x 10 months last year) on your 2002 return. You refinance your home again in January 2003. You pay no points with the January refinancing. Because you paid off the March loan, you can deduct the $1,050 ($1,080 - 30) of undeducted points from the March refinancing on your 2003 return. You could also deduct the remaining amount of points if you had sold the home.

This principle applies whenever you are deducting points paid over the life of the loan. So if you sell or refinance a vacation home or rental property, check to see if there are points you can deduct.

In summary, pay points when you buy or improve your primary home and deduct them immediately. Avoid paying points when you refinance or buy a second home. However, if you pay points to refinance your home or buy a second home, be sure to deduct them over the life of the loan and when you pay off the loan.

You Can Deduct The Interest When You Borrow Money To Buy Investments

If you borrow money to purchase investments, such as mutual funds, bonds, or stock, you can usually deduct the interest you pay on the loan. There are two limitations, however, on the amount of interest you can deduct.

First, you cannot deduct the interest on loans used to buy investments that produce tax-exempt income. In other words, if you borrow money to buy a municipal bond, you cannot deduct the interest paid on the loan.

Second, your investment interest expense deduction for the year cannot exceed your net investment income for the year. Net investment income is the amount of your investment income over your investment expenses, other than investment interest expense, for the year. Investment income includes dividends, interest, and short-term capital gains. Investment expenses include amounts paid for investment advice, investment publications, and safe deposit boxes. Investment expenses do not include broker's fees you pay when you buy or sell stock. These are added to the cost of your stock and reduce your gain or increase your loss when you sell the stock.

If part of the interest you pay is not deductible because it exceeds your investment income, the disallowed deduction is not lost. You can carry the amount forward to future years. The disallowed amount is then deducted in the year or years that your net investment income exceeds your investment interest.

> If you have $2,000 of net investment income and $2,400 of investment interest expense, you can deduct $2,000 of investment interest. The $400 ($2,400 - 2,000) you could not deduct is carried forward to the following year.

Investment expenses

In calculating your net investment income, your investment income is reduced only by the investment expenses you can deduct. If you cannot deduct your investment expenses because of the 2% of adjusted gross income (AGI) floor for miscellaneous deductions, you do not need to reduce your investment income by the expenses. In other words, your investment income is reduced only by expenses from which you receive a tax benefit.

> You have $1,800 of dividend income and total AGI of $50,000. You borrow money from your broker to purchase stock. Your investment interest expense is $1,700. Your only miscellaneous expenses are $500 for investment publications. Although it appears that your net investment income is $1,300 ($1,800 - 500) and $400 ($1,700 - 1,300) of your investment interest expenses will be disallowed this year and carried forward, this is not correct.
>
> Because your miscellaneous expenses must exceed 2% of your AGI, $1,000 ($50,000 x 2%), before you can take a deduction for the expenses, you cannot deduct your investment expenses. As a result, you do not have to reduce your investment income by the investment expenses. Your net investment income is $1,800, so you can deduct the entire $1,700 of investment interest expense.

Long-term capital gains

Long-term capital gains, including capital gain distributions from mutual funds, are not automatically included in investment income. You must elect to include long-term capital gains in the calculation of your net investment income. If you make the election, your long-term capital gains are taxed as if they are ordinary income. In other words, you must sacrifice the maximum 20% rate of tax on long-term capital gains to generate an investment interest expense deduction at ordinary rates.

Congress changed the law to prevent you from taking advantage of the difference in rates between ordinary income and long-term capital gains. Without the change, you could deduct interest expense at your ordinary tax rate of 27%, 30%, 35%, or 38.6%. At the same time, you could have your long-term capital gains taxed at a 20% tax rate.

For the most part, planning with this election is straightforward. If your net investment income is more than your investment interest expense without including your long-term capital gains, do not make the election to include your long-term capital gains in your investment income. This way you benefit from the 20% maximum tax rate on the capital gains.

The difficult choice occurs when your long-term capital gains are taxed at a rate lower than your ordinary tax rate. If your investment interest expense deduction is limited because you do not have enough investment income, you must choose between an investment interest expense deduction today or an investment interest expense deduction in a future year. Your decision depends on the amount of long-term capital gain that will be taxed at your ordinary tax rate if you make the election; and the amount of interest deduction that you will lose this year and carry over to next year if you do not make the election. Your decision also depends on how much investment income you expect in the future.

You are in the 30% tax rate bracket. You have investment income of $2,000 and a long-term capital gain of $3,000. Your itemized deductions include investment interest expense of $2,700.

If no election is made, you will pay tax of $600 (20% x $3,000) on the long-term capital gain. There is no tax on the net investment income of $2,000 because it is offset by $2,000 of the investment interest expense. You have an investment interest expense carry-over of $700 ($2,700 - 2,000). The $700 carry-over could reduce your tax by $210 ($700 x 30%) in the following year if you have enough investment income.

If you make the election to tax $700 of the $3,000 long-term capital gain at ordinary rates, all of your investment interest expense is deductible in the current year. You pay tax of $460 (($2,000 + 700 - 2,700) x 30%) + (20% x 2,300 (the remaining long-term capital gain)) on your income. You save $140 ($600 - 460) this year, but you no longer have an investment interest expense carry-over. Thus, over the two year period, you may pay additional tax of $70 ($210 (savings by not making the election and using the investment interest carry-over next year) - 140 (savings by making the election and deducting all of your investment interest this year)).

If you are certain your investment income next year will be more than your investment interest expense and your investment interest expense carry-over, you should not make the election. If you are not certain, it may be a good idea to make the election. By making the election, you can deduct your investment interest expense this year when you know you can take the deduction.

Keep Records Of Your Cash Charitable Contributions

Charitable contributions are one of the most common itemized deductions. You can deduct contributions made to qualified organizations. Charitable organizations, such as churches, schools, disaster-relief organizations, and public charities like the United Way and Red Cross, are the best known qualified organizations. Other permissible organizations include governmental units, war veterans organizations, fraternal lodges, private foundations, and nonprofit cemetery companies. If you are unsure if the organization qualifies, ask one of its officers, check Internal Revenue Service Publication 78 (available free by calling 1-800-TAX-FORM), or check www.irs.gov/bus_info/eo/eosearch.html. Contributions you make to needy individuals are not deductible.

You can deduct whatever you give the organization as long as you do not receive something in return. So, if you contribute $200 to your church, your deduction will be $200. If you are in the 27% tax rate bracket and itemize deductions, you will save $54 in Federal taxes. Thus, the contribution only costs you $146 ($200 - 54).

If you receive something in return for your contribution, such as a dinner, you must reduce your contribution by the value of what you receive. The organization is required to tell you the value of what you receive so you can calculate your tax deduction. For example, if you give $100 to an organization which is having a party and you attend the party, your deduction is limited. If the value of the party is $60, you can deduct $40 ($100 - 60).

Contributions are deductible in the year you make them. If you write and mail a check on December 31, you can take the deduction that year. If you charge the contribution on your credit card, you can deduct it in the year you charge it since you are legally liable for it at that time. Pledges are not deductible until you pay the pledge.

Remember to check your year-end pay stub from your employer. One of the most commonly overlooked cash charitable contributions is the amount withheld from your paycheck for organizations such as the United Way.

If you pay cash to an organization, be sure to keep a record of the date, the name of the organization, and the amount. Some people actually save their church program if they put cash in the basket that week.

Your cancelled check serves as your proof to the IRS. However, if you contribute $250 or more at one time to one organization, you must receive a written receipt from the organization. You must get this receipt before you file your tax return or your deduction could be disallowed.

Frequently people donate their time to charitable organizations. The value of your services is not deductible. However, your out-of-pocket expenses count as cash charitable contributions. Remember to deduct the costs of the cakes you donate to the church bake sales and your scout uniforms if you are the leader. Also, if you drive to and from your volunteer work, you can deduct either the actual costs of your gas and oil or your mileage at 14¢ per mile.

If you are a foster care parent, you can deduct the amount you pay to support a foster child to the extent it is more than the state or governmental agency reimburses you.

NOTE: If your contributions exceed 20% of your adjusted gross income, your deduction may be limited. You may encounter these limitations in years when you give significant charitable contributions or in years when you have low income.

Document Your Noncash Charitable Contributions To Get The Maximum Deduction

When you give property to a charitable organization, you must determine the fair market value of your donation. This is the *"price at which the property would change hands between a willing buyer and a willing seller, neither being under any compulsion to buy or sell and both having reasonable knowledge of the relevant facts."*

Noncash contributions of $5,000 or less

If you make a contribution of property to a charity, you should get a receipt from the organization. You need a receipt for contributions of $250 or more. The receipt should list the organization's name, the date and location of the donation, a description of the property, and the estimated value of the property.

For property contributions of $500 or less, you simply report the amount of the contribution on your Schedule A. For property contributions over $500, you must include Form 8283 with your return.

When you are cleaning out your closets with the idea of donating items to charity, make a list and take a picture of the items. You might also use your camcorder. This will help substantiate your contribution and remind you to deduct the full value of the contribution. It is especially important for large quantities and for items in good condition. Internal Revenue Service Publication 561 is helpful in determining the value of donated property (available free by calling 1-800-TAX-FORM).

Noncash contributions of more than $5,000

If you donate property worth more than $5,000, you must still get the receipts and provide the information mentioned above. For property other than publicly traded stock, you must also get a qualified appraisal of the property and attach an appraisal summary to your return.

If you donate over $10,000 of non-publicly traded stock, you must get an appraisal of the stock.

Give Appreciated Property To Charity

Donating appreciated property to charity can produce substantial tax savings. Appreciated property might include art, antiques, real estate, and stock. It does not include ordinary income property, such as inventory or a work of art you created. Generally, to take full advantage of this tax benefit, you must have owned the property more than one year before you give it away.

Giving appreciated property to charity is better than selling the property and donating the sales proceeds.

You own art worth $2,000. You bought the art five years ago for $500. If you sell the art and donate the proceeds from the sale, you get these results:

Contribution of cash after the sale	$2,000
Tax rate	x 27%
Tax savings	$ 540
Taxable gain ($2,000 - $500)	$1,500
Tax rate	x 27%
Tax cost	$ (405)
Net tax savings	$ 135

By selling the property and contributing the proceeds to charity, you receive a $2,000 tax deduction for the cash contribution. However, you are taxed on the $1,500 gain from the sale. Thus, your net tax savings is only $135.

If, instead, you donate the art directly to the charity, you will receive a tax deduction for the full fair market value of the art.

Contribution	$2,000
Tax rate	x 27%
Tax savings	$ 540
Taxable gain	$ 0
Net tax savings	$ 540

The tax savings are significantly better when you contribute the art directly to the charity because you avoid the tax on the gain from the sale.

Some people sell property to charities at a bargain price to help recover their cost of the property. Such sales are treated as part charitable contribution and part sale. The tax savings from bargain sales are less than the savings from donating the property directly to charity.

Do not give depreciated property to charity

Giving property that has gone down in value to charity is a bad idea. You cannot deduct the loss. You are better off selling the property and donating the proceeds from the sale to the charity. This allows you to donate the same amount to the charity, deduct the charitable contribution, and also recognize a loss on your tax return, as long as the item is either business or investment property such as stock.

You bought stock two years ago for $10,000. It is now worth $7,000. You are in the 27% tax rate bracket. If you give the stock to charity, you can only deduct $7,000. Your tax savings is $1,890 ($7,000 x 27%).

However, if you sell the stock for $7,000, you can deduct the $7,000 proceeds you give the charity and you can recognize a loss of $3,000 ($7,000 sales price less $10,000 cost). Your tax savings from the donation is still $1,890 ($7,000 x 27%). However, you also have the tax savings of $810 ($3,000 x 27%) from deducting the loss.

Know What Qualifies As A Casualty And Take The Maximum Deduction For The Loss

Casualties must be sudden, unexpected, or unusual in nature. Fires, floods, thefts, hurricanes, and car accidents are examples of casualties.

To determine the amount of your casualty loss, subtract the money the insurance company gives you from your basis in the property. Generally, your basis is what you paid for the property plus any improvements. If your basis is more than the decrease in the value of the property, you can only deduct the decrease in the value of the property.

For personal casualty losses, such as losses on your home or your car, you can only deduct the amount of the loss which is more than the following:

$100 per occurrence AND
10% of your adjusted gross income (AGI).

You total your car in an accident. You receive $9,000 from the insurance company for the car you recently bought for $15,000. You have income for the year of $50,000. Your casualty loss deduction is:

Value of car before accident	$15,000
Insurance reimbursement	9,000
Loss	6,000
Less $100	(100)
Subtotal	5,900
10% of AGI of $50,000	(5,000)
Deductible loss	$ 900

Business casualty losses are fully deductible and are not reduced by the $100 per occurrence or the 10% of AGI limitations that apply to personal casualty losses. Business casualty losses are losses on property you use in your business, such as machinery and buildings.

Continuing the above example, if your car is used 50% in business, your loss deduction is:

	50% PERSONAL	50% BUSINESS
Value of car before accident	$7,500	$7,500
Insurance reimbursement	4,500	4,500
Loss	3,000	3,000
Less $100	(100)	N/A
Subtotal	2,900	3,000
10% of AGI	(5,000)	N/A
Deductible loss	$ 0	$3,000

If you receive more insurance proceeds than your basis in your property, you have a casualty gain. If the damaged property is your home, you can defer this gain by buying a new home with the insurance proceeds within two years after the end of the year of the casualty.

Your vacation home, which you bought for $75,000, is destroyed in a fire in April of 2002. You have replacement value insurance, and the insurance company gives you $100,000. You have a $25,000 casualty gain ($100,000 insurance proceeds less $75,000 basis). You can include the $25,000 gain in your income in 2002 and pay tax on it. Alternatively, if you buy a new home or rebuild your old one and spend $100,000 (or more), you can defer the $25,000 gain until you eventually sell the home. Your basis in your new home is $75,000 ($100,000 cost of new home less $25,000 deferred gain). To qualify for this deferral, you must buy the new home by December 31, 2004 (two years after the end of 2002, the year that you received the insurance proceeds).

Sometimes an insurance company will reimburse you for living expenses when you cannot use your home because of a casualty. To avoid paying tax on part of these reimbursements, you must show that what you spent on living expenses is more than what you would normally spend.

Amend your prior year return if you suffer a loss from a disaster

If you have a casualty loss from a Federal disaster, you can choose to either deduct the loss that year or deduct the loss in the previous year. Careful planning can increase your deduction.

To qualify for this special disaster loss treatment, the President must declare the area a Federal disaster area. Federal disaster areas are listed in the Internal Revenue Bulletin, published by the government.

Generally, you must elect to amend your prior year return before the due date of your tax return for the year of the loss. This date is usually April 15th. Once you make this election, you cannot change your mind unless you do so within 90 days.

Some factors to consider when deciding whether to amend your prior year return include:

- Ability to get your refund more quickly. If your loss occurs in May of 2002, amending your 2001 return should get you your refund within 90 days of the date you file your amended return. However, if you deduct the loss on your 2002 return which you file on April 15, 2003, you generally will not get your refund until late May, 2003.
- Difficulties in computing the amount of your loss. You may be unable to get the information to file an amended return for the prior year before it is too late to make the election.
- Comparison of your income for the prior year and the current year. If you have significantly more income in the prior year, your personal casualty deduction will be less. This is because only your loss over $100 and over 10% of your income is deductible. In determining which year you should take the deduction, you also need to consider your tax rate brackets.

As mentioned above, you can defer a casualty gain by buying new property with the insurance proceeds. If the destroyed property is your main home, and if your home is located in a "Presidentially declared disaster area," you have four years after the end of the year you receive the insurance proceeds to invest the money you receive from insurance in a new home.

NOTE: On January 23, 2002, President Bush signed the Victims' Tax Relief Bill. This new law provides tax relief for victims of September 11, the Oklahoma City bombing, and the anthrax attacks.

Bunch Your Miscellaneous Deductions Into One Year

There are countless miscellaneous deductions. They fall into two broad categories — those that must be over 2% of your adjusted gross income (AGI) to be deductible; and those that are not subject to the 2% limitation.

Checklist of common miscellaneous itemized deductions that are subject to the 2% of AGI limitation

Employee expenses

- Unreimbursed employee expenses for meals (50%), entertainment (50%), long distance phone calls, cell phone fees, travel, education, and car expenses
- Professional dues and subscriptions
- Union dues
- Small work tools
- Work uniforms
- Job hunting costs, such as employment agency fees and resume expenses

Investment expenses

- Legal, accounting, and tax return preparation fees
- Investment counsel fees
- Asset management fees
- Custodial fees for IRA's and Keogh plans
- Business and investment books, including the cost of this book
- Investment subscriptions
- Cost of computer software and on-line services used to track investments
- Safe deposit box rentals

Checklist of miscellaneous itemized deductions that are not subject to the 2% of AGI limitation

- Gambling losses to the extent of gambling winnings (See Tax Saving Idea #3)
- Work expenses of disabled employees
- Federal estate tax on income in respect of a decedent
- Repayments of amounts under a claim of right if more than $3,000
- Amortizable bond premium
- Short sale expenses
- Your unrecovered investment in a pension or annuity contract
- Your share of the interest, taxes, and business depreciation of a cooperative housing corporation

The most common miscellaneous deductions must be over 2% of your AGI before you get a deduction. As a result, many people do not get a deduction. Here are three strategies to increase your deduction for miscellaneous expenses.

First, use the checklist above so you will include all your potentially deductible expenses. Remember that not all of the expenses are subject to the 2% limitation.

Second, bunch your expenses in one year. People who can take deductions for miscellaneous expenses are usually paying work-related expenses, getting a graduate degree, or going through a divorce. These large expenses usually put them over the 2% limitation making their other miscellaneous expenses deductible. Thus, if you are getting your MBA or paying for tax-related advice in a divorce, pay as many other miscellaneous expenses as you can in the same year.

Another bunching strategy is to alternate years when you pay recurring expenses such as dues, subscriptions, small tools, and work uniforms. For example, you can pay your *Wall Street Journal* subscription for 2002 in January of 2002. You can also pay your 2003 subscription in December 2002. Thus, you have bunched these expenses in 2002 and increased the likelihood you will get a deduction.

Third, if you have a small business, deduct these expenses on Schedule C of your return rather than Schedule A, if possible.

NOTE: Your miscellaneous itemized deductions are not deductible for the alternative minimum tax computation. See Tax Saving Idea #28.

Deduct Your Moving Expenses When You Move Because Of A New Job

If you move because of a job change, generally you can deduct your moving expenses. To qualify, there are two tests that you must meet. These tests are the distance test and the time test.

Distance test

To qualify under the distance test, your new job must be at least 50 miles farther from your old house than your old job was. In the following example, you would meet the distance test.

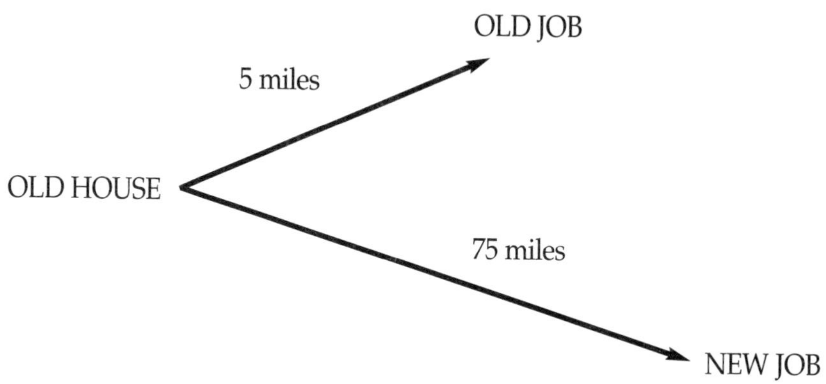

Under the distance test, the location of your new house is not important. Therefore, it does not matter how far your new house is from either your old job or your new job.

If you are moving and your new job is your first job, you can meet the distance test if the job is at least 50 miles from your old house.

Time test

The second test you must meet to deduct your moving expenses is the time test. This test depends on whether you are an employee or are self-employed.

- <u>If you are an employee</u>. You must work full-time at least 39 weeks in the 12 months after arriving at your new home.

- If you are self-employed. You must work full-time at least 39 weeks in the first 12 months AND at least a total of 78 weeks during the first 24 months after arriving at your new home.

If you move before you find a job, you must find a job within 13 weeks and you must stay employed for the next 39 weeks to meet the time test.

You do not have to meet the time test in the following circumstances:

- you die,
- you become disabled,
- you are transferred to another location by your employer, or
- you are fired for reasons other than willful misconduct.

NOTE: If both you and your spouse move and you file a joint tax return, only one of you must meet the time test.

Deductible expenses

You can deduct moving expenses even if you do not itemize deductions. The moving expenses are an adjustment in computing your adjusted gross income (AGI). Alternatively, if your employer reimburses deductible moving expenses, your employer may exclude these amounts from your income.

You can deduct most of your direct expenses. Direct expenses include:

- Moving household goods and personal effects. This includes the costs of packing and transporting your belongings. Remember to deduct the costs of extra insurance and storage of your belongings while they are in transit (up to 30 days before your belongings arrive at your new house). Also, costs to move your cars, boats, and pets are deductible.
- Travel expenses. This includes the cost of your family's transportation and lodging while traveling. You cannot deduct any meals. If you fly, your plane fare and taxi cab fees are your transportation costs. If you drive, you have a choice. You can either deduct the actual amounts you pay for car expenses or 13¢ (12¢ for 2001) per mile.

You can choose whether to deduct your moving expenses in the year you pay them or the year your employer reimburses you. You make the choice when you file your original tax return or by later amending your tax return.

Your wages are subject to the 7.65% FICA rate, and you are in the 33% (27% Federal plus 6% state) tax rate bracket. Your employer reimburses you $6,500 of moving expenses. You pay the following moving expenses:

Moving household goods	$ 3,000
Travel and lodging while moving	500
Meals while moving	150
Travel for house hunting trips	500
Meals for house hunting trips	250
Pre-move temporary living expenses	1,000
Qualified real estate expenses	2,000
Total	$ 7,400

Your employer may exclude from your income $3,500 ($3,000 moving household goods + $500 travel and lodging while moving). Thus, your tax on the reimbursement is $1,220 (($6,500 reimbursement - $3,500 exclusion) x (7.65% + 33%).

To make you whole for your moving expenses, your employer could "gross up" your reimbursement for the additional taxes you owe. In other words, rather than reimbursing you $6,500, your employer could pay you $8,556 ($6,500 + ($1,220/(1 - (7.65% + 33%)))).

NOTE: Your employer should indicate any reimbursed moving expenses on your Form W-2.

Exemptions
and
Filing Status

Give The Exemption Deduction To The Family Member Who Will Benefit Most

Exemption deductions can lead to significant tax savings. You can usually claim an exemption deduction for yourself, your spouse, and your dependents. The tax savings from a $3,000 exemption deduction at the various marginal tax rates is:

Marginal Tax Rate	*Tax Savings From A $3,000 Exemption Deduction*
10%	$ 300
15%	450
27%	810
30%	900
35%	1,050 (may be less if AGI is more than $103,000)
38.6%	1,158 (may be less if AGI is more than $103,000)

Although these tax savings may seem small, they are more than 10% of the total tax for married couples and heads of household with $40,000 of taxable income. The savings could be more if you are single, because claiming an additional exemption deduction might qualify you for head of household filing status.

You can claim an exemption deduction for yourself if someone else does not claim you as a dependent. If you are married and file jointly, you can claim an additional exemption deduction for your spouse. If you are married and file separately, you can still claim an exemption deduction for your spouse if your spouse has no gross income and is not claimed as a dependent on someone else's return.

You can also claim an exemption deduction for each of your dependents. To claim someone as a dependent, you must meet five tests: support, relationship, gross income, married filing jointly, and citizenship.

1. The support test. You must provide over half the support of your dependent. Support includes food, clothing, the fair rental value of housing, wedding expenses, allowances, and property such as TV sets or automobiles you buy for the person. It does not include scholarships your child receives to attend school.

2. The relationship test. Your dependent must be someone who is related to you or someone who lived with you the entire year. Relatives include: ancestors such as parents and grandparents; descendants such as children and grandchildren; brothers and sisters, aunts and uncles, nieces and nephews; and relatives by marriage (in-laws). Adopted children and half brothers and sisters also count as relatives.

3. The gross income test. Your dependent cannot have income of more than $3,000 in 2002 ($2,900 in 2001). However, your children who are under the age of 19 or are full-time students under the age of 24 can have more income than $3,000 ($2,900 in 2001) and still be claimed as dependents. Your children are full-time students if they are full-time students for at least some part of five months during the year. Thus, your child who graduates in May is a full-time student.

4. The married filing jointly test. You cannot claim an exemption deduction for someone who files a joint return with his or her spouse. This rule does not apply if the person files a separate return from his or her spouse or if the couple is filing a return simply to get a refund where no tax is due.

5. The citizenship test. Your dependent must be a citizen or resident of the United States or a resident of Mexico or Canada.

You must satisfy all five of the tests described above for each dependent. It is not necessary that your dependent be alive the entire year. A dependent might be born or die or both during the year. If you satisfy the five tests with respect to the person, you can claim the person as your dependent. In the case of a divorced couple's child, see Tax Saving Idea #95.

Although the IRS does not normally object unless two people claim an exemption deduction for the same person, the tax law does not give you the option. The person who satisfies the five tests claims the dependency exemption. If you satisfy the five tests for claiming your son as your dependent, your son is your dependent. He cannot claim his own dependency exemption. If you do not provide over half of your son's support, your son earns too much gross income, or your son files jointly with his spouse, then you cannot claim your son as your dependent.

There are several situations when a family, through planning, can give the exemption deduction to the family member who will receive the most tax savings from the deduction. The most common example is the struggle between a parent and child for the child's exemption when the child starts to provide his or her own support.

> Your daughter is single, in college, living at home between semesters, and working part-time. She is in the 10% tax rate bracket. She would save $300 if she claims the exemption deduction. You are in the 30% tax rate bracket. You would save $900 if you claim the exemption deduction. Thus, your family comes out ahead by $600 ($900 - 300) if you claim the exemption deduction. You can avoid a struggle if you give your daughter the $300 she would have saved if she had claimed the exemption. You keep the $600 savings.

Planning may be necessary to achieve this result. You and your children may need to figure out how much support your children have received to ensure that you provided over half. If your child is 19 to 23 years old and earns more than $3,000 ($2,900 in 2001), he or she may need to stay in school so you can meet the gross income test.

Another situation is when a group of people share someone's support. Grandparents and parents may be sharing the support of a child. Children may be sharing the support of a sibling or parent. Because of the group effort, no one provides over half the support of the person, and no one in the support group can claim the exemption deduction. In this case, the exemption deduction remains with the person who may have no income and thus receives no savings from the deduction.

In these situations, you can salvage the tax benefit of the exemption deduction by using a multiple support agreement (Form 2120) to designate one person as the provider of over half of the support.

> Your mother is a retired widow with little income. You and your brothers and sisters are sharing her support. None of you individually provide more than half of your mother's support. Consequently, none of you can claim your mother as a dependent. Your mother will claim her own dependency exemption even though she may receive no tax savings from claiming the deduction. If you and your brothers and sisters complete a multiple support agreement, you can designate which one of you is going to take the exemption deduction. From year to year, you can take turns claiming your mother's exemption deduction.

There are three additional points to remember about multiple support agreements. First, if you provide more than 10% of the person's support and, except for not providing over half the support, you could claim that person as a dependent, you must sign Form 2120. Your signature indicates your agreement to allow someone else to claim the exemption.

Second, multiple support agreements satisfy only the support test. You must also satisfy the other four tests to claim a dependency exemption — relationship, gross income, not married filing jointly, and citizenship.

Third, claiming someone as a dependent by means of a multiple support agreement will not allow you to claim head of household filing status.

There are other situations when a family might benefit from exemption planning. If newlyweds are not yet self-supporting, they could file separately so one or both of the parents could claim their exemptions. An elderly couple supported by their children might file separately, invest in tax-exempt bonds so they meet the gross income test, or take other steps so one or two of the children can claim their exemptions.

Several notes of caution are in order here. First, watch out for the emotions attached to the dependency exemption. Children might perceive the parents' desire to claim the dependency exemption as a refusal to let go. A child's desire to claim the dependency exemption may be a declaration of independence. Elderly parents may not want to give up their exemptions because it suggests they are dependent on their children. Although it is just a tax deduction and the family saves money by having someone else claim the deduction, this may be a situation where nontax factors carry greater weight.

Second, there may be nontax, monetary factors to consider. Claiming your child as a dependent may affect your child's chances of getting college grants and other financial aid. Many financial aid equations look to parental support when the child is claimed as a dependent. It does not make sense to save $600 by letting the parents claim the exemption if it will cost the child $3,000 in grants. Claiming elderly parents as dependents may affect their ability to qualify for other financial support, such as Medicaid. Before claiming a young adult or elderly parent as a dependent, consider these factors.

Finally, make sure the person who will claim the exemption deduction actually receives the greater tax benefit. If your income is over $103,000 ($99,725 for 2001), your exemption deduction may be phased out. This means you may begin to lose your tax savings from the dependency exemption if your income is over this amount. For children or elderly parents, losing the exemption deduction might reduce their standard deduction. After all factors are considered, the child or elderly parent may receive the greater tax benefit from the exemption deduction.

Choose The Best Filing Status Each Year

The five possible filing statuses are:

- single,
- head of household,
- married filing jointly,
- married filing separately, and
- qualifying widow(er) with dependent child.

Your filing status has a tremendous impact on the amount of tax you ultimately owe. Your filing status affects the income from Social Security benefits you report, the individual retirement account contributions you can deduct, the standard deduction you can take, and the credit for child and dependent care you can claim. Most importantly, your marginal tax rate varies based on your filing status.

As a general rule, your marital status on the last day of the year determines your filing status. You are single if you are not married on the last day of the year. Even if you divorce on December 30th, you are single as long as you are not married on the last day of the year. There is an exception if your spouse died during the year. In this case, you are considered married for the year of your spouse's death even though you are single on the last day of the year.

Single people may be able to reduce their taxes by using head of household filing status. To qualify as a head of household, you must provide a home for your child, foster child, parent, or other relative. Providing a home means you pay over half the cost of keeping up a household. Costs include mortgage payments, rent, utilities, and repairs.

Depending on your relationship to the person, the person may have to live with you for more than six months during the year, qualify as your dependent, or both. The chart below shows which requirements you need to meet.

	Lives with you	Qualifies as your dependent
Child or grandchild	X	
Foster child	X	X
Married child or grandchild	X	X
Parent		X
Other relative	X	X

In other words, you may qualify as a head of household if your child lives with you for more than six months of the year even if you cannot claim your child as a dependent. Furthermore, your child's temporary absences from your home for vacation, school, business, and illness count as time in your home. You may also file as head of household if you provide over half the cost of your parent's home and can claim your parent as a dependent. Your parent does not need to live with you.

You are married if you are legally married on the last day of the year or if your spouse died during the year. It does not matter if you are single for most of the year. If you are married, you generally have the choice of filing jointly or separately. It is also possible you can file as a head of household if your spouse does not live in your home for the last six months of the year and you provide the main home for yourself and your child. See Tax Saving Idea #94.

Qualifying widows and widowers with dependent children can use the beneficial married filing jointly tax rates for two years after the spouse's year of death. To qualify, you must provide over half the cost of keeping up your home, and your dependent child must live in your home for the entire year. Like the rules for head of household, your child's temporary absences for vacation, school, business, or illness count as time in your home.

NOTE: Even though you use the married filing jointly tax rates, you cannot claim an exemption deduction for your deceased spouse in the years following the year of your spouse's death.

Choosing the proper filing status is important. Consider the impact of filing status on the following four taxpayers with $80,000 of income in 2002.

	Single	Head Of Household	Married Filing Jointly	Married Filing Separately
Income	$ 80,000	$ 80,000	$ 80,000	$ 80,000
Standard deduction	(4,700)	(6,900)	(7,850)	(3,925)
Exemptions (2)	(6,000)	(6,000)	(6,000)	(6,000)
Taxable income	$ 69,300	$ 67,100	$ 66,150	$ 70,075
Tax*	$ 15,113	$ 13,130	$ 11,663	$ 16,228
Marginal tax rate	30%	27%	27%	30%

Depending on the filing status, the tax on $80,000 of gross income can range from $11,663 to $16,228. Differences in the standard deduction amounts and the marginal tax rates cause this variance.

To plan with filing status, you must know when it is to your advantage to claim a different filing status. If you are single, your choices are usually limited to filing single or the more favorable head of household. If you are married, your choices are usually married filing jointly or married filing separately.

Marriage May Not Be The Answer

A frequently asked question to tax advisers is, "If we get married, will we pay more or less tax?" The answer depends on the incomes of the two people. If the couple has one income, then the couple will generally pay less tax if they marry. If the two people earn approximately equal incomes, they will generally pay less tax if they stay single.

Excerpts from the 2002 Tax Tables

Taxable Income	Single	Married Filing Jointly
$18,800	$ 2,524	$2,224
$30,000	4,453	3,904
$41,200	7,477	5,584
$57,000	11,743	9,193
$60,000	12,553	10,003

The singles penalty

Consider the excerpt from the Tax Tables shown above. If you are single with $60,000 of taxable income, you will pay $12,553 of tax. To reduce your tax to $9,193, you can marry someone with no income and no deductions. Your taxable income decreases by $3,000 because of your spouse's exemption deduction. The tax on $57,000 for a married couple filing jointly is $9,193, a savings of $3,360 ($12,553 - 9,193). This disadvantage of being single is called the singles penalty.

The marriage penalty

In many cases, the tax system is unfair to married couples. Look again at the table above. If two single people each have $30,000 of taxable income, they pay tax of $8,906 ($4,453 x 2). If these two single people marry and file jointly, they pay $10,003, which is $1,097 ($10,003 - 8,906) more than if they remain single. This difference in tax is the result of the tax rate schedules that apply to the single and married filing jointly filing statuses. Single people are in the 15% tax rate bracket until their taxable income reaches $27,950. Then they start to pay tax at a 27% tax rate. You would think that a married couple would start paying tax at the 27% tax rate at twice that amount, $55,900. Instead, the 27% marginal rate starts at $46,700 for married couples filing jointly. The married couple in our example pays more tax because more of their income is subject to the 27% tax rate as opposed to the 15% tax rate.

At this point, you might ask, "How can there be both a singles penalty and a marriage penalty?" The answer is the tax system favors the traditional, one income family. When a two earner couple marries, they are pushed into higher tax rates because they both have income.

Again consider the above excerpt from the Tax Tables. A married couple with $60,000 of taxable income pays $10,003 in tax. Two single people together pay approximately the same tax if one has $41,200 of taxable income and the other has $18,800 of taxable income. The tax on $41,200 is $7,477 and the tax on $18,800 is $2,524, for a total of $10,001. In this example, one person has about 70% of the total income of $60,000 and the other has about 30% of the $60,000. This 70/30 breakpoint is typical, although the actual amount varies with income level. When the lower earning spouse earns less than 30% of the couple's taxable income, the couple is generally better off tax-wise being married. When the lower earning spouse earns more than 30% of the couple's taxable income, the couple is more likely to be subject to the marriage penalty.

There are other biases against married couples in the tax system. For example, the standard deduction for single filers is $4,700. For married filing jointly couples, the standard deduction is $7,850, not $9,400 ($4,700 x 2). The taxation of Social Security benefits for a single filer starts at $25,000 of modified adjusted gross income. For a married couple, the taxation of Social Security benefits starts at $32,000, not $50,000 ($25,000 x 2). The starting point for reducing itemized deductions begins at $137,300 for both single and married filing jointly filers. There are many more examples.

Despite the marriage penalty built into our tax system, you should not get married or divorced for tax reasons. This is an example of "Do not let the tax tail wag the dog." If you are going to marry, you might think about the timing of your marriage. Postponing your wedding date from December to January might save you money if each of you earn approximately the same amount of income. On the other hand, moving your wedding date up from January to December might reduce your tax if one of you earns significantly more than the other.

Couples should also not get divorced for tax reasons. You hear many stories about couples divorcing near the end of the year and remarrying shortly after the start of the year to reduce their taxes. The IRS considers such efforts a sham. If the couple is audited, not only will they be treated as married and owe the additional tax, they will also owe interest and penalties.

NOTE: The 2001 tax law changes will help reduce the marriage penalty beginning in 2005 with the following tax law changes:

- Standard deductions for joint couples will be increased to twice the amount of singles phased in over 5 years beginning in 2005.
- The 15% tax rate bracket for joint couples will be expanded to twice the size of singles over 4 years beginning in 2005.

If You Are Single, File As A Head Of Household If You Can

Filing as a head of household is better than filing single for three reasons. First, the higher tax rates apply at higher levels of income. For a single person, the 27% tax rate bracket begins at $27,950 of taxable income. For a head of household, the 27% tax rate bracket begins at $37,450. So, for a head of household, $9,500 ($37,450 - 27,950) more income is taxed at the lower 15% tax rate.

Second, your standard deduction is higher if you can file as a head of household. The standard deduction for a single person is $4,700. The standard deduction for a head of household is $6,900. Thus, a head of household gets an additional $2,200 ($6,900 - 4,700) of deduction.

Third, the level at which you begin phasing out your exemption deductions is higher. Phase out means you may begin to lose your tax savings for the dependency exemption if your income is over a set amount. A single person begins losing exemption deductions at $137,300 of income. A head of household begins losing exemption deductions at $171,650 of income. Thus, a head of household can have $34,350 ($171,650 - 137,300) more income before losing exemption deductions.

The people who most commonly claim head of household filing status are:

- Single parents with custody of a child,
- Single individuals supporting a parent,
- Single foster parents,
- Widows and widowers, and
- Abandoned spouses who have custody of a child.

If one of these descriptions applies to you and you are filing single, look into filing as a head of household.

An example of the taxes you can save by filing head of household rather than single is shown below.

You are single, earn $55,000, and provide over half the support of your parents. Your father receives nontaxable social security benefits and $16,000 from a pension. Your mother receives no income. You would like to claim an exemption deduction for your mother on your return so you can file as head of household. To do so, however, your father must agree to sacrifice the exemption deduction for his wife and file married filing separately.

A comparison of the alternatives is shown below.

	Alternative 1 You do not claim the exemption		Alternative 2 You claim the exemption and file head of household	
	You	Your father	You	Your father
Income	$55,000	$16,000	$55,000	$16,000
Standard Deduction	(4,700)	(9,650)	(6,900)	(4,825)
Exemption	(3,000)	(6,000)	(6,000)	(3,000)
Taxable income	$47,300	$ 350	$42,100	$ 8,175
Tax*	$9,124	$ 36	$6,380	$ 926
Total family tax	$9,160		$7,306	

*Tax amounts are from the 2002 Tax Tables. Using the Tax Rate Schedules to do the calculations will produce a slightly different amount.

To convince your father to do this, you may need to give him $890 ($926 - 36), the additional tax he will have to pay. Despite losing your mother's standard deduction and additional standard deduction for being over 65, you still come out ahead by $1,854 ($9,160 - 7,306) if you claim your mother's exemption and file as a head of household. You save money because as a head of household you have a higher standard deduction. Also, more of your income is taxed at the lower 10% and 15% tax rates rather than the 27% tax rate.

Many families benefit from this strategy, but there are nontax reasons people do not use this strategy. Some parents feel that filing separately says something about the condition of their marriage and that being claimed as a dependent on a child's return publicizes their dependence on the child. Although tax returns are confidential, it is important to respect your parents' feelings.

NOTE: The above example and discussion illustrate the savings if a child claims a parent as an exemption and qualifies for head of household filing status. Similar savings are possible if you qualify for head of household by providing a home for your child.

Tax Credits
and
Payments

Reduce Your Tax With The Child Tax Credit

You can claim a tax credit of up to $600 for each qualifying child under age 17. A qualifying child is any child, grandchild, stepchild, or foster child that you can claim as a dependent. The credit is phased out by $50 for each $1,000 (or part thereof) of adjusted gross income (AGI) above $110,000 for married filing jointly couples, $75,000 for single and head of household filers, and $55,000 for married filing separately couples.

> You are married with two children under age 17. You and your spouse have AGI of $114,250 and taxable income of $90,000. Your tax before the credit is $18,103. Your child tax credit is partially phased out because your adjusted gross income exceeds $110,000. You can claim a credit of $950 (($600 x 2) - (($114,250 - 110,000)/$1,000 (4.25 is rounded up to 5)) x $50)). Your tax liability is reduced to $17,153 ($18,103 - 950) by the child tax credit.

If you have one or two children, generally the child tax credit is nonrefundable. This means the credit can only reduce your actual tax (before considering your withholdings, estimated payments, and the earned income credit) to zero. After 2001, if your tax liability is less than your credit, the excess credit up to 10% of your earned income over $10,000 is refundable.

If you have three or more children or if you are eligible for the earned income credit, you may qualify for the supplemental child tax credit. This credit is refundable up to the amount of Social Security and Medicare taxes withheld from your pay and self-employment tax you pay. This means you may receive a refund even if you had zero tax. You use Form 8812 to calculate this supplemental child tax credit.

NOTE: The tax credit per child is scheduled to increase to $700 in 2005, $800 in 2009, and $1,000 in 2010.

Reduce Your Tax With The Dependent Care Credit

If you have children, take advantage of the dependent care credit. Credits are valuable because they directly reduce your tax.

For the dependent care credit, also known as the child care credit, you must pay day care expenses for your dependent while you are at work. Your dependent must be under age 13 or physically or mentally disabled. If your spouse is physically or mentally disabled, expenses for your spouse's care also qualify.

If your child turns 13 during the year, you can claim the expenses up to the date of his or her birthday. Also, you can claim the full amount of the credit. You do not need to prorate the credit in that year.

The types of expenses eligible for the credit include expenses which allow you or your spouse to remain employed and are attributable in part to the care of your dependent. Typical expenses include day care services, nursery schools, baby sitters, and maids. However, if your dependent stays at a camp overnight, these expenses will not qualify. Also, you generally cannot pay one child of yours to care for another and have it qualify for the dependent care credit.

The maximum expense you can use for the credit is $2,400 ($3,000 in 2003) if you have one qualifying dependent and $4,800 ($6,000 in 2003) if you have two or more qualifying dependents. If your earned income or your spouse's earned income is less than this amount, you can only claim the credit on the smaller amount. However, there is an exception to this rule if your spouse is a full-time student. In such cases, your spouse is treated as earning $200 ($250 in 2003) per month if you have one dependent, and $400 ($500 in 2003) per month if you have two or more dependents. Under this rule, you can claim a credit on your entire expense up to the maximum.

The percentage of your credit is based on your adjusted gross income. The credit gets smaller as your income increases. You use the following chart to determine your percentage. The chart also shows the maximum credit for your income level.

2002

Adjusted Gross Income		Applicable	Maximum Credit	
Over	But Not Over	Percentage	1 Child	2 Children
$ 0	$10,000	30%	$720	$1,440
10,000	12,000	29%	696	1,392
12,000	14,000	28%	672	1,344
14,000	16,000	27%	648	1,296
16,000	18,000	26%	624	1,248
18,000	20,000	25%	600	1,200
20,000	22,000	24%	576	1,152
22,000	24,000	23%	552	1,104
24,000	26,000	22%	528	1,056
26,000	28,000	21%	504	1,008
28,000	and over	20%	480	960

2003

Adjusted Gross Income		Applicable	Maximum Credit	
Over	But Not Over	Percentage	1 Child	2 Children
$ 0	$15,000	35%	$1,050	$2,100
15,000	17,000	34%	1,020	2,040
17,000	19,000	33%	990	1,980
19,000	21,000	32%	960	1,920
21,000	23,000	31%	930	1,860
23,000	25,000	30%	900	1,800
25,000	27,000	29%	870	1,740
27,000	29,000	28%	840	1,680
29,000	31,000	27%	810	1,620
31,000	33,000	26%	780	1,560
33,000	35,000	25%	750	1,500
35,000	37,000	24%	720	1,440
37,000	39,000	23%	690	1,380
39,000	41,000	22%	660	1,320
41,000	43,000	21%	630	1,260
43,000	and over	20%	600	1,200

You earn $25,000 and your spouse earns $15,000. You have 2 children under age 13 and you pay $6,000 of child care expenses. In 2002 you can claim a credit of $960 ($4,800 maximum expenses allowed x 20% credit based on your earned income).

In 2003, you can claim a credit of $1,320 ($6,000 maximum expenses allowed x 22% credit based on your earned income).

To the extent that you take advantage of a dependent care assistance program at work, you cannot take advantage of the dependent care credit. See Tax Saving Idea #66.

Some people must decide between a deduction for medical expenses and the dependent care credit. To the extent you use the expenses to compute a dependent care credit, you cannot deduct the expenses as medical expenses. If you treat the expenses as medical expenses, then you cannot use them to calculate your dependent care credit. You should compute your tax both ways, and choose the one that saves you more.

In 2002, you are married with $40,000 of income and $10,000 of itemized deductions before considering your medical expenses. Your spouse is disabled and requires nursing care during part of the time you are at work. You pay $6,500 for the care. The care qualifies for either the medical expense deduction or the dependent care credit.

	Deduct Medical Expense	Claim As Dependent Care Credit
Income	$ 40,000	$ 40,000
Itemized deductions:		
Medical ($6,500 - (40,000 x 7.5%))	(3,500)	
(($6,500 - 2,400) - (40,000 x 7.5%))		(1,100)
Other	(10,000)	(10,000)
Exemptions	(6,000)	(6,000)
Taxable income	$ 20,500	$ 22,900
Tentative tax	$ 2,479	$ 2,839
Dependent care credit ($2,400 x 20%)	0	(480)
Tax	$ 2,479	$ 2,359

In this case, claiming the dependent care credit saves you $120 ($2,479 - 2,359) of tax. If your income and medical expenses had been higher, you might have saved more by deducting the medical expenses rather than claiming the credit.

Increase Your Refund With The Earned Income Credit

If you have a low-income year, take advantage of the earned income credit (EIC). The earned income credit is a refundable credit which allows you to claim a refund larger than the amounts your employer withheld from your earnings or other amounts you paid in. Originally, the earned income credit was allowed to return FICA taxes withheld from your wages. It has evolved into a negative income tax system providing refunds to taxpayers reporting low income.

You can claim the earned income credit as long as your earned income or modified gross income, whichever is greater, is less than specified amounts and you have less than $2,550 of disqualified income. Disqualified income includes capital gain income, interest, dividends, tax-exempt interest, and nonbusiness rents and royalties.

The credit is based on earned income. Earned income includes wages, salaries, tips, net earnings from self-employment, military subsistence allowances, parsonage allowances, the value of meals and lodging provided by your employer, excludable employer-provided dependent care benefits, and union strike benefits. It does not include interest and dividends, welfare benefits, veteran's benefits, pensions and annuities, alimony, social security benefits, workers' compensation, unemployment compensation, or taxable scholarships and fellowships.

Modified gross income is your adjusted gross income reduced by certain capital losses, losses from trusts and estates, losses from nonbusiness rents and royalties, and half the net losses from a trade or business.

You find the amount of the credit in a table the IRS publishes in your tax return instructions.

You are single, have two children, and file as a head of household. In 2001, your only income was wages of $23,350 from which your employer withheld $500 of income tax and $1,786 ($23,350 x 7.65%) of FICA. Your taxable income is $8,000 ($23,350 - 6,650 (standard deduction) - 8,700 (three exemptions of $2,900 each)). Your income tax is $4 ($1,204 - 1,200 child tax credit). Your earned income credit from the IRS Table is $1,842, considerably more than the FICA withheld. Your income tax refund is $2,338 ($1,842 (earned income credit) + 500 (withholding) - 4 (tax liability)).

There are three common misconceptions about the earned income credit. The first misconception is that you have to be a single parent to claim the earned income credit. The earned income credit is available to married taxpayers who file jointly and single taxpayers. Although the earned income credit is greater if you have children, it is also available if you do not have children. To qualify, you must be a U.S. resident for over half the year, not claimed as a dependent on someone else's tax return, and between the ages of 25 and 65.

The second misconception is that the lower your income, the greater your earned income credit. The earned income credit starts out low and peaks based on the amount of your earned income. After the credit peaks, it is phased out based on your earned income or your modified gross income, whichever is greater, as you can see from the following chart.

	EIC if $1 of income	Income when EIC is maximized	Maximum EIC	Income level when EIC is phased out
Workers with no children	$ 2	$4,910 - 6,150	$ 376	$ 11,060
Workers with one child	9	7,370 -13,520	2,506	29,201
Workers with two children	10	10,350 -13,520	4,140	33,178

The third misconception is that you have to wait until you file your tax return to benefit from the credit. If you have at least one child, you can elect to receive advance payments of up to 60% of your earned income credit through your paychecks. You can use Form W-5 to notify your employer of your desire to receive these advance payments.

Change Your Tax Planning Strategy When You Are Subject To The Alternative Minimum Tax

The alternative minimum tax (AMT) is a separate tax system. Its purpose is to ensure that people with large amounts of income and deductions pay at least a minimum amount of tax. This purpose is accomplished by recomputing your regular taxable income. You add back regular tax deductions and change exemption deductions. Then, using the AMT rates, you recompute your tax. If the recomputed tax is greater than your regular tax, the difference, called the alternative minimum tax, is added to your regular tax. Because the AMT adds back deductions allowed in the regular tax calculation, the AMT is often called the "tax on loopholes."

You have regular taxable income of $70,000. Your regular tax is $15,323. For your regular tax calculation, you have $40,000 of deductions that are not allowed for AMT. Your AMT is calculated as follows:

Regular taxable income	$ 70,000
+ Some deductions allowed for regular tax	40,000
- AMT exemption	(35,750)
= AMT Taxable income	74,250
x AMT Tax Rate	x 26%
= Tentative Minimum Tax	19,305
- Regular Tax	15,323
= Alternative Minimum Tax (unless $0 or less)	$ 3,982

Your total tax is $19,305: $15,323 of regular tax plus $3,982 of AMT.

The AMT rate is 26% on AMT income up to $175,000 ($87,500 if you are married filing separately) and 28% on AMT income over that amount. Because the 26% AMT rate is close to the 27% regular tax rate that applies to many people, the AMT applies to many people.

Most people who pay AMT have regular tax deductions that are disallowed by the AMT. Here is a list of some common deductions that you must add back to your regular taxable income when calculating AMT:

- Personal exemptions
- Tax-exempt interest income from certain bonds
- Accelerated depreciation
- State and local income taxes
- Real estate and personal property taxes
- Miscellaneous itemized deductions
- Incentive stock options
- Depletion

If you have large amounts of the above deductions, you may be subject to the AMT.

The AMT exemption you can deduct is based on your filing status.

Married filing jointly	$49,000
Single or a head of household	$35,750
Married filing separately	$24,500

When your income reaches a certain level, you begin to lose your AMT exemption. This phase-out causes your AMT rate to be higher than the stated 26% or 28% rates. You reduce your AMT exemption by 25¢ for every $1 that your AMT income exceeds the following:

Married filing jointly	$150,000
Single or a head of household	$112,500
Married filing separately	$ 75,000

If it appears the AMT will apply to you, you should change your tax planning strategies. First, instead of accelerating deductions into the current year, you should defer them to a later year. Your goal is to raise your regular tax to the point that it equals your AMT. For example, since your state and local taxes are not deductible for the AMT, you should wait until January to pay your fourth quarter estimate. In this way, you increase your regular tax and decrease the likelihood that the AMT will apply.

Second, if the AMT applies to you this year but will not apply to you next year, increase your income this year. The AMT rate is 26% or 28%, while your regular tax rate may be higher.

Third, the law lets you make certain elections to avoid the AMT. For example, to eliminate the adjustment for accelerated depreciation, you can elect to depreciate your business equipment and real estate under a different method. These alternative methods allow the same amount of depreciation but at a slower rate. Thus, you have a higher regular tax and a smaller AMT add back. If you expect to be subject to the AMT for several consecutive years, these elections can help you reduce your tax.

Fourth, when you are subject to the AMT, be sure to take the alternative minimum tax credit the next year. If you pay the alternative minimum tax (AMT), you may be eligible for a credit. This credit reduces your regular tax in future years. You can use the credit to the extent your regular tax exceeds your AMT for that year.

The AMT you pay does not always produce a credit. Many AMT items are considered "exclusion" items. These items do not produce a credit. Examples of items that do not produce an AMT credit are:

- State and local taxes
- Real estate and personal property taxes
- Tax-exempt interest income from certain bonds
- Depletion

"Deferral" type items produce a credit. These are items that create timing differences over several years. Examples of items that produce an AMT credit are:

- Depreciation you claim on business or rental property
- Intangible drilling costs you claim for preparing land to drill for oil and gas
- Incentive stock options

Your credit is the amount of your AMT reduced by what your AMT would have been if you had no deferral items. For example, if your AMT is $20,000 and your AMT not including the deferral items is only $17,000, you have a $3,000 ($20,000 - 17,000) credit. You can use this credit to the extent your regular tax exceeds your AMT in a future year. Thus, in many cases, if you pay the AMT you are prepaying your tax for the future.

When You Adopt A Child, Be Sure To Claim The Adoption Credit

If you adopt a child, take advantage of the adoption credit. Credits are valuable because they directly reduce your tax.

You can claim up to a $10,000 ($5,000 for 2001) adoption credit for a child under the age of 18 on the date of the adoption or for a person who is physically or mentally incapable of self-care. You can claim up to a $10,000 ($6,000 for 2001) adoption credit for a U.S. citizen or resident child with special needs as determined by the state. The credit is available for each child you adopt.

Generally, you claim the credit in the year following the year you pay the expenses. So, if you incur expenses in 2001, you would claim the credit on your 2002 tax return. However, if you pay expenses in the year the adoption becomes final or in a later year, you can claim those expenses in the year you pay them.

The types of expenses eligible for the credit include:

- Adoption fees,
- Court costs,
- Attorney fees, and
- Other expenses directly related to a legal adoption.

The types of expenses not eligible for the credit include:

- Expenses in violation of state or Federal law,
- Expenses for a surrogate parenting arrangement, and
- Expenses for the adoption of your spouse's child.

Expenses for a foreign adoption only qualify if the adoption becomes final. When you adopt a foreign child, the year the adoption becomes final is the year you can claim the credit.

If your adjusted gross income (AGI) is less than $150,000 ($75,000 for 2001), you can claim a credit for all expenses you pay up to $10,000 ($5,000 for 2001, or $6,000 in the case of a child with special needs for 2001). If your AGI is between $150,000 and $190,000 ($75,000 and $115,000 for 2001), the credit is phased out ratably. So, if your AGI is $170,000 ($95,000 for 2001) which is halfway between income limitations, you would be able to claim a credit of $5,000 ($2,500 in 2001, or $3,000 in the case of a child with special needs for 2001). If your AGI is over $190,000 ($115,000 for 2001), you will be unable to claim any credit.

> Alex and Cindy begin the adoption process in 2001. During 2001, Alex and Cindy incur expenses of $4,500. During 2002 when the adoption is finalized, they incur an additional $2,500. Their AGI is $60,000. The 2001 expenses of $4,500 are eligible for the credit in 2002. Also, the 2002 expenses of $2,500 are eligible for the credit in 2002 since the adoption was finalized that year. If Alex and Cindy's AGI in 2002 is $165,000 instead of $60,000, their credit is $4,375 (($7,000 x ((190,000-165,000)/(190,000-150,000))) due to the phase-out of the credit.

Beginning in 2002, if the child you adopt is a U.S. citizen or resident and is a "special needs" child as determined by the state, you can claim a $10,000 credit in the year the adoption becomes final. Beginning in 2003, you can claim the full $10,000 credit in the year the adoption of a child with special needs is finalized, even if your qualified adoption expenses are less than $10,000.

Employers can offer an adoption assistance program. These programs allow your taxable income to be reduced by $10,000 ($5,000 for 2001, or $6,000 in the case of a child with special needs for 2001). Similar income limitations that apply to the adoption credit apply to adoption assistance programs. If you have over $10,000 ($5,000 for 2001, or $6,000 in the case of a child with special needs for 2001) of expenses, your employer can reimburse up to $10,000 of qualified adoption expenses, and you can claim the adoption credit for the remaining expenses, up to $10,000 ($5,000 for 2001, or $6,000 in the case of a child with special needs for 2001). If you have less than $10,000 ($5,000 for 2001, or $6,000 in the case of a child with special needs) of qualified adoption expenses, you can either claim the adoption credit for expenses or you can use your employer's adoption assistance program. You cannot claim a credit and use the adoption assistance program for the same expense. Generally, it is better to claim the credit since this directly reduces your tax.

NOTE: The $10,000 adoption credit amount will be adjusted for inflation beginning in 2003.

Stay On The IRS's Good Side By Following The Rules For Your Household Help

When you hire household help, such as a nanny, maid, or baby sitter, you may need to withhold and pay certain Federal and state employment taxes. You are not subject to these rules if:

- your help is employed by an agency or another person,
- your help is a household employee age 18 or younger during any part of the year, unless the help's principal job is household employment,
- your help is your spouse or your child under age 21,
- your help is an independent contractor, or
- you pay less than $1,300 to the person in a calendar year (for Federal unemployment tax purposes, you are exempt if your total household help wages for all employees are less than $1,000 per calendar year quarter).

If the person is your employee, here is what you need to do. There are two requirements for the initial setup. First, complete and file Federal Form SS-4 to get an employer identification number.

Second, check with your state's unemployment office to find out if you need to pay state unemployment tax. If so, file the necessary forms with the state unemployment office to receive a state unemployment number and an experience rating.

When you hire a new employee, the employee should complete Form I-9, Employment Eligibility Verification Form.

On every check you write to your employee, you should generally withhold Social Security tax if you pay this employee more than $1,300 in a calendar year. You, as the employer, must also match the amount of Social Security tax. For example, if your employee earns $2,000 and you withhold $153 ($2,000 x 7.65%) from your employee, you must also pay $153, for a total of $306. The only exception is if you pay your employee more than $80,400 during 2001 or $84,900 during 2002. You can, however, pay your employee's share of the Social Security tax. If you withhold Social Security tax but it turns out that no taxes are due, you must repay your employee.

This might happen if you end up paying your employee less than $1,300 during the year.

You do not need to withhold amounts for Federal or state income taxes unless your employee asks you to and you agree to do so.

Report the Social Security, Federal Unemployment, and any Federal income tax on Schedule H when you file your individual tax return. You must pay the taxes, including both the employee's half and your matching half of the FICA, through your estimated taxes or wage withholding.

You must also prepare Federal Form W-2 if:

- you withhold Social Security tax (because you pay your employee more than $1,300),
- you withhold Federal income tax, or
- you pay your employee more than $600.

One copy of Federal Form W-2 goes to your employee and one copy goes to the Social Security Administration along with Federal Form W-3. Give Form W-2 to your employee by January 31st, and mail the copy to the Social Security Administration by February 28th.

You must notify your employee about the earned income credit if you do not withhold Federal income tax. The notice is on Copy C of Federal Form W-2, or you can use Internal Revenue Service Notice 797. If your employee is eligible, you may need to include advance payments of the earned income credit on your employee's paycheck.

You could be subject to penalties if you do not follow the rules for your household help. This includes penalties for not filing returns, not depositing taxes, and not furnishing information statements to employees. You could also be subject to public scrutiny like the political nominees who have brought more public awareness to this issue.

The following pay record will help you keep track of each paycheck and help you summarize the information you are required to keep.

Pay Record For Household Help

Employee Name: **Year:**

Social Security Number:

Period Covered	Check Date	Check #	Gross Pay	6.2% FICA	1.45% Medicare	Total Withholding	Net Pay
Subtotal Jan. – Mar.							
Subtotal April – June							
Subtotal July – Sept.							
Subtotal Oct. – Dec.							
TOTAL YEAR							

Using A Form W-4, Set Your Withholding To The Amount Of Tax You Expect To Owe

Form W-4 is one of the many forms you complete on your first day of a new job. The Form W-4 sets the amount of Federal income tax that is taken out of your paycheck. Although you can change your Form W-4 at any time, there are some times when you must adjust your Form W-4.

Your goal should be to have the actual amount of your tax withheld. If you have too much withheld, you are decreasing your net paycheck and allowing the government to use your money interest-free. If you have too little withheld, you may need to write a big check on April 15th, and a penalty could apply.

Your Form W-4 remains in effect until you file a new form. Whenever your tax situation changes, you should complete a new form. For example, if you buy a house, have a baby, or incur large medical expenses, you probably need to change your Form W-4 to make sure the correct amount is withheld.

You must complete a new form within 10 days of the following:

- When you get divorced or legally separated, or when your spouse changes to claiming his or her own exemption on Form W-4
- When you no longer expect to provide over one half of the support of one of your dependents
- When your dependent will receive income of $3,000 in 2002 or more, unless your dependent is under age 19 or a student under age 24
- When you lose the right to claim the number of withholding allowances you previously claimed

To determine your withholding allowances, estimate your income and income tax and properly complete Form W-4. You can use the worksheets the IRS provides on the form. These worksheets provide a step-by-step approach for calculating the correct number of allowances to claim. Remember that each allowance is equal to an exemption amount of $3,000. You can use this amount as a shortcut for determining the number of allowances to claim.

If you are single, pay alimony of $6,300, make a deductible IRA contribution of $2,000, pay interest on your home mortgage of $4,000, and pay $1,400 of real estate taxes, your number of personal allowances to claim is calculated as follows:

Alimony	$ 6,300
IRA	2,000
Home mortgage interest	4,000
Real estate taxes	1,400
Total deductions	13,700
Less standard deduction	(4,700)
Subtotal	9,000
Divide by	3,000
Result (drop any fraction)	3
Add 1 exemption for yourself	1
Add 1 exemption for being single with only 1 job	1
Total number of allowances	5

If you have income other than your wages, you may want to have additional amounts withheld from your wages. This approach will save you the time and expense of filing quarterly estimated tax payments. To do this, put the additional amount you want to have withheld on Line 6 of Form W-4.

Two-earner married couples with total income more than $46,700 may wish to claim fewer withholding allowances so more tax is withheld. Generally, the payroll tax withholding tables withhold at a 15% rate to the extent that each spouse's income is less than $46,700. However, when you combine the incomes of both spouses on a joint return, the tax rate on income over $46,700 is 27%. Thus, claiming fewer exemptions causes additional tax to be withheld, helping to make up for this tax rate difference.

NOTE: File a new Form W-4 with your employer to change the amount of withholding. Your employer keeps your Form W-4 unless you claim more than 10 exemptions, in which case your employer must send your Form W-4 to the IRS. However, if you can justify more than 10 exemptions, generally you should claim them. If you do not claim them, you may have too much tax withheld from your wages.

Make Estimated Tax Payments To Avoid Underpayment Penalties

When your Federal income tax withholding is not enough to cover your Federal income tax, you should make estimated tax payments. "Quarterly payments" is another name for these payments, although the due dates are not quarterly. Usually people who are self-employed, have investment income, or receive retirement income need to make quarterly payments. Generally, if you only have wage income, you do not need to make quarterly payments.

If you do not make estimated payments and you owe more than $1,000 on April 15th, you might owe penalties. To avoid these penalties, you must have withholding or pay quarterly payments of at least 90% of your tax. You can also avoid the penalties if your withholding and quarterly payments are more than 100% of the amount of your tax liability from the previous year. This 100% rule does not apply if your income is more than $150,000.

Use the following chart to determine if you should make quarterly payments.

Do you need to make estimated tax payments? If so, how much?

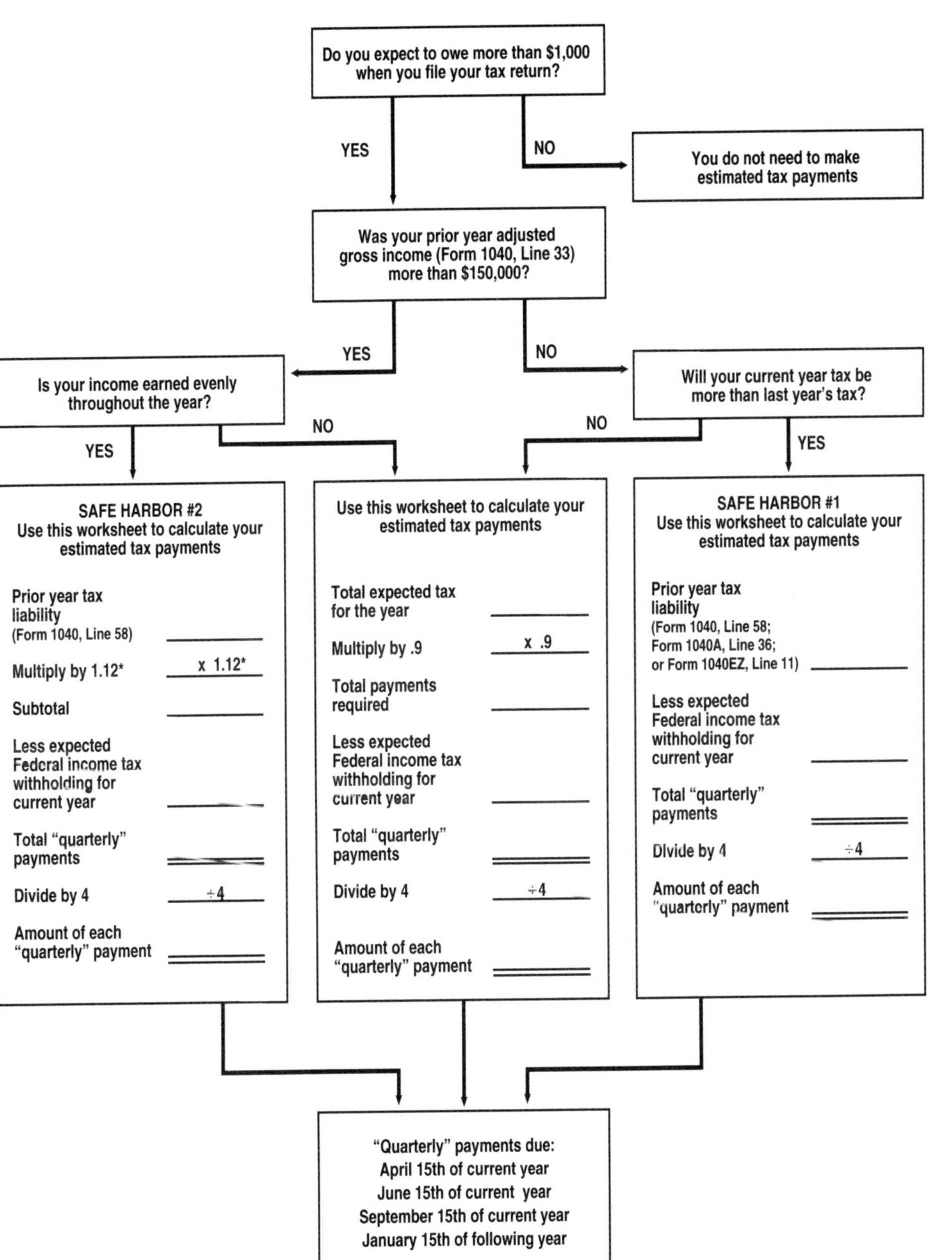

* During 2003, use 1.10 times 2002 tax liability.

If you expect to owe more than $1,000 when you file your tax return, you should make quarterly payments. Generally, you calculate your expected tax quarterly based on your income and deductions through set periods throughout the year. These periods are listed in the instructions for Form 2210.

Your quarterly payments are due on the following dates:

- April 15th of the current year
- June 15th of the current year
- September 15th of the current year
- January 15th of the following year

You may have a choice if you will owe more than $1,000 and do not want to make quarterly payments. Even if it is near the end of the year, you can increase your withholding on your wages. Do this by completing a new Form W-4 and giving it to your employer. The IRS treats your withholding as being withheld evenly throughout the year. In this way you can avoid a penalty for not withholding enough early in the year.

If you do not make quarterly payments and you owe more than $1,000, you should complete Form 2210. This form allows you to see if you meet any exceptions to the penalty. If you do not meet any exceptions, you compute the penalty. The amount is similar to interest on the balance due using the IRS's interest rates. The penalty is not deductible, but neither is the interest you pay if you borrow the money to pay your quarterly payments.

If you miss the payment date for a quarterly payment, you should make the payment as soon as possible. The penalty only applies from the due date of the payment to the date you actually make the payment.

NOTE: If your income varies throughout the year, you may wish to calculate the amount of your estimates quarterly. You can use the IRS Form 2210 Schedule AI (Annualized Income Installment Method) to make these calculations.

If You Cannot Pay The IRS, Request A Payment Plan

If you cannot pay your tax when it is time to file your tax return, you can request a payment plan. The IRS adopted this policy to encourage more people to file even if they do not have the money to pay.

To request a payment plan, you file Form 9465, Installment Agreement Request, with your tax return. You can also send this form to the IRS if they send you a notice of tax due and you are unable to pay. This form requires basic data, such as your name, address, Social Security number, telephone number, and the amount of your proposed monthly payment. The IRS will try to give you a decision on your proposed plan within 30 days.

The IRS will not tell you what minimum amount or what percentage of your amount due you must propose to pay. However, if the IRS feels your request is too low, they will contact you. Generally, your amount due must be less than $25,000 for you to qualify for the new simplified payment plan request procedures. The IRS will charge you $43 if they approve your payment plan.

When the IRS accepts your payment plan, you must pay at least the agreed upon amount every month and you must pay it on time. If your payment is late, the IRS may terminate your agreement. If you know you will not be able to pay your full payment on time, you should let the IRS know in advance. You should also let them know how much you will be paying and when you expect to pay the missed amount.

The cost of a payment plan with the IRS is interest plus the late payment penalty. As of the printing of this book, the interest rate is 6% compounded daily and the late payment penalty on approved installment plans is .25% per month. Thus, you end up paying about 9% (6% + (.25% x 12 months)). You cannot deduct this interest.

Instead of delaying your payment and paying interest to the IRS, consider borrowing money on a home equity loan. If the interest qualifies as residence interest, you can deduct the interest as an itemized deduction.

Additionally, the interest rate on your home equity loan may be lower than the IRS's rate.

The IRS allows you to pay your tax by credit card. Private-sector companies handle the credit card payments and generally charge fees and/or interest. As of the printing of this book, IRS-approved credit card companies include American Express, Discover, and MasterCard. To pay by credit card or determine the fee, call or access online one of the following service providers:

Official Payments Corporation
1-800-2PAY-TAX
www.officialpayments.com

PhoneCharge, Inc.
1-888-ALLTAXX
www.About1888ALLTAXX.com

The IRS also allows you to pay your taxes electronically at www.eftps.gov. To use this service, you must first enroll. Generally, you must initiate the payment by 8:00 p.m. ET at least one calendar day prior to the due date.

Education
Planning

Use A Qualified Tuition Savings Plan To Save Even More For College

Many states have established qualified tuition plans, also known as Section 529 plans because of the Internal Revenue Code Section that authorizes them. Each state has different rules. Beginning in 2002, schools can establish prepayment tuition plans. These plans encourage savings for post-secondary education. The tax benefits can be highly advantageous, and there are very few restrictions on establishing such savings plans.

If you set up a qualified tuition plan, you are the account owner. You name a beneficiary, without regard to the beneficiary's relationship to you or the beneficiary's age. If your beneficiary will not use any or all of the funds for education, you may designate a new beneficiary. The new beneficiary must be a member of the same family of the original beneficiary. You can also choose to withdraw the money for your own benefit.

The amount you put into a qualified tuition plan is considered a gift. Thus, if the amount you contribute, along with other gifts you give to the beneficiary during that year, is more than $11,000, you may be subject to the gift tax. See Tax Saving Idea #98. However, you can make a special election for gift tax purposes to treat amounts you contribute to a qualified tuition plan as spread over a five-year period. In other words, you can contribute $55,000 for a beneficiary, as long as you make no other gifts to that beneficiary for five years and have no gift tax consequences.

The maximum contribution you can make into a plan is set by each state or school. Many states have contribution limits in excess of $100,000. You can choose to contribute money to a state's qualified tuition plan even if neither you nor the beneficiary lives in that state.

Each state designates a professional money manager to invest the funds. Many states provide investment options when you initially establish the account. Some investors consider the conservative investment options to be a disadvantage, although the trend among plan managers is to allow investors more options. You can change your investment selection by rolling the account into another account as often as once every 12 months.

Distributions, including the earnings, from qualified tuition plans are tax-free as long as you use the money for qualified expenses. Distributions from prepayment tuition plans will be tax-free for qualifying expenses beginning in 2004.

A beneficiary can generally choose to attend any accredited college, trade school, or graduate school at any time, even if that school is in a different state than the plan.

Qualified expenses include tuition, certain room and board costs, mandatory fees, and books. If you make withdrawals for nonqualified expenses, the earnings are generally subject to a 10% penalty, and the earnings are taxable to you (the account owner). If nonqualified withdrawals are made because the beneficiary dies or becomes disabled, or because the beneficiary receives a scholarship, the 10% penalty will not apply. However, income tax on the earnings will still be due. Alternatively, you can designate a new beneficiary who is a family member of the original beneficiary. Family members include brothers, sisters, parents, children, spouse, and first cousins.

You or your child can also claim the HOPE or Lifetime Learning credit in the same year you pay expenses from the qualified tuition plan. See Tax Saving Ideas #38, #39, and #40.

You are single, have adjusted gross income of $150,000, and would like to start a college savings program for your child with $20,000. You select your state's qualified tuition plan that allows you to deduct $8,000 from your state income.

You contribute $20,000 to a qualified tuition plan, naming your child as beneficiary. You elect to spread your contributions over five years for gift tax purposes. Thus, you have not made a taxable gift, since you are electing to treat your gift as $4,000 ($20,000 divided by 5) for each of the next five years.

If your state tax rate is 6%, you will save $480 ($8,000 maximum deduction x 6%) of state income tax.

Six years from now, if the account is worth $30,000 and the plans pays $18,000 for qualified education expenses, the following results:

- Your child reports no taxable income.
- You report no taxable income.
- You pay no penalty.

The advantage of saving in a qualified tuition plan is the tax-free growth of your account and the tax deduction that may be offered by your state.

> You are in the 33% (27% Federal and 6% state) tax rate brackets. You save $10,000 per year and earn a 10% rate of return for your child who will start college in ten years. With a qualified tuition plan, you will have $159,374 for college in ten years. If you save in a taxable account, such as a mutual fund, you will have $136,222 (15% less) for college in ten years. The benefit you receive is even larger if your state offers a tax deduction for your contribution.

NOTE: The rules for each state are different. You should check the rules for the plan you are evaluating before making an investment. Each state has program booklets and Web sites to explain its program.

NOTE: If you roll a qualified tuition plan to a family member and that family member is in a younger generation, then the generation-skipping gift tax could apply.

NOTE: If you take distributions out of your qualified tuition plan and out of your Coverdell Education Savings Account in the same year totaling more than your qualified expenses, you must allocate your expenses among the distributions.

Your Scholarships May Be Tax-Free

Scholarships and fellowships generally are not included in your income. Amounts you receive from the Federal government, universities, and businesses are not taxable as long as the payments are aid to you and not a payment to you or your parents for services rendered to the payer.

Beginning in 2002, if you receive a scholarship from the National Health Services Corps or the Armed Forces Scholarship Program, the scholarship will be tax-free even if you must provide services to receive the scholarship. This tax-free scholarship applies primarily to tuition and fees and does not include room and board.

There are two conditions that you must satisfy to keep your scholarship tax-free. First, you must be a candidate for a degree at an educational institution that maintains a regular faculty, offers a curriculum, and has a regularly enrolled body of students.

Second, the amount you can exclude includes tuition and related expenses such as fees, books, supplies, and equipment required for your courses. You cannot exclude the value of room and board.

> You receive a $1,000 Pell grant from the Federal government, a $4,000 scholarship from State University, a $5,000 scholarship from ABC Corporation, a $2,000 student loan from First Bank, and $1,500 from a government-subsidized work/study job. For the year, your tuition is $6,000. You pay $1,800 for books and other school-related expenses. Your room and board is $5,000.
>
> The $10,000 of scholarships ($1,000 + 4,000 + 5,000) exceeds your tuition and related fees of $7,800 ($6,000 + 1,800) by $2,200 ($10,000 - 7,800). Thus, the $2,200 is taxable to you. The compensation from the work/study job is taxable to you. The student loan is not taxable because you must eventually repay it.

Many nonprofit educational institutions, such as universities, offer tuition waivers to the families of employees and graduate assistants. Although these programs are compensatory in nature, the value of the education received is not taxable as long as the tuition waiver policy does not discriminate in favor of highly compensated employees and the courses are taken by the employee, the employee's spouse, or the employee's dependent children. Generally, the exclusion is only available for education below the graduate level, but for graduate teaching and research assistants, the exclusion also applies to graduate courses.

There are several issues related to scholarships which frequently arise. First, if your scholarship is taxable, the income is treated as earned income. Consequently, you may have a larger standard deduction and be eligible for a deductible or Roth IRA contribution. See Tax Saving Ideas #5, #80, and #81. The scholarship income is not treated as self-employment income subject to the self-employment tax.

Second, scholarships are not considered support for purposes of determining who may claim the student as a dependent. Scholarships a child receives are simply ignored in the support calculation. This provision allows parents to continue claiming their children after they start college even though the financial aid the children receive is greater than the amount the parents provide in support.

Third, payments for educational expenses that are not tax-free scholarships may be deductible if they are job-related or excludable under an employer's educational assistance plan. See Tax Saving Idea #67.

Fourth, amounts you receive as a scholarship may reduce the amounts you can claim as a HOPE Scholarship credit or a Lifetime Learning credit. See Tax Saving Ideas #38 and #39.

You Can Use Coverdell Education Savings Accounts To Save For College And Let Your Money Grow Tax-Free

You can put $2,000 per child into a Coverdell Education Savings Account (ESA), previously called Education IRA. Similar to the Roth IRA (see Tax Saving Idea #81), you do not get a deduction at the time of contribution. However, the funds grow tax-free and are not taxed when you withdraw them to pay qualified education expenses.

The child is the owner of the ESA, and contributions may not be made to the account after the child reaches age 18. Anyone with income less than $110,000 ($220,000 if married filing jointly) may contribute to the account on behalf of the child, but contributions cannot exceed $2,000 per child per year.

By the time the child reaches age 30, the balance in the ESA must have been:

- withdrawn tax-free and penalty-free to pay for qualified education expenses,
- distributed to the child subject to tax and penalty, or
- rolled over tax-free and penalty-free by the child to the ESA of a family member.

Family members include the child's children, siblings, aunts and uncles, nieces and nephews, and the spouses of these individuals. If the child dies before reaching age 30, the balance in the ESA must be distributed within 30 days after the date of death to the child's estate.

Contributions to an ESA are phased out above certain adjusted gross income levels. For married filing jointly filers, the phase-out occurs between $190,000 and $220,000. For other filers, the phase-out occurs between $95,000 and $110,000.

Thus, you should carefully consider who should contribute the funds to the child's ESA and which type of account you wish to fund. If your income is above the phase-out levels, perhaps a grandparent, other relative, or friend with lower income can contribute to your child's ESA with money you give them. Money you or anyone else contributes to an ESA is not subject to gift tax.

Your child can take tax-free distributions from an ESA if the child uses the money for qualified education expenses. These expenses include post-secondary tuition, fees, books, and supplies even if the child is less than a half-time student. Room and board are also qualified education expenses if the child carries at least half of the normal workload for the course of study. Beginning in 2002, qualified expenses also include qualified elementary and secondary education expenses, such as tuition, fees, academic tutoring, and special needs services, as well as computers or Internet access fees during any school years of the ESA beneficiary.

Another restriction on the use of the ESA for 2001 is that if you use tax-free ESA earnings for education, you cannot use either the Lifetime Learning credit or the HOPE Scholarship credit. In other words, if the parents claim HOPE Scholarship and Lifetime Learning credits for 2001 for the child while the child is in college and graduate school, the ESA accumulations may go unused. If the parents have more than one child in college or graduate school, they can use the credits for one child and have that child roll the ESA to an ESA of another sibling. See Tax Saving Ideas #38 and #39 for more information on Lifetime Learning credits and HOPE Scholarship credits.

Beginning in 2002, you may claim the HOPE Scholarship credit or the Lifetime Learning credit for some educational expenses and use tax-free ESA earnings for educational expenses for which no credit is taken.

If you start contributing $2,000 per year at a 10% rate of return when your child is born, you will accumulate $102,318 by your child's 19th birthday. ESAs offer a way to accumulate income tax-free, similar to a retirement account. Furthermore, with the generous rollover provisions, you can shift these tax-free accumulations from family member to family member, even down to the next generation, as long as the funds are ultimately used for qualified education expenses.

You contribute $2,000 per year to your child's ESA for the six years before your child starts college. After the six years, the account balance is $16,000 ($12,000 of your contributions and $4,000 of tax-free earnings). Your child has $21,000 of higher education expenses in the first year of college.

If your child uses the $16,000 account to pay part of the expenses, your child will not be taxed on the $4,000 of earnings. Prior to 2002, if you as the parent claim a HOPE Scholarship credit for your $5,000 ($21,000 - 16,000) payment, your child will be taxed on the $4,000 of earnings, but will not be subject to a 10% early withdrawal penalty. After 2001, your child will not be taxed on the earnings and you can claim the education credit.

If your child withdraws the entire $16,000 and has only $10,000 of college expenses:

- Your child would not be taxed on your $12,000 of contributions.
- Your child would not be taxed on the portion of the earnings used for qualified education expenses of $2,500 ($4,000 x 10,000/16,000).
- Your child would owe tax and a 10% penalty on the amount that was not used for higher education expenses of $1,500 ($4,000 total earnings less $1,500 tax-free).

NOTE: Beginning with 2002 ESA contributions, you have until April 15 to make the contribution for the previous year. If you make an ESA contribution between January 1st and April 15th of the following year, you must indicate that you want the contribution to apply to the prior year or it will automatically be applied to the current year. ESA contributions for 2001 must have been made by December 31, 2001.

You Can Deduct Interest On Higher Education Loans

In 1986, Congress started eliminating deductions for personal interest. In an interesting reversal of that trend, Congress now allows you to deduct interest on student loans. You do not need to itemize deductions to benefit from the education interest deduction.

The deduction is allowed for interest you pay on loans you use to pay for qualified higher education expenses for you, your spouse, or your dependent at the time the loan was incurred. These loans could have been taken out at any time, for example, three years ago when you were in college. Qualified higher education expenses include:

- tuition,
- room and board, and
- other educational expenses, such as books and supplies.

The student must be or must have been attending college, junior college, graduate school, or certain postsecondary vocational schools at least half-time for the expenses to qualify.

The maximum deduction is capped at $2,500 per year and is subject to certain phase-outs.

The deduction phases out for married taxpayers filing jointly with incomes between $100,000 and $130,000 ($60,000 and $75,000 for 2001). For single taxpayers, the phase-out occurs between $50,000 and $65,000 ($40,000 and $55,000 for 2001). These phase-out levels will be adjusted for inflation starting in the year 2003.

In addition, for 2001, you can only deduct interest you pay during the first 60 months that interest payments are due on the loan. Months in which no interest payment is required, such as when the repayment of the loan is deferred because of graduate school, do not count against the 60-month period. For 2002 and thereafter, the 60 month limitation no longer applies.

Finally, education loans are not limited to the traditional student loan. Although loans from related parties, such as relatives, trusts, and more than

50%-owned businesses, do not qualify, any loans, including refinanced loans, used to pay for education expenses are treated as education loans.

If you used a home equity loan to pay for the education expenses, you cannot deduct the interest twice — once as student loan interest and also as home equity interest. To the extent that you are within the caps, the phase-out range, and the 60-month period, it may be preferable to deduct the interest as an education loan. Otherwise, remember that interest you pay on home equity loans you use to pay education expenses is still deductible as an itemized deduction and is not subject to the education loan limitations.

You are single with $46,000 of income in 2001 and $53,000 of income in 2002. You completed graduate school three years ago and are in your third year of 10 years of payments on your student loans from college and graduate school. You pay $3,500 of interest in 2001 and $3,300 of interest in 2002. For 2001, you can deduct education loan interest of $1,500 ($2,500 x (($55,000 - 46,000)/15,000)). For 2002, you can deduct education loan interest of $2,000 ($2,500 x (($65,000 - 53,000)/15,000)). If your income continues to rise, your interest deduction will continue to be limited by the cap and phase-outs. If you refinance your student loans using a home equity loan, you could deduct a portion of your interest payments as an education loan and the remaining portion as a home mortgage interest itemized deduction.

You Can Claim Lifetime Learning Credits For Continuing Education Courses

You can offset the costs of higher education with two credits — the Lifetime Learning credit and the HOPE Scholarship credit. See Tax Saving Idea #39 for information on the HOPE Scholarship credit.

The Lifetime Learning credit provides for a broader range of learners than the HOPE Scholarship credit, since the HOPE Scholarship credit is only available for the first two years of postsecondary education. Full-time or part-time students in undergraduate, graduate, professional, or continuing education programs at a higher education institution may use the Lifetime Learning credit.

The Lifetime Learning credit provides a nonrefundable credit equal to 20% of up to $5,000 ($10,000 beginning in 2003) of qualified expenses you pay. This credit is per taxpayer return, not per student like the HOPE Scholarship credit.

Qualified expenses include tuition and fees necessary for the enrollment or attendance of you, your spouse, or any of your dependents at a higher education institution. Expenses do not include books, sports fees (unless they are part of the degree program), activity fees, insurance expenses, transportation costs, or room and board. You must reduce your qualified expenses by scholarships, grants, and other tax-free educational benefits, but you do not need to reduce your qualified expenses by gifts, bequests, or inheritances. Higher education institutions include accredited postsecondary educational institutions that offer degree programs and are eligible to participate in student financial aid programs, i.e., colleges, community colleges, and many vocational schools.

There are limitations on using the Lifetime Learning credit and the HOPE Scholarship credit. First, the credit is phased out if you are single with adjusted gross income (AGI) between $41,000 and $51,000 or married filing jointly with AGI between $82,000 and $102,000. These amounts are adjusted annually for inflation.

Second, if you are married filing separately, you cannot claim either the Lifetime Learning credit or the HOPE Scholarship credit.

Third, for 2001, you may elect only one of the following with respect to one student: (1) the HOPE Scholarship credit, (2) the Lifetime Learning credit, or (3) tax-free distributions from a Coverdell Education Savings Account (ESA). However, if you have more than one student at the same time, you can use the HOPE Scholarship credit or tax-free ESA distributions to pay for the expenses of one student and the Lifetime Learning credit to offset the expenses of the other student.

Beginning in 2002, you may claim the HOPE Scholarship credit or the Lifetime Learning credit for some educational expenses and use tax-free Coverdell Education Savings Account earnings for educational expenses for which no credit is taken.

NOTE: The effective rate of the Lifetime Learning Credit is 20%. If you are in the 27% tax rate bracket or higher, you may receive a greater tax benefit by claiming your education expenses as a business deduction on Schedule C or an employee business expense on Schedule A, if applicable to you. Education expenses you deduct as employee business expenses are subject to the 2% floor. Because of the credit phase-outs, self-employment tax, and miscellaneous itemized deduction limitations, you must decide the best way for you.

You are single with adjusted gross income (AGI) of $34,000. To maintain your license in your profession, you must attend 40 hours of continuing education. You attend a week-long continuing education program. Your tuition is $1,000, books are $100, room is $300, travel is $380, and meals are $200.

You may claim a Lifetime Learning credit of $200 (20% x $1,000 for the tuition). The $980 of books, room, travel, and meals do not qualify for the credit. However, if you are an employee who itemizes deductions, in addition to the credit of $200, you can deduct $200 (($100 books + 300 room + 380 travel + (200 x 50%) deductible meals) - (34,000 AGI x 2%)) giving you an additional $30 ($200 x 15%) of tax savings.

If you are self-employed, your total tax rate on your business income is 30.3% (15% income tax rate plus 15.3% self-employment tax rate). Rather than claiming the credit, you could deduct the education as a business deduction on Schedule C. Your tax savings from the deduction would be $570 (($1,000 tuition + 100 books + 300 room + 380 travel + (200 x 50%) deductible meals) x 30.3% total tax rate).

Use the HOPE Scholarship Credit To Significantly Reduce The Cost Of College

The costs of higher education may be offset with two credits — the HOPE Scholarship credit and the Lifetime Learning credit. See Tax Saving Idea #38 for information on the Lifetime Learning credit.

The HOPE Scholarship credit is available for a student's first two years of postsecondary education. Either the student or the parents may claim the credit. The maximum nonrefundable credit allowed for any year is 100% of the first $1,000 of qualified expenses plus 50% of the second $1,000 of qualified expenses. In other words, the maximum annual credit is $1,500 per student, and the maximum overall credit is $3,000 per student. The credit will be indexed for inflation.

To qualify for the HOPE Scholarship credit, the student must be carrying at least one-half of the normal workload for the student's course of study. Individuals convicted of a Federal or state felony offense related to a controlled substance cannot claim the HOPE Scholarship credit.

Similar to the Lifetime Learning credit, the HOPE Scholarship credit:

- Only applies to qualified expenses, including tuition and fees necessary for the enrollment or attendance of you, your spouse, or any of your dependents at a higher education institution. Expenses do not include books, sports fees (unless they are part of the degree program), activity fees, insurance expenses, transportation costs, or room and board. You must reduce your qualified expenses by scholarships, grants, and other tax-free educational benefits, but you do not need to reduce your qualified expenses by gifts, bequests, or inheritances. Higher education institutions include accredited postsecondary educational institutions that offer degree programs and are eligible to participate in student financial aid programs, i.e., colleges, community colleges, and many vocational schools.
- Is phased out if you are single with adjusted gross income (AGI) between $41,000 and $51,000 or married filing jointly with AGI

between \$82,000 and \$102,000. These amounts are adjusted annually for inflation.

- Cannot be claimed if you are married filing separately.

Furthermore, for 2001, you may elect only one of the following with respect to one student: (1) the HOPE Scholarship credit, (2) the Lifetime Learning credit, or (3) tax-free distributions from a Coverdell Education Savings Account (ESA). In other words, for 2001, you cannot claim the HOPE Scholarship credit if you use either the Lifetime Learning credit or tax-free distributions from an ESA to pay for the student's education expenses. However, if you have more than one student at the same time, you can use the Lifetime Learning credit or tax-free ESA distributions to pay for the expenses of one student and the HOPE Scholarship credit to offset the expenses of the other student.

Beginning in 2002, you may claim the HOPE Scholarship credit or the Lifetime Learning credit for some educational expenses and use tax-free Coverdell Education Savings Account earnings for educational expenses for which no credit is taken.

> You and your wife have AGI of \$70,000 and pay the expenses of your two children in college. Your son is ending his first year and starting his second year. Your daughter is starting graduate school in the fall. The tuition for your son for the year is \$3,000. Your daughter's graduate school tuition will be \$2,500.
>
> You may claim a HOPE Scholarship credit for your son of \$1,500 (100% of the first \$1,000 plus 50% of the second \$1,000). You may claim a Lifetime Learning credit of \$500 (\$2,500 x 20%) for your daughter's first semester of graduate school. In other words, you can reduce your taxes by \$2,000 of the \$5,500 you pay in higher education expenses for the year.
>
> If you and your wife have AGI of \$92,000, your HOPE Scholarship credit would be reduced to \$750 (\$1,500 x (\$92,000 - 82,000/\$20,000)) because of the phase-outs, and your Lifetime Learning credit would be reduced to \$250 (\$500 x (\$92,000 - 82,000/\$20,000)).

The planning strategies for the HOPE Scholarship credit and the Lifetime Learning credit focus on timing your tuition payments so you receive the \$3,000 maximum HOPE Scholarship credit during your child's first two years of school. Because most college students start in the fall following graduation from high school, the HOPE Scholarship credit is usually available for two of the first three years following graduation. If tuition payments in the first semester are not at least $2,000, leading to a $1,500 credit, it may be advisable to claim the Lifetime Learning credit for the first semester and claim the HOPE Scholarship credit for the second and third years.

For both the HOPE Scholarship credit and the Lifetime Learning credit, it may make sense to pay spring semester tuition in the December before the semester begins. For the HOPE Scholarship credit, this could bunch two semesters into the high school graduation year.

In the example on the preceding page, you could claim a $500 Lifetime Learning credit for paying your daughter's fall graduate school tuition. You could increase the Lifetime Learning credit to $1,000 ($5,000 x 20%) if you pay her spring tuition in December rather than in January.

NOTE: If available, you can use scholarships, Schedule C business education deductions, or Schedule A employee business expenses for amounts over $2,000.

Allow Your Child To Claim Either The HOPE Or Lifetime Learning Credit

You can use either the HOPE or Lifetime Learning Credit to help offset the costs of higher education. However, there are limitations on using the HOPE and Lifetime Learning Credits. These credits phase out if you are single with adjusted gross income (AGI) between $40,000 and $50,000 or married filing jointly with AGI between $80,000 and $100,000. These amounts will be adjusted for inflation starting in the year 2002. See Tax Saving Ideas #38 and #39.

If you would lose part or all of these education credits due to the income limitation, you may wish to allow your dependent child to claim the credits. In this situation, you must be willing to forego claiming your child as a dependent on your tax return. Although you sacrifice the dependency exemption, your child could be able to claim the HOPE or Lifetime Learning credit. To benefit from this tax saving opportunity, your child must have a tax liability before the credit. Additionally, your child needs to meet the income limitations.

> You are married and file jointly with your spouse. Your AGI is $110,000. You pay $2,500 of tuition for your dependent daughter, who is a freshman in college. Your daughter has AGI of $17,000 from a part-time job and interest on her savings account.
>
> Here are the tax savings if you forego claiming your daughter as a dependent and your daughter claims the HOPE credit:

	Alternative 1 You claim the dependency exemption		Alternative 2 You do not claim the dependency exemption and your daughter claims the HOPE credit	
	You	Daughter	You	Daughter
AGI	$110,000	$ 17,000	$110,000	$ 17,000
Standard deduction	(7,850)	(4,700)	(7,850)	(4,700)
Dependency exemptions	(9,000)	(0)	(6,000)	(0)
Taxable income	$ 93,150	$ 12,300	$ 96,150	$ 12,300
Tax	$ 18,953	$ 1,549	$ 19,763	$ 1,549
HOPE credit*	(0)	(0)	(0)	1,500
Net tax**	$ 18,953	$ 1,549	$ 19,763	$ 49
Total family tax	$ 20,502		$ 19,812	

Thus, by foregoing the dependency exemption and allowing your daughter to claim the HOPE credit, your family saves $690 ($20,502 - 19,812). Remember to consider the state tax savings or cost on the dependency deduction.

If your daughter provides more than 50% of her support, she would be able to claim her dependency exemption. In this case, her taxable income would be $9,300 ($12,300 as shown in alternative 2 less $3,000 dependency exemption). Her tax would be $1,099 less the HOPE credit of $1,099, which is limited to her tax, and her net tax would be $0. This would increase the family savings in the example to $739 ($690 + $49).

*HOPE credit is 100% of the first $1,000 of qualified expenses plus 50% of the second $1,000 of qualified expenses.

**Tax amounts are from the 2002 Tax Tables. Using the Tax Rate Schedules to do the calculations will produce a slightly different amount.

NOTE: This idea works especially well when the parents lose the benefit of the dependency exemptions due to the phase-out.

Deduct Your Education Expenses When The HOPE Credit Is Not Available

You may be able to deduct education expenses depending on your filing status and your adjusted gross income (AGI). Qualifying expenses include tuition and related fees, but not books or room and board. Use the following charts to determine your maximum deduction.

Maximum Deduction for Single Taxpayers

AGI Per Year	2002 and 2003	2004 and 2005
Less than $65,000	$3,000	$4,000
$65,001 - 80,000	No deduction	$2,000
Greater than $80,000	No deduction	No deduction

Maximum Deduction for Married Filing Jointly Taxpayers

AGI Per Year	2002 and 2003	2004 and 2005
Less than $130,000	$3,000	$4,000
$130,001 - 160,000	No deduction	$2,000
Greater than $160,000	No deduction	No deduction

You can deduct education expenses for you, your spouse, and your dependents even if you are paying the expenses with nontaxable income from a qualified tuition plan or a Coverdell education savings account. However, if you claim a HOPE or Lifetime Learning credit for the year, you cannot also deduct the education expenses of the student for whom you are claiming the credit. Also, you cannot deduct the education expenses if you file married filing separately.

Deducting education expenses is particularly beneficial if you have too much income to claim the HOPE and Lifetime Learning credits (See Tax Saving Ideas #38 and #39). Furthermore, if your combined Federal and state tax rate is higher than 20%, you will probably receive more benefit by deducting the education expenses than by claiming the Lifetime Learning credit.

> In 2002, you and your spouse have $55,000 of adjusted gross income. You pay $5,000 in tuition and related fees for your dependent child who is a senior in college, $2,800 for your dependent child who is a sophomore in college, and $4,000 for yourself in pursuit of a graduate degree. You can claim a $1,500 HOPE credit for your sophomore's expenses, a $1,000 Lifetime Learning credit for your senior's expenses, and a $3,000 deduction for your own expenses.
>
> If you only had expenses for your two children, you would be forced to choose between the Lifetime Learning credit and the education expense deduction for your senior's expenses, because you could not claim both the deduction and the credit for the same student. If your tax rate is 22% (15% Federal plus 7% state), you would choose to deduct the expenses, since the Lifetime Learning credit is only 20%.
>
> If your income was $120,000, you could claim the $3,000 education expense deduction but not the credits, because your income makes you ineligible to claim the credits.

Investments

You Can Deduct Your Capital Losses Against Your Capital Gains

People buy investments for many reasons, such as income, hedge against inflation, status, and personal pleasure. Investments include stocks, bonds, mutual funds, U.S. Savings Bonds, certificates of deposit, and rental property.

Investments can give you two types of income. First, investments give you income such as interest, dividends, and rent. Usually, this income is taxed as ordinary income.

The second type of income from investments is the result of the investment's change in value. When investments increase in value and are sold, the increase in value is a realized capital gain. Of course, the risk of owning investments is that the investment may go down in value. When you sell an investment at a loss, you have a realized capital loss.

You combine your realized capital gains and losses from all your investments to figure your net capital gain or loss. The gain or loss from the sale of an investment that has been held one year or less is short-term. If the investment has been owned for longer than one year, the gain or loss from the sale is long-term.

Short-term and long-term capital gains and losses offset each other.

Short-term gain	$ 2,000	Long-term gain	$ 7,000
Short-term loss	(4,000)	Long-term loss	(1,000)
Net short-term	(2,000)	Net long-term	6,000

Net long-term capital gain = $4,000 ($6,000 - 2,000).

If this netting process results in short-term gain, the gain is taxed as ordinary income at rates as high as 38.6% (39.1% for 2001). If the netting process results in long-term gain, as it did above, the gain is generally taxed at a maximum tax rate of 20% (10% [8% for five-year property] if you are in the 15% tax rate bracket) rather than at ordinary income tax rates. Congress allows this special treatment for long-term capital gains to encourage investing.

NOTE: Long-term gains from the sale of collectibles, such as antiques and art, or qualifying small business investment company stock acquired at original issue after August 10, 1993, are taxed at a 28% rate. Long-term gains from the sale of depreciable real estate may be taxed at a 25% rate. Use the following chart to help determine the appropriate tax rate. (See Appendix G for the full chart.)

CAPITAL GAINS
FOR MOST NONCORPORATE TAXPAYERS

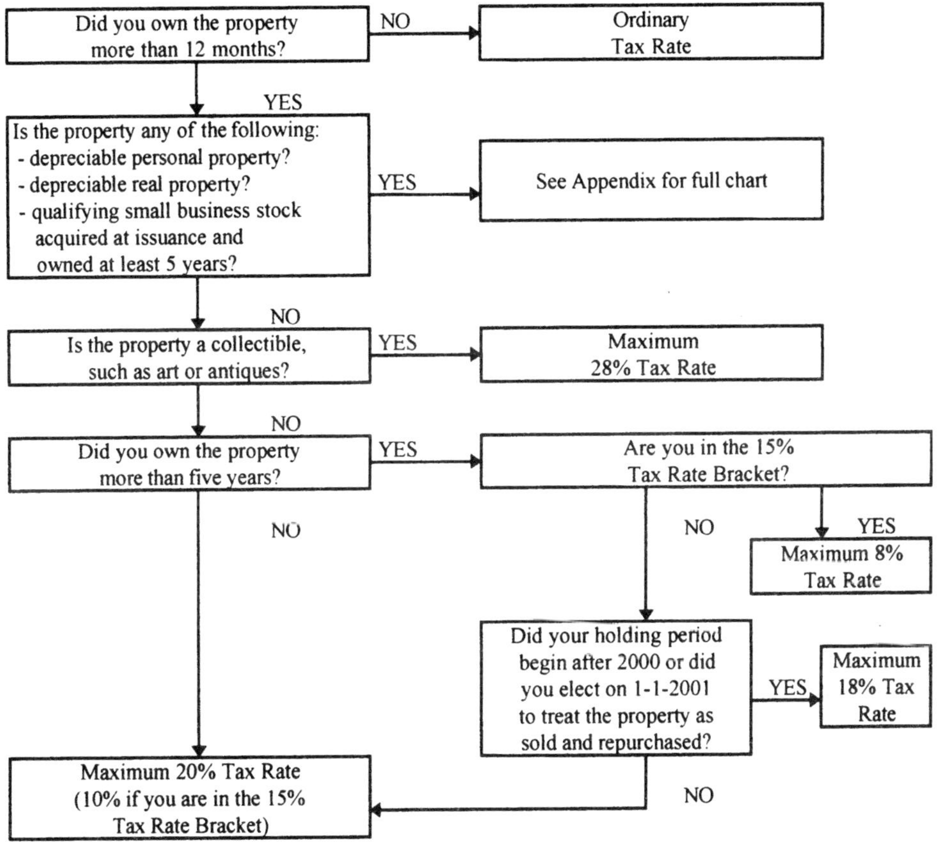

If the netting process results in a short-term or long-term capital loss, you can deduct the loss at ordinary rates up to a maximum of $3,000 per year. Losses over this amount are carried forward to future years.

In other words, long-term capital gains receive favorable treatment. Capital losses, because of the $3,000 limitation, receive unfavorable treatment. In years when you have capital losses over $3,000, avoid the deferral of your deduction by considering selling investments that have increased in value.

However, "do not let the tax tail wag the dog." In other words, you should not sell an investment you would not otherwise sell just for the favorable tax treatment.

You have owned the following stocks for 3 years:

Stock	Value Of Stock Today	Cost Of Stock
A	$2,000	$1,500
B	500	5,000
C	3,000	2,000

You sell Stock A and B. This gives you a net long-term capital loss of $4,000 (Stock A ($2,000 - 1,500 = 500 gain) plus Stock B ($500 - 5,000 = 4,500 loss)). You can only deduct $3,000 of this loss. The remaining $1,000 of long-term capital loss is carried forward to next year.

However, if you sell Stock C before the end of the year, you can deduct the full loss this year. Selling Stock C will give you a long-term capital gain of $1,000 ($3,000 - 2,000). This makes your net long-term capital loss $3,000 ($4,000 - 1,000) rather than $4,000.

However, if you think Stock C is a good investment, you should not sell it just to avoid the $1,000 carryover. Unless you die, you can deduct the $1,000 loss at some time whether you sell Stock C or not.

Special election for 2001

Beginning in 2006, the maximum long-term capital gains tax rate on most property you buy after 2000 and own at least 5 years will be 18%, rather than 20%. See Tax Saving Idea #45 for a special election that you may make on your 2001 tax return.

You Do Not Pay Tax On Investments That Appreciate Until You Sell Them

Some investments, such as bonds and certificates of deposit, give you current income that is taxed each year as you receive it. Other investments, such as land, give you little or no current income, but over time they may increase in value. This increase in value, also known as appreciation, is not taxed until the year you sell the investment. Postponing the time when you pay tax results in savings. By not selling the investment, you postpone the time when you pay the tax.

You are considering two investment options. Option 1 is a $20,000 certificate of deposit (CD) which pays 6% ($1,200) per year for two years. Option 2 is a $20,000 painting that you expect to appreciate at 6% per year. You are in the 34% (27% Federal and 7% state) tax rate bracket.

If you buy the CD: after tax, you will have $792 ($1,200 - ($1,200 x 34%)) of cash at the end of the first year. If you reinvest the $792 at 6%, you will receive $1,248 (6% x $20,792) of interest income in the second year. After tax, you will have $824 ($1,248 - ($1,248 x 34%)) in cash. When the CD matures at the end of the second year, you will have $21,616 ($20,000 + 792 + 824) from your investment.

If you buy the painting: after tax, the painting is worth $21,200 ($20,000 + (20,000 x 6%)) at the end of the first year. At the end of the second year, the painting is worth $22,472 ($21,200 + (21,200 x 6%)). If you sell the painting at the end of the second year, you will pay $840 in tax on gain of $2,472 ($22,472 - 20,000). After tax, you have $21,632 ($22,472 - 840) from your investment.

You receive $16 ($21,632 - 21,616) more from investing in the painting, which appreciates, than from the CD that pays income annually. This savings is entirely the result of paying tax on the CD income in the first year. The taxation of the interest from the CD in the first year decreases the value of your investment by $408. With the painting, this $408 is still invested.

> The $408 produces $24 of additional income in the second year. This $24 increases your after-tax wealth by $16 ($24 - (24 x 34%)).
>
> This savings is the result of deferring the payment of tax one year. If you hold the investments for ten years, you would save $948 by investing in the painting.

Examples of investments that can appreciate and do not pay income annually include:

- land,
- growth stocks that do not pay dividends,
- precious metals,
- antiques, and
- art.

There are other tax advantages of holding investments that appreciate. First, you can choose when to sell the investment. This flexibility allows you to choose a year when your tax rates are low.

Second, the tax rate on most investments that appreciate, including securities and land, is 20% (10% [8% for five-year property] if you are in the 15% tax rate bracket). The tax rate on gains from collectibles, such as precious metals, antiques, and art, is 28%. The interest income from a CD could be taxed at a rate as high as 38.6% (39.1% for 2001).

Third, you can give appreciated investments to people who have lower tax rates, such as your children. See Tax Saving Idea #98.

There may be disadvantages of holding investments, such as land, that appreciate. You might owe property taxes. The investment may not appreciate. The investment is illiquid, meaning it takes time to sell. You might also incur transaction costs, like brokerage commissions, to buy and sell the investment. With a CD, your investment is usually insured and you know when you buy the CD what return to expect.

Make Sure You Deduct All Of Your Costs When You Sell An Investment

You might think that the amount of gain or loss you have from the sale of an investment is the difference between the sales price and your purchase price. Generally, that is correct. However, there are adjustments you can make to the sales price (referred to in tax jargon as the "amount realized") and the purchase price (referred to as the "adjusted basis") that will save you money.

From your sales price you can subtract your expenses of selling the investment. These expenses might include:

- advertising,
- abstract of title,
- escrow fees,
- mortgage title insurance,
- recording fees,
- realtor's or broker's commissions, and
- legal fees.

The purchase price of the investment is also adjusted. To your purchase price, you can add expenses of purchasing the property, such as

- commissions,
- legal fees,
- recording fees,
- appraisal fees,
- closing costs, and
- improvements to the property.

The cost of the investment might also be reduced by adjustments such as depreciation.

You own a rental house that you bought for $60,000. You also paid $2,000 in legal expenses to record your ownership of the property and $15,000 to add a family room off the kitchen.

During the five years you own the rental house, you claim $12,000 in depreciation. This year you sell the investment for $100,000 and pay a realtor $8,000 to help with the sale. Many would look at this transaction and say that your gain is $40,000 ($100,000 - $60,000). However, your gain is actually much less. Your amount realized is really $92,000 ($100,000 - 8,000); and your adjusted basis in the property is $65,000 ($60,000 + 2,000 + 15,000 - 12,000). Consequently, you have a gain of $27,000 ($92,000 - 65,000), not $40,000.

Make A Special Election On Your 2001 Tax Return To Obtain A More Favorable Capital Gains Rate In The Future

The maximum long-term capital gains tax rate on most property you buy after 2000 and own at least 5 years will be 18%, rather than 20%. Thus, this 18% tax rate will first apply beginning in 2006. You can make a special election on your 2001 tax return to treat property you own as if you sold it and reacquired it on January 1, 2001 (January 2, 2001 for readily tradable securities, such as stocks). You may choose to make this election on a property-by-property basis.

You pay tax on any gain at your 2001 capital gains tax rate. If you own the property for an additional 5 years, any gain will be taxed at a maximum of 18%. There is no deduction for any loss.

You might consider making this election if:

- You are in the 15% tax rate bracket now and you expect to be in a higher bracket in the future;
- You have a minimal gain position in a stock and you expect to own the stock until at least 2006;
- You expect the stock to appreciate and you want to create a semi-installment sale by reporting the current gain in 2001 and the subsequent gain when you sell the stock;
- You have a minimal loss position in a stock, you expect the stock to appreciate, and you expect to own the stock until at least 2006 (remember that if you have a loss position on property and you make this election, you can never deduct that loss);
- You have unused capital loss carryovers that can be used to offset any capital gains as a result of this election; or
- You have investment interest expense carryovers (See Tax Saving Idea #14).

You should **NOT** make this election if:

- You believe Congress will reduce the maximum long-term capital gains tax rate from 20% to 18%; or
- You have a significant loss position in a property and you do not expect the stock to appreciate.

You are in the 30% tax rate bracket. You own the following stocks on January 1, 2001:

	Date Bought	Purchase Price	1/2/01 value
A	7-27-1960	$1,000	$100,000
B	8-4-1984	$1,000	$100
C	6-18-1994	$1,000	$1,100

You might consider making an election on your 2001 for Stock C. You will pay tax of $20 (($1,100 - 1,000) x 20% capital gains tax rate). If you sell the stock in 2006 and the value is more than $1,100, you will pay tax at only 18%.

You probably would not make the election on Stock A, since you would pay tax of $19,800 (($100,000 - 1,000) x 20%). You probably would not make the election on Stock B since your $900 ($100 - 1,000) loss would never be deductible.

NOTE: This election is only available on your 2001 tax return. You must file your 2001 tax return by its due date (including extensions). You may amend your timely filed 2001 tax return to make the election as long as you file within 6 months of the original due date of your tax return (excluding extensions). Thus, you generally have until October 15, 2002, to make a valid election.

You Do Not Have To Pay Tax On Nontaxable Dividends

Most dividends you receive on stock you own are taxable. However, some are not taxable.

The most common nontaxable dividends are:

Stock dividends and stock splits. These are additional shares of stock you get from a corporation. They are not taxable if they do not increase your percentage of ownership in the corporation. If you get a stock dividend or stock split, you must allocate the basis of your old shares between your old shares and your new shares. The holding period for the stock you receive from a stock dividend or a stock split goes back to the time when you bought your original shares. The holding period is important because it determines if you qualify for the 20% (10% [8% for five-year property] if you are in the 15% tax rate bracket) long-term capital gain tax rate. If the stock dividend or stock split is taxable, then your basis in the new shares is the fair market value of the stock when you receive it. The holding period for the new stock would then start on the date you receive the new stock.

> You own 100 shares of XYZ Company that you bought 2 years ago for $1,000 ($10 per share). XYZ Company declares a 2-for-1 stock split and you receive 100 additional shares of XYZ Company stock. This stock split is not taxable because all of the shareholders of XYZ own the same percentage of the corporation as they did before the stock split. They just own twice as many shares. Your new basis in your stock is $5 ($10/2) per share, for a total basis in your 200 shares of $1,000. Since you have owned your old stock for 2 years, you are treated as if you owned your new stock for 2 years. Thus, if you sell the stock at a gain, it will be a long-term capital gain.

Insurance policy dividends. These are rebates you get from premiums you paid on life insurance policies. They are not taxable unless the total rebates you receive are more than the premiums you paid for the policy.

Return of investment and liquidating dividends. Return of investment dividends are amounts you receive on stock you own when the company has no accumulated earnings. They are not taxable since taxable dividends must be paid from a corporation's earnings. Public utility stocks, besides paying dividends at a high rate of return, often distribute return of investment dividends that are not currently taxable. Liquidating dividends are distributions you receive in a partial or complete liquidation of the company. Both return of investment dividends and liquidating dividends are treated as a nontaxable recovery of capital and reduce your basis in your stock. Once your basis is reduced to zero, any future distributions are taxed as capital gains.

Patronage dividends. These are dividends you receive from cooperatives. The most common recipients are farmers and students. The dividends are treated as purchase rebates and reduce the cost of items purchased from the cooperative, such as feed or books. They may be taxable if you previously deducted the cost of the items.

The following dividends are taxable:

Dividends that are really interest income. Some income on deposits that are called dividends should be reported on Schedule B of your tax return as interest income. Examples include dividends from:

- cooperative banks,
- credit unions,
- savings and loans, and
- mutual savings banks.

On the other hand, the income from money market fund accounts, which is often called interest income, should be reported as dividend income. The proper reporting of interest and dividend income is important because misreporting this income can trigger a notice from the IRS when the IRS cannot match what you report with the information they have received. Responding to these notices is time consuming.

Capital gain distributions. These are distributions you get from your mutual funds. They are taxable as long-term capital gains. Many mutual funds make these payments in December. Capital gain distributions are taxable even if you reinvest the dividends and do not actually get the cash.

Reinvested dividends. Many publicly held corporations maintain dividend reinvestment plans which let you buy additional shares through reinvestment of dividends and, in some cases, through optional cash payments. The amount of dividends reinvested is treated as a dividend received and is taxable. The dividends are taxable even though you do not physically receive the cash or the stock.

You Can Select One Of Several Options For Calculating Gain Or Loss When You Sell Shares In A Mutual Fund

People invest in mutual funds for a variety of reasons. Mutual funds usually offer higher rates of return than certificates of deposit, are run by professional managers, reduce risk through diversification, and offer a smorgasbord of investment alternatives. Mutual funds usually have specific objectives. Some focus on common stocks or growth stocks while others invest in bonds, international securities, or precious metals.

Favorable tax rules apply to distributions from mutual funds and sales of mutual fund shares. Distributions from mutual funds may include:

- ordinary dividends,
- capital gain distributions,
- tax-exempt interest dividends,
- return of capital (nontaxable) distributions, and
- allocations of undistributed capital gain.

Ordinary dividends are treated as dividend income even if you receive them from a mutual fund that invests in interest-bearing accounts, such as a money market fund. This rule applies even if the dividends are reinvested and you do not receive any cash. If your dividends are reinvested, the basis of your newly acquired shares is the amount of the dividends reinvested. Some dividends represent interest from U.S. obligations, such as Treasury Bills, and are exempt from state taxation. Your mutual fund information will usually tell you if any of the income is from U.S. obligations.

Capital gain distributions represent net realized long-term capital gain. You report them as long-term capital gains no matter how long you own the shares in the mutual fund. You combine these distributions with your other capital gains and losses on Schedule D (Line 13).

Tax-exempt interest dividends are tax-exempt interest amounts you receive from a mutual fund. Tax-exempt interest dividends are exempt from Federal tax because they are from state and local bonds. The dividends may also be exempt from state tax if they are from your home state. Your mutual fund usually tells you the amount of tax-exempt interest from each state.

Although tax-exempt interest dividends are not taxable, you must show the amount of tax-exempt interest dividends received on your return. If you receive tax-exempt interest dividends, your Social Security benefits may be taxable and you may owe alternative minimum tax.

Return of capital distributions are not paid out of a corporation's earnings. Thus, they are not treated as ordinary dividends. Instead, they are nontaxable and reduce your basis in the shares of the mutual fund. If you have no basis in your mutual fund shares, you must treat the distributions as a capital gain. These distributions may be long-term or short-term depending on how long you have owned the shares.

Allocations of undistributed capital gain occur when a mutual fund retains long-term capital gains and pays taxes on them. You must still report these amounts as income even though you do not receive a distribution. You can take a credit for any tax paid by the mutual fund on the undistributed capital gain. Your basis in the mutual fund shares increases by the difference between the undistributed capital gain you include in your income and the tax credit that passes through to you. The mutual fund uses Form 2439 to report the amount of undistributed capital gain and any tax paid.

You receive Form 2439 from your mutual fund. The form shows that the mutual fund did not distribute a capital gain of $1,000 and paid tax of $280. You need to include the $1,000 as a capital gain and claim the $280 as a credit for taxes paid on your return. Your basis in your mutual fund shares increases by $720 ($1,000 - 280).

Losses inside the mutual fund reduce your income from the fund. This treatment is one of the tax advantages of owning mutual funds rather than stocks and bonds. If you have a net loss from the sale of a stock or bond, your deduction may be limited to $3,000 per year. However, when losses are incurred inside a mutual fund, the losses are indirectly allowed in full.

When you sell or exchange your mutual fund shares, you generally have a taxable gain or loss. Exchanges occur when you trade your shares for shares in another mutual fund. Gains or losses from exchanges of shares of one fund for shares in another fund are taxable even if the funds are part of the same family of funds.

Generally, the rules for determining gain and loss from the sales of shares in a mutual fund are the same as for other stock transactions. You compare your sales price to your basis. As with any security transaction, you can specifically identify the shares you sell. If you do not identify the shares you sold, you are treated as selling the shares you have owned the longest time first. This approach is called the first-in, first-out method.

For mutual funds, there is an important alternative method you can use to calculate your basis. You can average the cost of your shares. The government allows this method only for mutual funds because mutual fund shares are frequently acquired in different quantities, at different prices, and at different times.

There are two averaging methods: single-category or double-category. Under the single-category method, the average cost of your shares is calculated as follows:

The total basis of all your shares in the fund ÷ The total number of shares you own

If you use the single-category method, you are treated as selling the oldest shares first. If you owned the oldest shares longer than one year, you will have a long-term capital gain or loss from the sale of those shares.

Under the double-category method, your shares are split between long-term and short-term. The long-term average is calculated by dividing the total basis of all your shares owned longer than one year by the total number of those shares. The short-term average for shares owned one year or less is calculated similarly. If you use the double-category method, you can specify which category of shares — long-term or short-term — you sold. If you do not specify, your long-term shares are considered sold first.

Once you choose one averaging method to use for a mutual fund, you must always use that method for that specific fund. However, you can use a different method for other mutual funds.

Many mutual funds will provide you average cost basis information when you sell shares. Be sure to compare the average cost basis method to the other methods to assure it is appropriate for your situation.

You have considerable flexibility in determining the amount and type of gain and loss in the first year you sell a portion of your mutual fund shares because of these options.

You acquired three lots of 100 shares of Anchor Mutual Fund as follows:

100 @ $12 on 1/2/98
100 @ $16 on 1/2/99
100 @ $20 on 1/2/02

On April 5, 2002, you sell 150 shares for $15 per share. Depending on the method you use to determine your adjusted basis, you could end up reporting gain or loss.

If you use the first-in, first-out method, you have long-term capital gain (LTCG) of $250 (($15 x 150) - (($12 x 100) + ($16 x 50))).

If you use the specific identification method to identify the most recently bought shares as the first ones sold, you have a short-term capital loss (STCL) of $500 (($15 x 100) - ($20 x 100)) and long-term capital loss (LTCL) of $50 (($15 x 50) - ($16 x 50)). You can control the amount and type of gain or loss.

If you use the single-category averaging method, the average cost for all your shares is $16 ((($12 + $16 + $20) x 100)/300). Because the oldest shares are considered sold first, you would have a $150 LTCL (($15 x 150) - ($16 x 150)) under the single-category method.

If you use the double-category method, the average cost for the long-term shares is $14 ((($12 + 16) x 100)/200). The average cost for the short-term shares is $20. If you treat the short-term shares as sold first, then you would report $500 STCL (($15 x 100) - ($20 x 100)) and $50 LTCG (($15 x 50) - ($16 x 50)). If you treat the long-term shares as sold first, then you would report $150 LTCG (($15 x 150) - ($14 x 150)).

NOTE: Because of dividend reinvestments and undistributed but taxable capital gains, many people unintentionally pay too much tax when they sell their mutual fund shares. Be sure to keep accurate records and consider all of the activity in your mutual fund before calculating your gain or loss when you sell your shares.

With Taxable Bonds, You Can Choose When To Report Your Interest Income

Bonds are debts (IOU's) of corporations, the U.S. government, and state, county, and municipal governments. Bonds represent money you lend to the organization. You purchase bonds primarily for the interest you can earn. You may also buy bonds for the potential for appreciation (increase in value) due to changes in the market interest rate. The risk of owning bonds differs based on the financial strength of the bond issuer.

Generally, the interest income from bonds is taxable when you receive it. If you purchase a bond at par (the bond's eventual redemption price) and hold it until maturity, then you will recognize no gain or loss when the bond matures. However, bonds are often:

- not held until maturity,
- bought at a discount or premium rather than at par, and
- bought on the secondary market rather than when they were originally issued.

Consequently, bonds are often sold at a gain or loss.

Accrued interest

If you buy a bond on the secondary market, you will often have to buy accrued interest from the seller. This is because you generally buy the bond sometime between the dates the bond pays interest. You can deduct the accrued interest you pay against the first interest income payment you receive on the bond.

You buy a bond with a $10,000 par value on March 1, 2002 for $10,300. The bond pays 6% interest on January 1 and July 1. Since it is 2 months through the interest period, you must pay an additional $100 ($10,000 x 6% x 1/2 x 2/6 months) in accrued interest.

On July 1, you receive $300 ($10,000 x 6% x 1/2 year) in interest income. You deduct the $100 in accrued interest you paid from the $300 you receive. Thus, you have $200 in net interest income for 2002. When you report this on your tax return, be sure to list both the income of $300 and the deduction of $100 on Schedule B.

If you sell the bond on January 1, 2004 for $10,500, you will have a gain of $200 ($10,500 - 10,300). Since you owned the bond for more than one year, you have a long-term capital gain. Since you sold the bond on an interest payment date, you will not receive any payment for accrued interest. However, you will still receive your $300 in interest income.

Bond discounts

When the interest rate actually paid on a bond is lower than the market interest rate, the bond will sell or be issued at a discount. For example, if a bond that will mature at $10,000 is paying a 10% rate of return and the market rate is 12%, the bond will sell for less than $10,000 (a discount). The market (potential buyers) will drive the value of the bond down until the equivalent rate of return is 12%. The length of time to maturity, the taxability of the bond, and the riskiness of the issuer influence the actual amount of the discount.

Original issue discount (OID) bonds are offered at prices less than the amounts at which they will mature.

For example, you will pay $4,632 for a newly issued 8% OID bond that will mature in 10 years for $10,000.

The difference between $4,632 and $10,000 is taxable unless the bond was issued by a state or local government. It is interest income that you will recognize over the ten years until the bond matures. As the interest is recognized, your basis in the bond increases.

You will report $371 ($4,632 x 8%) in interest income in the first year. The basis of the bond increases to $5,003 ($4,632 + 371). In the second year, you will report $400 ($5,003 x 8%) in interest income, and the basis of the bond will increase to $5,403 ($5,003 + 400).

NOTE: Although you do not receive any cash, you must report this interest as income on Schedule B of your Form 1040.

OID bonds are appealing because they usually are affordable and offer good rates of return. However, because of the disadvantage of being taxed on income you have not yet received, you may want to own them in a nontaxable account, such as an individual retirement account (IRA) or a 401(k) plan.

Market discount bonds are bonds purchased at a discount from someone other than the issuer. In other words, you buy the bonds on the secondary market.

You will usually get interest income in cash each year from a market discount bond. You are taxed on this interest income. You also receive interest income from the discount as the bond gets closer to maturity. Unlike OID bonds, you do not report the income from the discount until the bond matures. You can elect to report the income currently, but most people choose to wait. This option of taxing the income now or waiting until the bond matures is a key advantage of investing in market discount bonds.

You buy an 8% bond for $9,503. The bond is selling at a discount because the market rate is 10%. The bond was originally issued in 1995 for $10,000. It will mature in 2004 for $10,000. You will receive and pay tax on $800 ($10,000 x 8%) in interest income each year. You also receive income from the discount of $497 ($10,000 - 9,503) when the bond matures. You can report the $497 as interest income in 2004 when the bond matures.

Alternatively, you can choose to report the $497 as interest income over the next three years ($150 for 2002, $165 for 2003, and $182 for 2004).

Bond premiums

Bond premiums are the opposite of bond discounts. A bond will sell or be issued at a premium when the interest rate actually paid on a bond is higher than the market interest rate. If a $10,000 bond pays 10% and the market rate is 9%, the bond will sell for more than $10,000 (a premium). The market (potential buyers) will drive the value of the bond up until the equivalent rate of return is 9%. As with bond discounts, the length of time to maturity, the taxability of the bond, and the riskiness of the issuer influence the actual amount of the premium.

Taxable bonds issued at a premium are tax-wise investments because you can choose either to spread the deduction for the premium over the life of the bond or to claim a loss in the amount of the premium when the bond matures. Spreading the deduction over a number of years is called amortization. For tax-exempt bonds, you must amortize the bond premium. You do not have the choice you have with taxable bonds.

Most people choose to spread the premium deduction over the life of the bond because the deduction reduces the amount of interest income they report each year.

You purchase an 8% bond for $5,185 in 2002. The bond is selling at a premium because the market rate is 6%. The bond was originally issued in 1999 for $5,000 and will mature in 2003 for $5,000. In 2002, you will receive $400 ($5,000 x 8%) from the bond issuer. However, you only have to report $311 of the $400 as taxable interest because you can claim an amortization deduction of $89 ($400 - ($5,185 x 6%)). For 2003, you would only report $304 of the $400 as taxable interest ($400 - (185 - 89)).

Alternatively, you can choose to report interest income of $400 for 2002 and $400 for 2003. You would then claim a long-term capital loss deduction in 2003 of $185 ($5,185 - 5,000) for the unamortized premium.

Depending on the issuer, bonds are a moderately safe investment that usually pay a rate of return higher than CDs. When you buy bonds, take advantage of the opportunities you have to deduct accrued interest and premiums and to defer interest income from discounts.

You Can Defer And Possibly Exclude Interest Income From U.S. Savings Bonds

U.S. Government Savings Bonds (Series E before 1980 and Series EE after 1979) are a popular, low-risk investment. They are issued at a price less than face value (a discount) and are redeemable for fixed amounts that increase at stated intervals. You do not receive actual interest payments. When you redeem savings bonds, you report the difference between the purchase price and the redemption amount as interest on your Federal return. U.S. Savings Bond interest is not subject to state income tax.

There are several special advantages of Series E and EE savings bonds. First, you can defer paying tax on the interest until the bond matures. Alternatively, you can elect to report the interest income each year.

Because of this choice, savings bonds are an ideal planning tool for young and old. Parents often buy savings bonds for young children. By choosing to report the interest each year while the income is sheltered by the child's $750 standard deduction, parents assure the income will not be taxed when the child redeems the bond. Generally, when the child finally redeems the bond, the child has enough earnings to be subject to tax. Thus, you avoid paying tax on the interest. If the child's income is subject to tax at the parent's marginal tax rate because the child is under age 14 and has over $1,500 of investment income, the election to report interest each year is not made. Instead, you defer payment of the tax on the savings bond income until the savings bond is redeemed. Similarly, the elderly usually defer reporting the income from savings bonds until they retire and are subject to lower tax rates.

A second advantage of savings bonds is that you can further defer the taxation of Series EE bonds by exchanging them within one year of maturity for Series HH bonds. Although the interest on the Series HH bonds is taxed each year, the previously accrued but not-yet-taxed interest on the Series EE bonds is deferred until the Series HH bonds mature.

Educational savings bonds

You can exclude the interest from Series EE bonds issued after 1989 if the bonds are redeemed to pay higher education expenses. You must be at least 24 years old and use the redemption proceeds to pay the higher education expenses — tuition and fees at an educational institution — for your dependent, your spouse, or yourself.

If the redemption proceeds (both principal and interest) you get are more than your education expenses, you can only exclude part of the interest. Furthermore, the exclusion is phased out (reduced proportionately) at the following levels of modified adjusted gross income. Modified adjusted gross income is your adjusted gross income plus the interest income from the Series EE bonds.

	2001 Phase-Out Range	2002 Phase-Out Range
Single or Head of Household	$55,750 - 70,750	$57,600 - 72,600
Married filing jointly	$83,650 - 113,650	$86,400 - 116,400

These phase-out amounts are adjusted annually for inflation. Once your income is above this range, you are not eligible for the exclusion. Married couples filing separately are not eligible for the exclusion at all.

You bought Series EE bonds in 1999 for $6,000. In 2002, you pay higher education expenses of $6,435 with the $7,150 ($6,000 of principal and $1,150 of interest) in redemption proceeds from these qualified savings bonds. You are married, file jointly, and have modified adjusted gross income of $90,000. On your Federal return, $911 of the $1,150 is nontaxable. First, only $1,035 (($6,435 ÷ 7,150) x 1,150) is eligible for exclusion because the redemption proceeds are more than the higher education expenses. Second, the exclusion is further reduced by the phase-out. Of the $1,035, only $911 ($1,035 x ((116,400 - 90,000)/(116,400 - 86,400))) is actually excluded. Thus, $239 (($1,150 - 1,035) + ($1,035 - 911)) is taxed as ordinary income.

On your state return, the entire $1,150 in interest is nontaxable.

You Can Buy Municipal Bonds And Not Pay Tax On The Interest Income

Interest income from most bonds issued by state and local governments is exempt from Federal income tax. Some bonds, called private activity bonds, are subject to Federal income tax or the alternative minimum tax. This happens when the proceeds are used to finance nonessential governmental activities such as a sports arena or an industrial park.

Although the interest from state and local government bonds is exempt at the Federal level, states generally tax the interest from these bonds. However, states usually do not tax the interest from bonds issued within that state.

Your broker can tell you if your bond is a private activity bond or is taxable by your state.

Many investors think that tax-exempt bonds are investments for the wealthy. Tax-exempt bonds are appealing to high tax rate bracket investors, but they are also advantageous to investors with middle incomes. To determine if a tax-exempt bond is advantageous for you, you need to compare the after-tax yield of the taxable and tax-exempt bonds.

> You are in the 27% Federal tax rate bracket and the 5% state tax rate bracket. You are thinking about investing in a tax-exempt bond that has a yield of 4% and is exempt from Federal regular and alternative minimum tax and from state tax. A comparable taxable bond yields 5.7%.
>
> The equivalent taxable yield of 5.9% can be approximated by dividing the tax-exempt bond yield by one minus the Federal and state marginal tax rates (4/(1 - (.27 + .05)) = 5.9%).
>
> If the bonds are of comparable quality, you should purchase the tax-exempt bond. If the bond had not been exempt from state tax, the equivalent yield would have been 5.5% (4/(1 - .27)) and the taxable bond would have been preferable.

You can use the table below to determine whether a tax-exempt bond will pay you a better return than a taxable investment. The table considers only Federal tax. A taxable investment must pay a higher rate than the yield shown if the tax-exempt bond you are comparing is also exempt from state tax.

Equivalent yield on a taxable bond

	Yield on a tax-exempt bond			
Federal Tax Rate bracket	4%	6%	8%	10%
10%	4.4%	6.7	8.9	11.1
15%	4.7	7.1	9.4	11.8
27%	5.5	8.2	11.0	13.7
30%	5.7	8.6	11.4	14.3
35%	6.2	9.2	12.3	15.4
38.6%	6.5	9.8	13.0	16.3

If you are in the 15% tax rate bracket and you are comparing a tax-exempt bond that pays 6% to a taxable investment that pays 6.5%, you will pick the tax-exempt bond because it pays an equivalent yield of 7.1% compared to the taxable investment of 6.5%.

NOTE: If you are receiving Social Security benefits, tax-exempt interest income may cause your benefits to be taxed. See Tax Saving Idea #4 to determine if your Social Security benefits are taxable.

You Can Use Options To Defer Gains

Options are contracts that grant you the right to buy (referred to as a call option) or sell (referred to as a put option) property at a set time and price. The property covered by the contract might be property listed on an exchange including stock, commodity futures, or a broad-based stock index, such as the Standard and Poor's 500 Index. The option might also cover unlisted property, such as real estate.

Investors buy and sell options for many reasons. For example, a buyer who wants to buy land might use an option to hold the land until the buyer has the money to buy the land. Options are also used as a hedge to decrease risk. A farmer might buy an option to "lock in" a selling price for wheat the farmer is growing. Finally, many investors speculate in options, buying and selling them as stock is bought and sold.

The tax treatment of options varies depending on whether you are the seller or the buyer of the option and whether the option expires, is exercised, or is sold or exchanged.

You own 100 shares of OMB stock. You receive $500 for selling a call option to Buyer. The call option allows Buyer to buy 100 shares of OMB stock before a set date (October 19) at a set price ($110 per share).

If the option expires because the stock price does not reach $110, then you have short-term capital gain of $500 and Buyer has a short-term capital loss of $500.

If Buyer exercises the option and buys the stock, you increase your sales proceeds by the amount received for the option, and Buyer treats the amount paid for the option as part of the purchase price. In other words, you are treated as receiving $11,500 ($500 + (110 x 100 shares)) for the OMB stock. Buyer is treated as having paid $11,500 for the stock.

Calls and puts fluctuate with the market. Their price is affected by the value of the underlying property, the amount of time before the option expires, and all the factors that influence the securities markets. If you sell the option, then both you and the buyer treat the gain or loss as you would any other property transaction. If, in the example above, the price of the OMB call option drops to $300, then Buyer might close the transaction by selling an identical call option to someone else. Buyer would have a capital loss of $200 ($300 - 500).

The transaction described in the example is a common investment strategy, called a covered call. You own the OMB stock. By selling the call, you receive $500. If the option expires, you are $500 ahead, less the tax on the gain. Many investors use this strategy to increase the return on their stock.

The risk of a covered call is that the price of the OMB stock may go over $110. Then, you might be forced to sell the OMB stock to Buyer. You could avoid this forced sale by buying an option identical to the one you sold. If the price is different, you will have a loss. However, you will not need to sell the stock because the two options cancel each other.

Another common strategy allows you to defer gain from the sale of stock. This strategy uses a put option. If you buy a put option, you can force the seller of the option to buy the stock at a set price on a certain date.

You own 100 shares of GDM stock. You purchased the stock for $75 per share on December 28, 2002. On December 1, 2003, GDM is trading for $95 per share. Fearing that the price might drop, but not wanting to recognize the gain in 2003, you buy a put option for $100 that allows you to make the seller of the put buy the stock for $95 per share on January 20, 2004.

If the stock is trading at $95 or above on January 20, 2004 you will let the put expire, recognizing a $100 short-term capital loss.

If the stock is trading at $91 per share on January 20, 2004, you will exercise the put. The seller of the put is forced to buy the GDM stock for $9,500 ($95 x 100 shares). You are treated as receiving $9,400 (($95 x 100) - 100 (paid for the put)) for the GDM stock. You have a short-term capital gain of $1,900 ($9,400 - 7,500) which you report for 2004, not 2003. You cannot use puts to convert short-term capital gains to long-term capital gains.

Using puts this way is an effective strategy to defer gains to the following year and to reduce the risk of holding a volatile stock.

Many people shy away from options because they hear they are risky. The two strategies described here are not as risky as some because you cannot be forced to buy stock. With covered call options, you receive money for selling the option, but you might lose some gain if you are forced to sell your stock because the price of the stock goes over the option price. When you buy a put option, you pay the cost of the option, but you are protected from a decrease in the price of the stock.

You are taking a risk when you:

- sell call options and do not own the stock,
- buy call options for speculation, or
- sell a put option.

Many people do it, but you might end up buying stock you cannot afford.

You Can Deduct Your Losses From Worthless Stock

You can deduct your basis in a stock or bond that has become worthless. You treat the security as if it was sold on the last day of the year in which it became worthless.

Usually the loss is a long-term capital loss. However, if the stock is small business stock, it may qualify for ordinary loss treatment.

You may have just learned that the stock you bought eight years ago became worthless five years ago. Normally you can only amend tax returns you filed in the last three years. However, in the case of worthless securities, you can amend tax returns you filed in the last seven years.

The stock or bond must be entirely worthless to take the deduction. Suffering a significant decrease in value is not enough. You can prove that the stock or bond is entirely worthless by proving that the stock or bond had value in the year before the loss year. Generally, an identifiable event must have caused the loss in the deduction year. These events might include:

- the company went bankrupt,
- the officers of the company cannot be found, and
- letters to the company are returned with no forwarding address.

You bought stock in XYZ Company in 1998 for $5,000. In 2003, you learn that the company went bankrupt in 1999. You can amend your 1999 tax return to deduct your loss on the stock. The loss will be a capital loss unless it is qualifying small business stock. You can deduct up to $3,000 of net capital losses each year. So, unless you had other capital gains in 1999, you can deduct $3,000 on your 1999 tax return. You can also amend your 2000 tax return to deduct the remaining capital loss of $2,000 ($5,000 total loss less $3,000 loss deducted in 1999). It is helpful to attach a copy of the bankruptcy notice to your amended 1999 and 2000 returns to support your deductions.

Investing In Small Business Stock Has Its Advantages Whether You Sell The Stock At A Gain Or A Loss

Congress encourages investment in small business stock, also known as Section 1202 stock. First, if you acquire qualified small business stock at issuance and hold the stock for five years, you are taxed on only 50% of the capital gain. Your maximum tax rate on the gain is 28%, but after the exclusion, your maximum effective tax rate is 14% (28% x 50%). See Tax Saving Idea #42. Second, if you sell the qualified small business stock, you can avoid paying tax on any gain by reinvesting the proceeds in additional qualified small business stock. You must have owned the original small business stock for at least six months. You have 60 days after the sale to buy new qualified small business stock.

To be qualified small business stock, the stock must be issued after August 10, 1993, and the total assets of the corporation at start-up cannot exceed $50,000,000. Furthermore, only certain businesses qualify. For example, the company must be an active business and cannot just hold investment assets, such as stocks, bonds, and real estate. Additionally, the company cannot engage in a service-type business, such as accounting, law, engineering, and medicine, or be in the business of banking, insurance, farming, or operating a motel or restaurant.

> You buy $125,000 of qualified small business company stock. After five years, you sell the stock for $205,000. You have $80,000 ($205,000 - 125,000) of long-term capital gain. Fifty percent of the $80,000 gain is tax-free, and the remaining 50% is taxed at a 28% rate. Thus, your tax is $11,200 ($40,000 x 28%).
>
> You can avoid recognizing the $80,000 gain by reinvesting the $205,000 in new qualified small business stock within 60 days.

NOTE: If you exclude 50% of the gain on the sale of qualified small business stock, 42% of the excluded gain is an item of tax preference for the alternative minimum tax. See Tax Saving Idea #28.

If you sell your business at a loss or if it becomes worthless, ordinary loss treatment is crucial. You cannot deduct net capital losses greater than $3,000 in the current year. You can carry them over to future years, but each year they are subject to the $3,000 maximum capital loss deduction. On the other hand, ordinary losses are not subject to the $3,000 annual limit.

Section 1244 of the Internal Revenue Code was enacted to help small businesses attract financing. Under Section 1244, you can deduct up to $50,000 ($100,000 if you are married and file a joint return) of loss as ordinary loss rather than capital loss. Only the first $1,000,000 of money and property put into a corporation for stock qualifies for the ordinary loss treatment. Also, more than half the corporation's gross receipts for the past five years must be from business operations, not dividends, interest, rents, royalties, or gains from the sale of securities.

> You are single. You start a corporation that sells furniture. You invest $200,000. You sell the stock for $110,000 three years later. You lost $90,000 ($200,000 – 110,000). If the stock qualifies as small business stock under Section 1244, you can deduct $50,000 as ordinary loss and $3,000 as capital loss. A long-term capital loss of $37,000 ($90,000 - 50,000 - 3,000) is carried over to future years. However, if the stock does not qualify as small business stock under Section 1244, you can only deduct $3,000, with an $87,000 carry-over to future years.
>
> NOTE: If you marry before the end of the year you sell the stock, you can deduct the full $90,000 loss as an ordinary loss, since a married couple filing a joint return can deduct up to $100,000.

You Can Deduct Your Nonbusiness Bad Debts As Short-Term Capital Losses

If you loan money to a friend or family member and you are not repaid, you can deduct the unpaid amount as a nonbusiness bad debt. Nonbusiness bad debts receive short-term capital loss treatment. Because the loss is treated as a capital loss, the maximum amount you can write off for the year is $3,000. Any excess loss is carried over to future years subject to the $3,000 maximum deduction per year.

You claim the deduction in the year the debt becomes worthless. Although it is not necessary for you to initiate legal proceedings against the borrower or for the borrower to declare bankruptcy, those events usually indicate that you cannot collect the debt. Other indicators of worthless debt include the disappearance of the borrower or notification in writing from the borrower that the debt will not be repaid.

When you loan someone money, the most important thing you can do is have the person sign a note. The note should show the amount of money loaned, the date of the loan, a reasonable interest rate, and the date the loan is to be repaid. Both you and the borrower should sign the note showing your agreement with the terms.

Many people are reluctant to get documentation for a loan because they are afraid of offending the borrower. Often, the borrower is a close friend, relative, or significant other. It is with these close relationships that it is most important to have a signed loan document. When the IRS disallows deductions for bad debts, it is usually because they view the loan as a gift. They will argue that because of the close relationship and lack of documentation, you did not intend to collect the loan. Furthermore, if the need arises, it is easier to collect a loan through the courts if you have a signed note.

NOTE: If you are in the business of making loans for a profit or you have accounts receivable in your business, you can deduct the bad debts as ordinary losses. This treatment is better than the short-term capital loss treatment of nonbusiness bad debts.

You Can Reduce Your Tax By Investing In Rental Real Estate

Although the deduction of most "passive" losses is limited, you can reduce your taxable income by deducting up to $25,000 of losses from rental real estate. In 1986, Congress stepped up its attack on tax shelters (investments that produce tax losses) with the enactment of the "passive loss rules." Before 1986, many people invested money in tax shelters, such as real estate ventures, oil and gas operations, and farming businesses. The people did not get personally involved in the tax shelters, but they did use the losses from the tax shelters to reduce the tax on their salary and investment income.

The passive loss rules stop you from using losses from tax shelters to reduce your income from wages, interest, and dividends. If you have a loss from a passive investment (an investment that you spend less than 500 hours per year managing), you can only deduct the loss if you have income from another passive investment. Any losses you cannot deduct in the current year are suspended and carried over to the following year. The loss is deductible in a future year when you have passive income or sell the passive investment. In other words, the passive loss rules do not take away your loss; they just postpone the deduction to a future year.

With the rental real estate exception, you can deduct a loss equal to your passive income plus $25,000 every year. Naturally, there are several conditions you must meet before you can take this rental real estate deduction. First, you must own more than 10% of the real estate investment for the entire year. Thus, if you are a limited partner in a real estate partnership and you own 5% of the partnership, you cannot use the special $25,000 deduction.

Second, you must "actively participate" in the rental of the real estate. Active participation is not measured in hours. It is determined by the decisions you make. If you approve new tenants, decide rental terms, collect and deposit rent checks, and approve expenditures for repairs and improvements, you actively participate in the rental of the real estate.

Third, the $25,000 loss you can deduct is reduced by one half of your adjusted gross income (AGI) over $100,000. In other words, if your AGI is less than $100,000, you can use the full $25,000 special deduction. If your AGI is between $100,000 and $150,000, the $25,000 loss you can deduct is reduced by 50% of your AGI over $100,000. Thus, if you have $130,000 of AGI, your loss deduction is limited to $10,000 ($25,000 - ((130,000 - 100,000) x 50%)). Finally, if your AGI is more than $150,000, you cannot use the $25,000 exception at all ($25,000 - ((150,000 - 100,000) x 50%) = $0). Any losses that you cannot deduct because of this AGI limitation are suspended and carried over for deduction in future years.

You are single with $75,000 in AGI. You own a duplex that you rent to two tenants. You actively participate in the management of the rental property. Your income and deductions for the year are described below:

Rental income		$ 24,000
Deductions:		
Interest	(16,200)	
Real estate tax	(4,000)	
Insurance	(1,000)	
Repairs and miscellaneous	(2,000)	
Depreciation (200,000 x 3.636%)	(7,272)	
Total deductions		(30,472)
Loss from rental		(6,472)
Tax rate (Federal and State)		x 32%
Tax savings		$ 2,071
Cash flow from the duplex:		
Rental income		$ 24,000
Tax savings		2,071
Less:		
Principal (assumed)		(1,200)
Interest		(16,200)
Real estate taxes		(4,000)
Insurance		(1,000)
Repairs and miscellaneous		(2,000)
Net cash flow		$ 1,671

On paper, the rental of the duplex shows a loss of $6,472. However, the loss is the result of your depreciation deduction of $7,272. Depreciation is an expense you can deduct for the wear and tear on your rental property. You can depreciate a residential rental property over 27.5 years. The deduction has nothing to do with an actual change in the value of the property. Also, except for the initial purchase price of the property, depreciation does not require a cash outlay.

Your cash flow, after considering the tax savings from the loss you deduct on your tax return, is a positive $1,671. If you pick the right property,

- you have an investment that is giving you cash,
- your tenants are paying the mortgage and other expenses for you, and
- the value of the duplex is increasing.

If you are a real estate professional, such as a developer, and operate your rental properties as a business, you can deduct the full amount of your real estate losses. In other words, you avoid the $25,000 limitation discussed above. To qualify, you must:

- spend more than half of your time in real property trades or businesses, and
- spend more than 750 hours during the year in real property trades or businesses.

Avoid Tax By Trading Your Property For Similar Property

When you are ready to sell your property, you may want to trade it for similar property to avoid paying tax on the gain in that year. Such trades are called like-kind exchanges, tax swaps, or 1031 exchanges. With a qualifying exchange, you can defer the gain until you sell the new property.

To qualify as a like-kind exchange, you must use the property you give and the property you receive either for business or investment purposes. Business property includes business equipment or a warehouse, and investment property includes a rental home or appreciating land. You can trade a business property for another business property, a business property for an investment property, an investment property for a business property, or an investment property for another investment property. Property you use personally, such as your car or home, does not qualify for like-kind exchange treatment. Inventory, foreign real estate, partnership interests, and securities also do not qualify for like-kind exchanges.

If you trade personal property, such as a truck you use in your business, you must receive the same type of property (another truck). You cannot trade the truck for dissimilar property, such as a computer.

The rules are more relaxed for real estate. For example, you can trade a warehouse for an apartment building. You can also trade improved real estate, such as a building, for unimproved real estate, such as raw land.

With like-kind exchanges, the gain or loss does not go away forever; it is postponed. Eventually you may recognize the gain or loss, since you must adjust your basis in your property for the postponed gain or loss. You also consider how long you owned the property you gave in the like-kind exchange when you later sell the property you received to determine whether your gain or loss is long-term or short-term.

You own an apartment building that is worth $100,000. You purchased the building 10 years ago for $90,000. You deducted depreciation of $30,000, so your basis in the building is now $60,000.

Ted owns land that he acquired 20 years ago for $125,000 that is now worth $100,000.

You and Ted exchange your properties. You will not recognize your gain of $40,000 ($100,000 of land value you receive minus your $60,000 basis in the apartment building), and Ted will not recognize the loss of $25,000 ($100,000 of apartment building minus $125,000 basis in the land).

Your basis in the land is $60,000 even though its fair market value is $100,000, and your holding period is 10 years. Your $40,000 ($100,000 - 60,000) gain is postponed. If you later sell the land for $110,000, your taxable gain will be $50,000 ($110,000 - 60,000). Ted's basis in the apartment building is $125,000, and Ted's holding period in the building is 20 years. Ted's $25,000 ($100,000 - 125,000) loss is postponed. If Ted later sells the building for $105,000, Ted's deductible loss will be $20,000 ($105,000 - 125,000).

In the above example, you probably preferred the like-kind exchange because it allowed you to postpone recognizing gain. However, Ted probably would have preferred to sell the property in order to recognize the loss. By working with a third party or an exchange organization, you can both accomplish your goals. Ted could sell the land to the third party, recognizing the $25,000 loss, and you could conduct the exchange with the third party, avoiding recognition of the $40,000 gain. In order for an exchange with a third party to qualify, it is important that you meet certain strict time limits. You must identify the property you will receive within 45 days, the exchange of the properties generally must occur within 180 days of the transfer of your property to the third party, and the deal must be structured properly (usually using an escrow agent).

Boot is taxable

Because the properties traded are seldom exactly equal in value, cash or other non-like-kind property, referred to as boot, is often traded as part of the exchange. If you pay boot as part of the exchange, you increase your basis in the property you receive by the amount of boot you pay. If you receive boot in the exchange, you must report your gain to the extent of the boot because the government now views you as having the ability to pay tax. You increase your basis by the amount of gain you recognize, but you reduce your basis by the amount of boot you receive. Thus, in many cases, your basis is unchanged.

You own a warehouse that is worth $100,000. You purchased the warehouse for your business five years ago for $85,000. You deducted depreciation of $15,000, so your basis in the building is now $70,000. Sally owns land that she acquired 20 years ago for $30,000 that is now worth $90,000.

You and Sally exchange your properties. Because your warehouse is worth more than Sally's land, Sally gives you the land and $10,000 ($100,000 - 90,000) cash.

Your potential gain from the exchange of the warehouse is $30,000 ($90,000 of land plus $10,000 cash minus your $70,000 basis in the warehouse). You will recognize gain of $10,000, the lesser of the $30,000 gain and the $10,000 boot. You will not recognize the remaining gain of $20,000 ($30,000 potential gain minus the $10,000 gain you must recognize because you received boot). Your holding period in the land is 5 years, and your basis in the land is unchanged at $70,000 ($70,000 basis in the warehouse minus $10,000 of boot plus $10,000 for the gain recognized). Another way to view this basis adjustment is that you have $90,000 of land, but still have $20,000 of gain to recognize from the exchange. Thus, your basis in the land is $70,000 ($90,000 worth of land minus the $20,000 of postponed gain).

Sally's potential gain in the land is $60,000 ($100,000 of warehouse minus the $10,000 boot and the $30,000 basis in the land). Sally will not recognize this $60,000 gain. Sally's holding period in the warehouse is 20 years, and Sally's basis in the warehouse is $40,000 ($30,000 basis in the land plus $10,000 boot). Another way to view Sally's basis adjustment is that Sally has a $100,000 warehouse, but still has $60,000 of gain to recognize. Thus, Sally's basis in the warehouse is $40,000 ($100,000 of warehouse minus $60,000 postponed gain).

When there is an outstanding loan on the property and it is assumed as part of the exchange, it is treated as cash (boot) received by the person who is relieved of the debt. In other words, you treat transfers of debt included in a like-kind exchange as cash and, thus, recognize gain. In the example above, if you take out a $10,000 loan on your warehouse, the net value of your warehouse is $90,000, the same as Sally's land. If Sally agrees to pay off your loan, Sally does not need to give you $10,000 to make the exchange fair. Nonetheless, you are still treated as receiving $10,000 cash meaning the tax consequences of the transaction as far as recognized gain and basis are the same as above for both you and Sally.

NOTE: Like-kind exchanges between related parties are taxable if either of the parties dispose of the property within 2 years of the exchange date.

Defer Your Gains From The Sale Of Property Using The Installment Method

When you sell property, you normally receive payment and report your gain or loss from the property in the same year. It is possible, using the installment method, to spread the gain over more than one year. With an installment sale, you do not receive all of the cash from the sale in the year you sell the property. Instead you receive a down payment in the year of the sale and receive a promissory note for payments in future years. Because you do not have the cash to pay the tax on the sale, the government allows you to defer reporting the gain. Thus, you pay tax on the gain when you receive the future payments.

The amount of gain you report each year is based on the amount of cash you receive during the year.

$$\frac{\text{Total gain}}{\text{Contract price}} \times \text{Cash received} = \text{Gain to be reported}$$

Your total gain is calculated by subtracting your basis in the property from your sales price. Your contract price is the amount of cash you will receive from the down payment plus the future cash payments on the promissory note. Cash received is the cash you receive for the year, not including interest income on the note. Any interest income you receive is taxed as ordinary income in the year you receive it.

NOTE: If you have a loss from an installment sale, you must recognize the entire loss in the year of the sale.

You sell land on January 1st that you bought ten years ago as an investment. You paid $20,000 for the land. You sell the land for $100,000. The buyer agrees to pay you $30,000 today and $35,000 per year for the next two years plus interest on the unpaid balance at 8%. In the first year, you receive:

Down payment $ 30,000

You have $80,000 ($100,000 - 20,000) of total gain on the sale of the land. The amount taxable in the first year is calculated as follows:

($80,000 ÷ 100,000) x 30,000 = $24,000

Thus, you must report $24,000 of long-term capital gain from the sale of the land in the first year.

In the second and third years, the amount of gain you will report is calculated as follows:

($80,000 ÷ 100,000) x 35,000 = $28,000

You will report the $80,000 ($24,000 + 28,000 + 28,000) of total gain over three years instead of reporting it all in the year of sale. You must also report the interest income you receive from the buyer in the years you receive it.

You can increase the amount of cash you get in the first year by reducing the contract price. The contract price is the amount of cash you will receive on the promissory note. If the buyer assumes a loan you have on the property, then the amount of cash the buyer will pay and the contract price decrease. When the total gain and the contract price are the same, every dollar received is taxed to you as gain. You can structure your sale so that the total gain and the contract price are the same by borrowing against the property before the sale and having the buyer assume the loan.

You sell land that you bought ten years ago as an investment. You paid $20,000 for the land. You sell the land for $100,000. Prior to selling the property, you borrow $20,000 from the bank using the property as collateral. The buyer agrees to assume the loan. The buyer also agrees to pay you $10,000 today and $35,000 per year for the next two years plus interest on the unpaid balance at 8%. In the first year, you receive:

Loan proceeds	$20,000
Down payment	10,000

Comparing this transaction to the above example, the buyer is still paying you $100,000 for the land ($20,000 (assumed loan) + 10,000 + 35,000 + 35,000). You still have $80,000 ($100,000 - 20,000) of gain from the sale of the land. However, the amount taxable in the first year is calculated as follows:

($80,000 ÷ 80,000) x 10,000 = $10,000

You still receive $30,000 in cash, but $20,000 came from the bank and only $10,000 came from the buyer. In the first year, you now report long-term capital gain of $10,000, a reduction of $14,000 ($24,000 - 10,000). You are not taxed on the cash you receive from the loan. At a 27% tax rate, you reduce your tax in the first year by $3,780 ($14,000 x 27%). You will pay this tax in the second and third years because all of the $35,000 received in those years is taxed. You still pay tax on a gain of $80,000, but the timing is different because the loan assumed by the buyer reduces the cash you receive from the buyer. You also must report the interest income you receive from the buyer in the years you receive it.

Installment sales are an important planning tool, but not all sales qualify for installment sale treatment. For example, you generally cannot sell inventory or stock using the installment sale method. Also, if you are selling property you have depreciated, you generally cannot defer the gain from the previously claimed depreciation.

There are also other requirements. You must charge a reasonable interest rate on amounts to be paid in the future. Furthermore, if you sell property to a relative who sells it within two years, you must report your remaining gain at that time.

Generally, you must use the installment sale method if your sale qualifies. However, you can elect not to use the installment sale method. This election may be a good idea if you expect to pay tax at higher tax rates in future years.

Homes

Compare The Pros And Cons Of Renting Versus Owning A Home

People buy homes for a variety of reasons. Some people look at a home as a place to live and focus on the nonfinancial advantages of owning it. These advantages include privacy, comfort, and neighborhoods.

Others look at a home as an investment and focus on the financial and tax aspects. They view a home as a hedge against inflation and see themselves building equity in a property that is increasing in value. They point to the tax advantages of home ownership, including:

- the deductibility of interest and taxes, and
- the opportunity to exclude gain from the sale of a home.

Despite these advantages, many people still choose to rent, citing the many disadvantages of home ownership. The disadvantages include:

- the initial cash outlay to purchase a home,
- illiquidity of the investment,
- the expense of repairs,
- the expense and cost in leisure time of maintenance,
- immobility,
- increasing real estate taxes, and
- market uncertainty.

Renters also point to the amenities available at many rental complexes, such as swimming pools, exercise rooms, hot tubs, and clubhouses.

It is no wonder so many people ask: "Should I rent an apartment or buy a home?" The answer depends on you and your goals. Do you want to buy a home for the comforts or to reduce your tax? Do you expect to move soon?

It is easy to overanalyze the decision. Nonetheless, as you analyze the financial aspects of the decision, there are some assumptions you need to watch.

Many people use a shortcut approach to show the tax advantages of owning a home. With the shortcut approach, you divide your monthly rent by one minus your income tax rate (monthly rent/(1 - tax rate)). This calculation shows the house payment you should be able to pay. In other words, if you are paying rent of $730 and paying tax at a 27% Federal tax rate, you will have cash flow similar to owning a home with a $1,000 house payment ($730/(1 - .27) = $1,000).

Although this approach makes the point that you can deduct part of your house payment, it goes too far. Not all of your house payment is deductible. Furthermore, if you claim the standard deduction, you are getting a deduction without making a cash payment. You only get itemized deductions by making cash payments. See Tax Saving Idea #5.

The best way to figure out how much tax you will save is to calculate your tax first as a renter and second as a home owner.

You and your spouse earn $70,000. You are currently renting an apartment for $730. You are looking into buying a home for $120,000. If you put $12,000 down, your house payment includes the following:

	Monthly		Annual
Interest*	$ 705 x 12	=	$ 8,460
Principal*	88 x 12	=	1,056
Real estate taxes	125 x 12	=	1,500
Hazard insurance	51 x 12	=	612
Mortgage insurance	31 x 12	=	372
Payment	$ 1,000 x 12	=	$ 12,000

*Interest and principal were calculated using an 8%, 30-year mortgage of $108,000. The allocation between principal and interest varies monthly. Thus, the principal was based on the decrease in the mortgage amount after five years.

Your Federal tax with and without the home is calculated below:

	Rent		Own
Income	$70,000		$ 70,000
Deductions:			
Interest	0		(8,460)
Real estate taxes	0		(1,500)
Other itemized deductions	0		(4,500)
Standard deduction	(7,850)		(0)
Exemptions	(6,000)		(6,000)
Taxable income	$56,150		$ 49,540
Tax	$ 8,963		$ 7,168
Tax savings		$ 1,795	

By buying the home, you reduce your tax $1,795, or about $150 per month. However, your cash outflow is $120 ($1,000 - 150 - 730) more per month if you buy the home.

The tax savings is not $270 per month as the shortcut approach would lead you to believe. The actual reduction is less because only the interest and tax portion, $830, of your $1,000 monthly house payment is deductible. Also, under the renting option, your standard deduction of $7,850 is more than your itemized deductions of $4,500. Thus, you are receiving $3,350 ($7,850 - 4,500) of deductions without a cash outlay when you rent.

You should also consider your cash flow over the time you own the home. Below is a comparison of cash flows from renting and buying for five years:

Cash flow	Rent	Own
Down payment	$ 0	$ (12,000)
Closing costs (assumed)	0	(2,000)
Monthly payments		
$730 x 60 months	(43,800)	
$1,000 x 60 months		(60,000)
Tax savings (1,795 x 5 years)	0	8,975
Sale of home		
Sale price if 3.5% appreciation	0	142,522
Mortgage payoff	0	(102,720)
Closing costs and commission	0	(12,000)
Earnings from cash savings from renting		
Earnings on down payment and closing costs (($12,000 + 2,000) at 6% after-tax)	4,735	0
Earnings on extra $120 cash flow (($1,000 - 150 - 730) x 60 months at 6% after-tax)	1,172	0
Net cash flow	$ (37,893)	$ (37,223)

This cash flow analysis suggests you are better off buying a home since you have less cash outflow if you buy the house. However, if you use a 3% increase in the value of the home instead of 3.5%, you would have been better off renting. You can get more sophisticated with the analysis, but your conclusion usually depends on your assumptions.

In the end, when it comes to deciding whether to rent or own, the answer frequently comes from the heart, not the head.

You Can Exclude Up To $500,000 Of Gain From The Sale Of Your Home

When you sell your home for more than you pay for it, you have a gain. You do not pay any tax on the gain if:

- you, or your spouse if you file a joint return, own and live in your home for at least two years of the five years before you sell your home,
- your gain is less than $250,000 ($500,000 if you are married filing a joint return), and
- you have not excluded gain on the sale of another house during the two years before you sell your current house.

Thus, in many cases, the full amount of your gain will be tax-free. The exclusion applies each time you sell a home, but generally no more than once every two years. However, if you depreciated your home for either business or rental use after May 6, 1997, the exclusion does not apply to the depreciation portion of the gain.

If you have not owned and lived in your home for the necessary two-year period, you may still be able to exclude your gain. If you sell your home because of your health, a change in your employment, or unforeseen circumstances (as determined by the Internal Revenue Service regulations), your available exclusion is based on the portion of the two years you meet the requirements.

> You are single and own the home that you have lived in for six months. Your employer is transferring you to a new location. You paid $120,000 for your home and you sell it for $190,000. The maximum amount you can exclude is $62,500 ($250,000 x 6 months/24 months). Since your gain is $70,000 ($190,000 sales price - $120,000 cost), you only pay tax on $7,500 ($70,000 gain - $62,500 exclusion). If you lived in your home for one year, you would not pay any tax on the $70,000 gain, since your exclusion would be $125,000 ($250,000 x 12 months/24 months).

Even though you can exclude up to $250,000/$500,000 of gain from the sale of your home, it is still important to keep records of your home improvements so that you can calculate your gain. These records are particularly important if you previously sold a home and rolled over the gain into your current home under the pre-May 7, 1997 rollover rules. In this case, you must reduce the basis in your current home by the gain you previously deferred. If you do have a gain from the sale of your home, be sure to include all of the improvements you made to your old home in the basis. Examples of improvements include:

- New room additions and modernizations of old rooms
- Landscaping
- Security systems and exterior lighting
- Decks, hot tubs, and swimming pools
- Carpeting and drapes
- Storm windows and doors
- Water and air filtration systems
- New furnaces, water heaters, and roofs

NOTE: This $250,000/$500,000 exclusion generally applies to homes sold after May 6, 1997. It replaces the old rules for rolling over the gain on the sale of your home and the one-time $125,000 exclusion of gain after age 55.

If Your Home Is Declining In Value, Convert It To Business Or Rental Use

Generally, if you sell your primary home for less than you paid for it, you cannot deduct the loss. However, you can deduct a loss if the property is rented out or used for business. Thus, if you are renting out your home or using part of your home for business when you sell it, you can deduct a loss. This principle of converting to business or rental use also applies to other property, such as cars and computers, that you use entirely or partly for business.

If you convert your home to business or rental use, you can depreciate the part of your home you use to produce income and claim a loss when you sell your home. The basis for depreciation and for calculating the loss is the lower of your home's basis or fair market value when you convert it to business use.

> You bought your home in 1994 for $80,000 ($70,000 for the home and $10,000 for the land). You tried without success to sell your home in 2001. Your home appraised for $75,000 ($65,000 for the home and $10,000 for the land) when you began renting it out in January 2002. On November 20, 2004, you sell your old home for $66,000.
>
> As part of your rental expenses, you can deduct depreciation expense on $65,000 (the lower of $65,000 or $70,000).
>
> Assume you claimed depreciation deductions of $6,200 during the three years of rental. You can deduct a loss of $2,800 ($66,000 - (75,000 - 6,200)) for 2004. By converting your home to rental property in 2002, you made it possible to claim depreciation and loss deductions you otherwise could not have claimed.

You Can Deduct Your Home Office Expenses

Generally, the only expenses you can deduct for your home are interest and real estate taxes. However, if you use part of your home for business, you can deduct part of your utilities, insurance, and repair costs. You can also deduct depreciation on the portion of your home you use for business. Depreciation is an expense you can deduct for the wear and tear on your home when you use your home to produce income.

You do not have to own your home to benefit from deductions for the business use of your home. If you rent a home, condo, or apartment, you can deduct the portion of your rent, utilities, and insurance that relates to the business use of your home. However, you cannot take a deduction for depreciation.

Here is how you can deduct business expenses for using your primary home.

- As your main place of business for any business you run. If you use a room, usually an office, in your home only for business on a regular basis, you can deduct the expenses related to the room. Thus, if you are a writer or an artist and you use your home office as your place of work, you probably can take a home office deduction. You also can use your home office as an administrative office and do your work someplace else, as long as you have no other fixed location to do administrative work. Thus, doctors (who perform their primary duties in hospitals), salespeople (who spend time in customers' offices), and painters and other tradespeople (who spend most of their time at job sites) can probably take a home office deduction.
- As a place to meet or deal with patients, clients, or customers in the normal course of your business. You must physically meet with people in your home office and not use the room for personal purposes. Making business phone calls from your home is not enough.
- As a place to store inventory you use in your business. If you regularly use an area of your home to store inventory that you sell from your home by mail or delivery, you can deduct expenses for

the portion of your home you use to store the inventory. Storing old records from a business you conduct elsewhere does not qualify.

- As a place to store product samples for your trade or business.
- As a day care facility. You must use your home regularly to provide day-care services for children, persons 65 or older, or persons who are physically or mentally incapable of caring for themselves. Your day care facility must be certified or exempt from certification. Generally, if you use your home to provide day care, your deduction is based on the portion of your home that is used, as well as the amount of time in a day the home is used.

You can also deduct the expenses of an unattached, separate building you use only for business. Barns and garages are examples of separate structures that frequently qualify.

To calculate your deduction, you first gather your home expenses. You can deduct all the expenses that relate directly to the business area of your home. Examples include the cost of repairs to the room and the cost of painting the room. You can also deduct the portion of your indirect expenses that relates to the business-use portion of your home. Indirect expenses include mortgage interest, real estate taxes, insurance, security, utilities, and repairs and maintenance.

Many people calculate the business-use portion by dividing the square footage of the business area by the total square footage of the home. It is also acceptable to base your business percentage on the number of rooms used for business compared to the total number of rooms in your home. Use the method that gives you the higher business-use percentage.

> You use a room in your home as an office. The room measures 14 x 16 (224 square feet). The room is one of eight rooms in your home. The total square footage of your home is 2,240 square feet. Using the square footage method, you can deduct 10% (224/2,240) of your indirect expenses. Using the number of rooms method, you can deduct 12.5% (1/8) of your indirect expenses. You can deduct more expenses using the number of rooms method.

If you own your home, you can also depreciate the portion of your home you use for business based on the business-use percentage. Multiply the cost of your home, not including land, by your business-use percentage. This is the business-use portion of your home. You can depreciate the business-use portion of your home over 39 years (31.5 years if you started to use your home for business before May 13, 1993).

Your deductions for the business use of your home cannot be more than the income from your business. If your deductible home expenses are greater than your business income, then two things happen. First, you must prioritize the home expenses you can deduct. The ones deductible first are itemized deductions that you can deduct anyway, such as mortgage interest and real estate taxes. Next are home expenses that usually are not deductible and do not affect the basis of your home, such as repairs and utilities. The last expense you deduct is depreciation.

Second, you carry forward the expenses you cannot deduct this year because you do not have enough income. You can use this carryforward against future income from your home business.

You are employed full-time and also operate a second business from your home. You use a room in your basement, which is 15% of the home's square footage, on a regular basis exclusively for your second business.

Your income from the second business is $10,000. Your business expenses, other than home office expenses, total $7,000. For the year, you pay the following home-related expenses:

- Real property taxes of $2,000,
- Mortgage interest of $8,000,
- Utilities and other operating expenses of $1,500, and
- Repair of the wall in your home office of $1,000.

You purchased your home for $120,000, of which $20,000 is allocated to land. Your business income and home office deductions are determined as follows:

Business income	$ 10,000
Less: Other business expenses	(7,000)
Subtotal	3,000
Less:	
Taxes (2,000 x 15%)	(300)
Interest (8,000 x 15%)	(1,200)
Subtotal	1,500
Wall repair	(1,000)
Utilities and other expenses (1,500 x 15%)	(225)
Subtotal	275
Depreciation (($100,000 x 15%)/39 years = $385) limited to remaining income	(275)
Net business income	$ 0

Depreciation expenses of $110 ($385 - 275) are not allowed in the current year. You can use the $110 of deductions to reduce your income from the second business in the following year if your income is greater than your deductions.

You calculate your home deductions using Form 8829. The deduction transfers to Schedule C of your Form 1040. The deductible home expenses reduce your self-employment tax and your adjusted gross income.

NOTE: The portion of your home you use for business is generally not eligible for the $250,000 ($500,000 if you are married filing a joint return) exclusion when you sell your home. An exception is if you do not use any portion of your home for business for at least two of the five years immediately before you sell your home. In that case, the $250,000 ($500,000 if you are married filing a joint return) exclusion can apply. Any gain up to the amount of depreciation you take on your home office is taxed at 25%, whether or not the $250,000 ($500,000 if you are married filing a joint return) exclusion applies. On the other hand, if you sell your home for a loss, you should use part of the home for business, because you can deduct losses on business property but not personal-use property. See Tax Saving Idea #60.

You Can Significantly Reduce Your Costs Of Owning A Vacation Home By Renting Out The Vacation Home

You can deduct the interest expense and real estate taxes on both your primary home and a second home. To qualify as a home, the property must have sleeping accommodations, cooking facilities, and a toilet. The second home for many people is a vacation home, such as a cabin at the lake, a condo in a ski resort, a beach house, a recreational vehicle, or a boat with living quarters.

You can significantly reduce the costs of owning a second home if you rent out the home. By renting the home to others, in addition to deducting interest and taxes, you can deduct part of the cost of utilities, insurance, and maintenance and repairs. You can also deduct depreciation expense for the part of the year you rent out the home. The disadvantage of renting out your vacation home is tenants do not take care of the home the way you would.

There are two sets of rules that apply to homes you use personally. First, if you rent out your primary home or second home for less than 15 days, you do not pay tax on the rental income and you cannot claim deductions.

> When the city's hotels were full for the Super Bowl, you rented your home to a family who came to see the game. You charged $2,000 for 8 nights. The $2,000 is tax-free. You are not required to report the income on your return and you cannot deduct any rental expenses.

The second set of rules applies if you rent out your home or second home for more than 14 days. The emphasis switches from how much you rent the home to your personal use of the home. If you use your home personally for more than 14 days or 10% of the rental days, whichever is greater, then you cannot claim expenses greater than your income. In other words, you cannot claim a loss from renting your primary home or second home if you personally use the home a lot.

If you use the home less than 15 days or 10% of the rental days, whichever is greater, you can deduct expenses in excess of your rental income. The home is treated as a rental home, and subject to the passive loss rules (see Tax Saving Idea #55), you can claim a loss.

In calculating your rental deductions, you cannot deduct expenses related to your personal use. You also must take the deductions in a certain order. The first deductions you can take are the ones you can take anyway, such as mortgage interest and taxes. The second deductions you can take are operating expenses, such as utilities, insurance, and repairs and maintenance. Finally, you can deduct depreciation.

To calculate your income or loss from renting out a home, you can use one of two methods — the Court Method or the IRS Method. The only difference between the two methods is the way they treat the deduction for interest and taxes. Under the Court Method, you determine the rental portion of interest and taxes by dividing the number of rental days by the 365 days in a year. Under the IRS Method, you determine the rental portion of interest and taxes by dividing rental days by the total of rental and personal-use days. Both methods are demonstrated in the example below.

You use your vacation home for 54 days during the year and rent it out for 146 days. Your rental income is $14,600 ($100 x 146 days). Your expenses are interest of $12,000, taxes of $2,000, utilities of $2,400, and insurance of $800. You bought the home for $150,000 ($130,000 for the home and $20,000 for the land).

	Court Method	IRS Method
Rental income	$ 14,600	14,600
Deductions:		
Interest and taxes		
(($12,000 + 2,000) x 146/365)	(5,600)	
(($12,000 + 2,000) x 146/(146 + 54))		(10,220)
Utilities and insurance		
($3,200 x 146/(146 + 54))	(2,336)	(2,336)
Income before deduction for depreciation	6,664	2,044
Depreciation expense		
(($130,000/27.5) x 146/(146 + 54))	(3,451)	
Limited to income of $2,044		(2,044)
Rental income	3,213	0
Deductions for interest and taxes on Schedule A		
($14,000 - 5,600)	(8,400)	
($14,000 - 10,220)		(3,780)
Total reduction in income	$ (5,187)	$ (3,780)
Difference	$ (1,407)	

In this example, you can deduct $1,407 more depreciation under the Court Method than under the IRS Method. At a 27% tax rate, you will save $380 ($1,407 x 27%).

The Court Method is advantageous here because your personal use is more than 14 days and 10% of your rental days. Consequently, your rental deductions cannot exceed your rental income. Because the Court Method allows you to prorate your deduction for interest and taxes over 365 days instead of the 200 (146 + 54) days of rental and personal use, your rental income is more than your rental deductions, including all of your depreciation expense. The interest and taxes that are not deductible as rental expenses are still deductible as itemized deductions on Schedule A.

Under the IRS Method, you allocate more of your interest and taxes to the rental property. As a result, your rental deductions are more than your income and $1,407 of your depreciation deduction is disallowed.

In this example, you are better off using the Court Method because your deductions are limited if you use the IRS Method. In many cases, however, you are better off using the IRS Method. The IRS Method shifts interest and taxes to deductions in arriving at adjusted gross income (AGI). If your rental deductions are not limited to your rental income because you did not personally use the home too much or you have more rental income than deductions, you save more tax by deducting interest and taxes as deductions in arriving at AGI. When you lower your AGI, you can deduct more medical and miscellaneous deductions. You may also reduce your state income tax since many states use AGI as the starting point for their tax calculations.

Decide which method is best for you in the first year you deduct rental expenses. You cannot switch methods from year to year. Most people use the Court Method because they want to use the home themselves.

How much does it cost to own a vacation home? Referring again to the example above, your cash flows are as follows:

Outflows: Interest	$ 12,000
Taxes	2,000
Utilities	2,400
Insurance	800
Principal paid on loan	
($100 per month assumed)	1,200
	18,400
Inflows:	
Rent	14,600
Tax savings using the Court Method	
($5,187 x 27%)	1,400
	16,000
Net cash outflow	$ 2,400

Ignoring the costs of acquiring the vacation home and using the rental assumptions above, it costs you $2,400 per year to own a vacation home you use personally for 54 days. If you did not rent out the vacation home, you would pay $14,620 ($18,400 - ((12,000 + 2,000) x 27%)) per year.

There are additional advantages of renting out vacation homes. You can deduct trip expenses, such as transportation, to maintain your home. Furthermore, days you spend maintaining your home do not count as personal-use days.

There are also some things to watch if you own a vacation home. Use of the vacation home by any family member counts as a personal-use day. Also, rental to anyone for less than a fair rental amount counts as a personal-use day.

Some people are very concerned about deducting losses from a vacation home. They keep the personal use of their vacation home under 15 days or 10% of the rental days, whichever is greater. Others use the vacation home as much as they want and view any rents they receive as reducing their costs of owning the home.

Move To A Low-Tax Or No-Tax State Before You Receive A Large Gain

If you anticipate a large retirement distribution or large gain from the sale of property, such as stock, move to a no-tax or low-tax state. Be sure to establish residency before you retire or sell the property. If possible, you should move a year or two before your retirement or property sale.

> You own stock with a basis of $2,000 that is now worth $202,000. If you sell the stock, you will have a $200,000 gain. If your state tax rate is 6%, you would save $12,000 by moving to a state with no income tax. If you are planning to retire and move, consider moving to a state with no income tax before you sell the stock.

If you are planning a move to avoid state tax on a retirement distribution or sale of stock, you must properly establish residency in your new state. Some considerations that indicate your state of residence are:

- Your mental determination that a particular place is your home
- Your registered place to vote
- Your position in the community
- Your manner of living
- Your social connections in the community
- Your financial connections in the community
- Your connections in your former community
- Your continuance to pay taxes in your former community

You should also consider taxes other than income taxes. Some states impose an intangibles tax on your investments. Some states have high property taxes. Some states have high sales taxes. When you decide to move, you should consider all factors, not just income taxes.

Fringe
Benefits

Save Money By Taking Advantage Of Fringe Benefits Your Employer Provides

Fringe benefits are noncash compensation you get from your employer, such as a company car, life or medical insurance, and free use of the company copier. Many fringe benefits are not included in your income. Thus, if you get something as a fringe benefit you would otherwise have to pay for, you increase your after-tax cash flow. In many cases, you also save Social Security tax. Your employer gets to deduct the fringe benefits, and in many cases, also saves Social Security tax.

You are single and do not itemize deductions. You have 2 job offers. Employer A will pay you $40,000 a year but does not provide health insurance. You will need to spend $3,600 a year to buy it. Employer B will pay you $36,400 and provide health insurance at no cost to you. The offers look comparable. However, here is a comparison of the money you will have after taxes:

	Employer A No Health Insurance	Employer B Health Insurance
Wages	$ 40,000	$ 36,400
Standard deduction	(4,700)	(4,700)
Personal exemption	(3,000)	(3,000)
Taxable income	$ 32,300	$ 28,700
Cash flow:		
Wages	$ 40,000	$ 36,400
Social Security tax		
($40,000 x 7.65%)	(3,060)	
($36,400 x 7.65%)		(2,785)
Income tax on taxable income	(5,074)	(4,102)
Cost of health insurance	(3,600)	0
Net cash you have after tax	$ 28,266	$ 29,513

Thus, by taking the job from Employer B who pays for your health insurance, you have $1,247 ($29,513 - 28,266) more cash available to spend. Also, Employer B saves $275 ($3,060 - 2,785) in Social Security payroll taxes.

Another example of a fringe benefit that is exempt from income and Social Security taxes is group-term life insurance. If your employer provides group-term life insurance to you of $50,000 or less, you are not taxed on the value of the insurance. However, if your coverage exceeds $50,000, you are taxed based on the following IRS table.

Use the number of thousands of dollars of coverage over $50,000 times the amount from the following table to determine the taxable amount. You use your age at the end of the year to make the calculation.

Cost per $1,000 of Insurance per Month

AGE	COST
Under 25	$ .05
25-29	.06
30-34	.08
35-39	.09
40-44	.10
45-49	.15
50-54	.23
55-59	.43
60-64	.66
65-69	1.27
70 and above	2.06

If you are 36 years old and your employer provides $75,000 of group-term life insurance coverage for the entire year of 2002, you will be taxed on $27 ((($75,000 - $50,000)/$1,000) x (.09 x 12 months)). If you are in the 27% tax rate bracket, your cost for this benefit is $9 ($27 x (27% (income tax) + 7.65% (FICA))). That is a small cost for $75,000 of life insurance coverage.

Generally, your employer will include this amount on your Form W-2. However, if you have 2 or more jobs at the same time, and your total coverage between both employers is more than $50,000, you must compute the taxable amount.

NOTE: Cafeteria plans often offer group-term life insurance as an option.

Participate In Tax-Free Health Insurance And Medical Reimbursement Plans

Health insurance provided by your employer is one of the most important fringe benefits. Sometimes your employer will pay the full amount of the insurance premiums, while other times you must pay part or all of the premiums. The insurance can cover you, your spouse, and children.

Generally, your employer can deduct the full amount of the health insurance premiums. When your employer pays the premium for you, you do not pay tax on the amount of the premiums. The premiums are not treated as compensation for Social Security tax purposes. Also, you do not pay tax on the amount of claims you file with the insurance company.

What is this benefit worth to you if your employer pays the premium? Here is an example. The monthly insurance premium for you and your spouse is $300. You are in the 27% tax bracket with income of $40,000.

Premiums paid for you		$3,600
Amount which would otherwise be deductible on your individual tax return as a medical expense:		
Adjusted gross income	$40,000	
7.5% "floor" limitation	3,000	
Amount of premiums	3,600	
Deductible amount on your individual tax return (excess of premiums over floor)		600
Amount received "tax-free"		$ 3,000
Income tax savings at 27% ($3,000 x 27%)		$ 810
Social Security tax savings ($3,600 x 7.65%)		275
Total tax savings		$ 1,085

Your employer saves money as well by not having to pay the matching Social Security tax on the $3,600 of premiums. Additionally, this is one of the easiest fringe benefits for your employer to provide. If your employer pays your health insurance premiums, all the company must do is pay the bill. The IRS does not require your employer to file any extra forms. Also, since it is a tax-free benefit, no adjustments are made on your Forms W-2 at the end of the year.

NOTE: If you are self-employed, are a 2% or more partner in a partnership, are a 2% or more member in a Limited Liability Company, or are a 2% or more owner in an S Corporation, you must include the amount of the premiums paid in your income. You may be able to deduct 70% (60% for 2001) of the premiums on your individual tax return as a deduction against your income even if your expenses are under 7.5% of your adjusted gross income. See Tax Saving Idea #76.

Medical reimbursement plans

If your employer has a written medical reimbursement plan, you do not pay tax on any reimbursements you receive for medical expenses for you, your spouse, or your dependents. However, you must pay tax on reimbursements if they exceed your actual medical expenses or are attributable to medical expenses you previously deducted.

NOTE: Small businesses may be able to take advantage of medical savings accounts (Archer MSAs) to pay health care costs. Archer MSAs are a test program for high-deductible health insurance plans. They are only available to the first 750,000 plans started before 2003.

You Can Increase Your Take-Home Pay By Taking Advantage Of Dependent Care Assistance Plans

With a dependent care assistance plan, you do not pay tax on the amounts set aside from your paycheck to pay a care provider for your dependent. The maximum amount you can exclude from income is $5,000 per year ($2,500 annually for a married individual filing separately).

If either you or your spouse earns less than $5,000, the amount you may exclude from income is limited to that spouse's earnings. However, there is an exception to this rule if your spouse is a full-time student or is disabled. In such cases, your spouse is treated as earning $200 ($250 in 2003) per month if you have one qualified dependent, and $400 ($500 in 2003) per month if you have two or more qualified dependents.

The qualification requirements are similar to the requirements for the dependent care credit. The expenses must be employment-related dependent care expenses. Also your dependent must be a child who is under age 13, a physically or mentally disabled relative, or your spouse who is physically or mentally disabled.

If your child turns 13 during the year, you can claim the expenses up to the date of his or her birthday. Also, you can claim the full amount of the expenses for reimbursement up to the $5,000 limitation. The limitation is not prorated in the birthday year.

Expenses which allow you or your spouse to remain employed and are attributable in part to the care of your dependent can be covered in a dependent care assistance plan. Typical expenses include day care services, baby sitters, and maids. However, if your dependent stays at a camp overnight, these expenses will not qualify. Also, you generally cannot pay one child of yours to care for another and have it qualify for this dependent care exclusion.

To the extent you take advantage of this dependent care assistance plan at work, you cannot take advantage of the dependent care credit on your tax return. See Tax Saving Idea #26. Often, taking advantage of the exclusion rather than the credit saves you more in tax.

You earn $50,000 and your spouse earns $20,000. If you have two children under age 13 and you pay $7,000 of child care expenses, you can claim a credit of $960 ($4,800 maximum expenses allowed x 20% credit).

If your employer has a dependent care assistance program, you can reduce your taxable income by $5,000 (maximum amount allowed under one of these plans), thus saving you $773 more than if you claim the credit:

Federal income tax savings at 27% tax rate bracket ($5,000 x 27%)	$ 1,350
Social Security taxes at 7.65%	383
Total savings	1,733
Tax savings from child care credit	960
Additional savings by using the dependent care assistance program	$ 773

NOTE: This strategy works if you have just one dependent or if you are in the 27% tax rate bracket or higher. However, if you have two dependents and are in the 15% tax rate bracket or lower, taking the credit might be to your advantage.

Many states do not allow a credit for dependent care expenses, but they do allow the exclusion from income. Thus, you save even more by taking advantage of your employer's dependent care assistance program.

NOTE: While the dependent care tax credit is scheduled to increase in 2003, no change in the excludable amount is scheduled for dependent care assistance plans. See Tax Saving Idea #26.

Go Back To School, Have Your Employer Pay For It, And Exclude Your Tuition Costs From Your Income

Education expenses can reduce your taxes in one of three ways. First, you can deduct job-related education expenses, along with your other miscellaneous itemized deductions, to the extent they exceed 2% of your adjusted gross income. Education expenses are deductible if they are job related, do not qualify you for a new business, and are not taken to meet the minimum educational standards for qualification in your business. The costs of obtaining an undergraduate degree do not qualify because they are usually meeting the minimum educational standards. The costs of obtaining a graduate degree, especially in business, do qualify unless the degree qualifies you for a new business, such as law or medicine. Examples of some of the costs you can deduct include tuition, books, supplies, car expenses, and travel costs.

Second, you can exclude job-related education expenses as a working condition fringe benefit. See Tax Saving Idea #68. Many employers used this approach when the educational assistance provisions temporarily expired in prior years.

Third, you can exclude education expenses under your employer's educational assistance program. This is generally the best approach. Check to see if your employer offers an educational assistance plan. If your employer does, you can exclude up to $5,250 from your income. Although meals, lodging, and transportation costs cannot be reimbursed, the costs that can be reimbursed tax-free include:

- tuition,
- books,
- supplies, and
- equipment.

Your employer can either pay the expenses directly to the school or reimburse you after you pay them. You need to have proof of your expenses, such as receipts for tuition and books.

Unlike the deduction for educational expenses, the subjects you are studying do not have to be business or job related. Thus, you can complete your college degree or take nonbusiness courses of interest to you. However, subjects considered a sport, game, or hobby are ineligible unless required as part of your degree program or related to your employer's business. Also, beginning in 2002, graduate courses also qualify for this exclusion.

Your savings include both income tax and Social Security tax. Additionally, many states do not tax educational assistance reimbursements, thus saving you even more.

You have $40,000 of income, are in the 27% tax rate bracket, and have $5,500 of educational expenses. If you claim the expenses as a deduction, you will save:

Education expenses	$5,500
2% floor ($40,000 x 2%)	(800)
Deductible education expenses	4,700
Income tax rate	27%
Tax savings	$1,269

If your employer reimburses $5,250 of your educational expenses under an educational assistance plan, you will save the following:

Federal income tax savings at 27% tax bracket	$1,418
Social Security taxes at 7.65%	402
Total savings	$1,820

The unreimbursed education expenses of $250 ($5,500 - 5,250) are considered a miscellaneous itemized deduction subject to the 2% floor. You receive no additional tax savings since 2% of your adjusted gross income of $800 ($40,000 x 2%) exceeds the $250.

You save $551 ($1,820 - 1,269) in tax by using your employer's educational assistance plan.

Take Advantage Of Other Tax-Free Fringe Benefits That Your Employer Offers

Look into other fringe benefits which you can receive tax-free. These benefits save you money since you do not have to pay for them and you do not pay tax on them. So, for every dollar of tax-free benefits you receive, you actually save a full dollar. Additionally, you will not have to pay Social Security tax on these benefits.

These fringe benefits fall into the following four major groups: no-additional-cost services, qualified employee discounts, working condition fringes, and de minimis fringes.

No-additional-cost services

The value of services you receive from your employer for which your employer incurs no additional costs is tax-free. The best example is the airlines which allow employees and immediate families to fly free on a stand-by basis. Another example is a hotel which allows employees to stay overnight free.

Qualified employee discounts

Discounts you receive from your employer are generally not taxable. For example, if you work at a department store and you can purchase items at a 25% discount, you do not pay tax on this fringe benefit. If you work for a company that provides a service rather than a product, such as dry cleaning, you can receive a tax-free discount of up to 20% off the normal price.

Working condition fringes

You do not pay tax on items your employer pays for you that you could otherwise deduct as business expenses. This is helpful in most situations since these "employee business expenses" are miscellaneous itemized deductions. You can deduct them only if you itemize deductions and only to the extent they exceed 2% of your adjusted gross income.

Examples of working condition fringe benefits include:

- Dues to professional organizations
- Subscriptions to professional journals
- Meals
- Entertainment
- Transportation
- Use of a company car to the extent it is business-related
- Bodyguards in sensitive situations
- Business travel including a Saturday night stay over if it makes the trip less expensive
- Job-related education expenses

Transportation fringes

You may exclude up to $185 ($180 for 2001) per month of employer-provided parking and up to $100 ($65 for 2001) per month in employer-provided transit passes or employer-provided van pooling.

De minimis fringes

Items that are so small that accounting for them would be an administrative burden are considered tax-free de minimis fringes.

Examples of de minimis fringes include:

- Photocopying
- Typing of personal letters by the company's secretary
- Use of company computers and printers for personal items
- Postage on occasional personal items
- Use of company materials, including reference materials
- Coffee and soda
- Birthday cakes
- Occasional lunch or supper money
- Company parties
- Company tickets to sporting and theater events
- Occasional long distance telephone calls

Most employers do not object to your use of the listed items. However, some companies consider it stealing. Be sure to work with your employer in using this fringe benefit.

Tailor Your Benefits With A Cafeteria Plan

Cafeteria plans, also called flexible spending accounts, allow you to choose your benefits. With this type of fringe benefit plan, you can choose between taxable items, such as cash, and nontaxable items, such as dependent care or medical expenses. This flexibility is especially advantageous if both you and your spouse work and have duplicate benefits.

If you choose cash from a cafeteria plan, you pay tax on the amount of cash you receive. If you choose a fringe benefit, however, you receive the value of the benefit tax-free. Many of the selections available in cafeteria plans are the benefits discussed in previous Tax Saving Ideas, such as medical reimbursements, dependent care reimbursements, and group-term life insurance.

Your employer can set up a cafeteria plan in many ways. Some give you a set amount each month to "spend." Some allow you to reduce your salary in exchange for a non-taxable benefit. Some provide a combination of giving you "spending" money and allowing you to reduce your salary.

The advantages to you are tax savings. This includes Federal income tax, Social Security tax, and in many cases, state and local income tax.

The potential disadvantage to you if you participate in a salary reduction cafeteria plan is that you must use the money set aside each year or you lose it. This so-called use-it-or-lose-it rule can be scary.

Generally, you can change the amount you reduce from your salary only at the beginning of each year. There are a few circumstances when you can change your election during the year, but these are limited. Examples of when you can change your elections include

- a change in your family status (marriage, divorce, or a new child),
- termination of employment, and
- a significant change in the cost or coverage of a benefit offered by your employer or your spouse's employer.

Take advantage of salary-reduction cafeteria plans. Dependent care is a somewhat predictable cost, so estimate what you pay in a year. There is a $5,000 limit on dependent care expenses. See Tax Saving Idea #66.

Medical expenses are a little more risky. Review your records during the past couple years to estimate your expenses. Remember to include annual physical examinations, prescription drugs not covered by your health insurance, prescription eyeglasses or contacts, and annual dentist visits.

There are two disadvantages to choosing disability insurance coverage through a cafeteria plan. First, if you pay the disability insurance premiums yourself, the benefits you receive during a period of disability are tax-free. However, if your employer pays the premiums or you pay the premiums with pre-tax money through a cafeteria plan, the benefits you receive during a period of disability are taxable. Second, the disability plan your employer offers may not be the plan you would choose based on its terms, particularly its definitions of disability, waiting period, benefit amount, and benefit period. Although you should determine whether you are adequately insured, most individuals take advantage of their employer's disability plan despite these disadvantages.

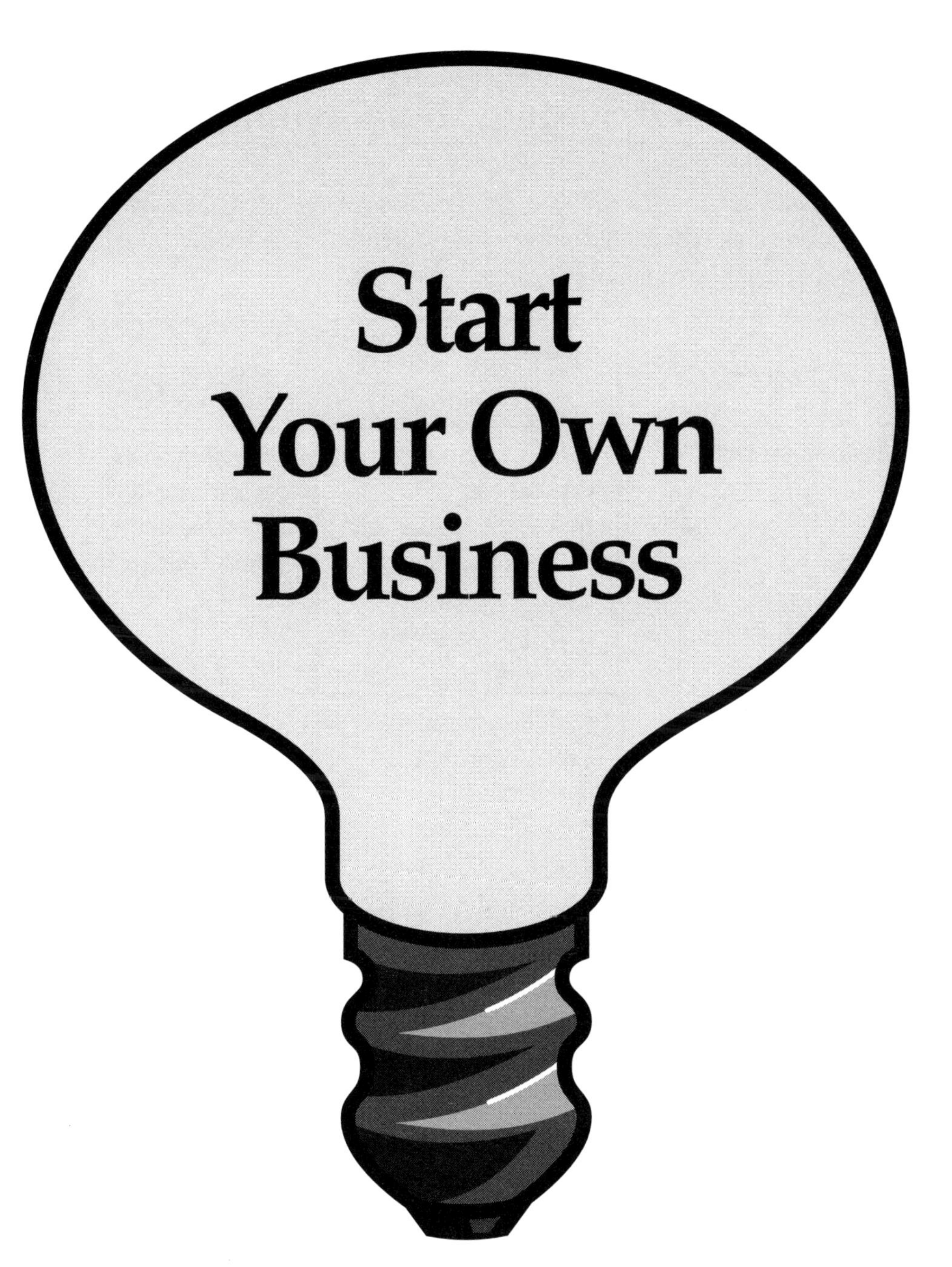
Start
Your Own
Business

Reap The Tax Benefits Of Starting Your Own Business

When you are self-employed, you have several tax advantages over employees. Take advantage of these opportunities. The following chart lists some of the tax advantages of being self-employed.

	Employee	Self-employed person
Business expenses	Employee business expenses are miscellaneous itemized deductions subject to the 2% of adjusted gross income (AGI) limitation	Self-employment expenses are deductible directly against your business income
FICA tax/Self-employment tax	Employee business expenses are not deductible in determining the amount of FICA tax your employer collects from you	Self-employment expenses reduce your income, and thus reduce your self-employment tax

Calculation of expense items based on your adjusted gross income (AGI)	Employee business expenses are not deductible in determining your AGI	Self-employment expenses reduce your AGI, which has a favorable effect on the calculation of your medical deductions, reduction of your itemized deductions, eligibility for Roth and deductible IRAs, and other calculations based on your AGI
Retirement plans	Eligible for employer-provided plans and IRAs	Eligible to start Keogh, SEP, or SIMPLE plans and also eligible for IRAs
Alternative minimum tax treatment	Employee business expenses are not deductible for alternative minimum tax — they are a tax preference item	Self-employment expenses are deductible for alternative minimum tax

However, there are some disadvantages of being self-employed. Some of these disadvantages are:

- Self-employment tax, although you are able to deduct half of your self-employment tax,
- Estimated tax payments,
- Preparation of Schedule C and possibly other business tax forms, and
- Increased likelihood of Internal Revenue Service audit.

Use The 20 Factors To Show You Are An Independent Contractor

Many businesses would rather pay independent contractors ("contract labor") than employees. This practice allows the company to avoid paying payroll taxes and to exclude the independent contractor from fringe benefit and retirement plans.

Many people would rather receive "contract labor" payments than wages. As discussed in Tax Saving Idea #70, this allows the person to deduct expenses in computing adjusted gross income.

The Internal Revenue Service has been focusing attention on independent contractors. The IRS thinks many independent contractors do not report all their income.

You can use the following 20 factors to structure your work arrangements with your customers and help prove you are an independent contractor. These factors are the tests applied by the courts in determining employment status. No single factor is controlling, nor is any particular weight given to any one of the factors.

20 Factors to Determine Independent Contractor Status

***Behavioral Control Factors** — These factors measure whether there is a right to direct or control how the work is done.*

1. Few instructions are given to you about how, when, and where you are to work.
2. Little training is provided by the company.
3. Your services are not integrated with the company's operations.
4. You are not required to perform the services personally.
5. You hire, supervise, and pay assistants.
6. Your relationship with the company is not continuing or is infrequently recurring.

7. You set your working hours.
8. You do not work full-time for the company.
9. You do not work at the company's location.
10. You set the steps in which the work will be done.
11. You are not required to submit written or oral reports.

***Financial Control Factors** — These factors measure whether there is a right to direct or control how the business aspects of the worker's activities are conducted.*

12. You are paid by the job rather than by the week or month.
13. You are not reimbursed for your business or traveling expenses.
14. You provide your own equipment and supplies.
15. You invest in the facilities you use for doing the work.
16. You can realize a profit or suffer a loss as a result of your services.
17. You work for many different companies at the same time.
18. Your services are available to the general public on a regular basis.

***Relationship Factors** — These factors measure how the parties perceive their relationship.*

19. You cannot be fired as long as you produce the requested work.
20. You cannot terminate your relationship with the company until your work is complete.

You are writing and implementing a marketing plan for ABC Company. You work 15 hours per week at ABC Company's office for $35 per hour. You use ABC Company's computers, copiers, and phones. For the rest of the week, you serve a variety of other companies on a project by project basis. You may be an employee of ABC Company because you provide the services personally, work at ABC Company's office, and use ABC Company's equipment.

If you wish to be an independent contractor, you may want to restructure your relationship. First, you might work at your office rather than at ABC Company's office. Second, you might use your own computer and equipment. Third, you might arrange to be paid on a project basis. Fourth, you might have a written agreement with ABC Company.

Avoid Having Your Business Classified As A Hobby

The Internal Revenue Service likes to disallow losses from small businesses. This is especially true for people with sideline businesses. If your business is not "engaged in for profit," your deductions are limited. The deductions you can take for "hobbies" include items you can deduct anyway plus other expenses up to the amount of your income from the hobby. If your business is classified as a "business," the deductions you can take are more liberal and your deductions can exceed your income. You report your business income and deductions on Schedule C of your tax return.

Having your business classified as a hobby can be disastrous if you have significant losses. In addition to losing your business loss deductions, you could lose some of your other deductions, such as deductions for your retirement plan contributions and your home office expenses.

The IRS assumes you have an actual business if you have profits for three or more years in a five year period. If your business is breeding, training, showing or racing horses of any kind, you must show a profit in two out of seven years. If you do not meet these tests, your business is still treated as a business if you can prove that you intend to make a profit.

The IRS Regulations list nine factors which are helpful in showing that you intend to make a profit. No single factor is controlling, nor is any particular weight given to any one of the factors.

Use the following nine factors to make sure the IRS does not reclassify your business as a hobby.

- The manner in which you conduct the activity
- Your expertise and the expertise of your advisers
- The time and effort you spend on the activity
- The expectations that the assets you use in the activity will appreciate in value
- Your success in similar activities
- Your history of income or losses with respect to the activity
- The amount of profits
- Your financial situation
- The elements of personal pleasure or recreation

You are an artist and sell the art you create. You have had losses on your tax returns for the past three years. You are at risk of having your business classified as a hobby. Make sure you are keeping financial records for your business, using experts to help you market your work, and devoting the time to the business needed to make it work. Otherwise, you could lose your deductions for the losses you claimed on your previous tax returns.

Deduct The Full Cost Of Your Equipment And Furniture Purchases

When you buy equipment and furniture, you must spread the cost over a period of years. This is called depreciation. For example, you can depreciate computers over 5 years and desks over 7 years. The tax law specifies the number of years of depreciation to take as well as the depreciation method to use.

Rather than depreciating purchases, you can choose to deduct (expense) up to $24,000 of business equipment and furniture purchases each year. Be sure to time your purchases to take advantage of this special deduction. The difference between depreciating and expensing equipment can be substantial.

You buy a copier for $10,000 in 2002. Your depreciation compared to the choice to expense the equipment is as follows:

YEAR	DEPRECIATION	ELECTION TO EXPENSE
2002	$2,000	$10,000
2003	3,200	0
2004	1,920	0
2005	1,152	0
2006	1,152	0
2007	576	0
Total	$10,000	$10,000

Under both methods you eventually deduct the full $10,000 cost of the computer. However, choosing to expense it in the first year allows you to match your expenses with your cash flow.

Special rules apply for the expensing of your major purchases.

- You must have taxable income from your business and employment of at least the amount you elect to expense.
- You must reduce the amount you expense if you buy more than $200,000 of major items in one year. If you are married and file separately from your spouse, you must split the $24,000 maximum amount. This amount is split 50/50 unless you choose otherwise.
- Once you elect to expense the items, you cannot change your mind. However, each year you have the choice.

It is usually not a good idea to expense a car. There are special rules for cars. If your car costs more than about $15,300, you will be subject to the luxury automobile rules. These rules limit the amount of depreciation you can deduct each year. See Tax Saving Idea #74.

NOTE: When you depreciate, rather than expense, your major purchases, beware of the alternative minimum tax. The alternative minimum tax uses a different method to depreciate your major purchases. Under the alternative minimum tax (AMT), your depreciation is usually spread over a longer period, giving you lower deductions in the early years you own the items. Depreciation of personal property for AMT purposes is calculated using the same number of years as the regular tax depreciation for assets you purchase in 1999 and later. However, the method you use to calculate the AMT depreciation will generally be different.

The maximum expense amount is as follows:

Taxable Year Beginning in	Maximum Expense
2001 and 2002	24,000
2003 and thereafter	25,000

Use Your Personal Car For Business And Deduct Your Car Expenses

When you use your car for business, you can deduct the related expenses. You can use 34.5¢ per business mile for 2001 and 36.5¢ per business mile for 2002, or you can deduct the business percentage of your actual expenses. The Internal Revenue Service (IRS) may adjust the mileage rate for 2003.

In either case, you should keep a record of your mileage. One method is to keep a log in which you track your business miles. Write down the following:

- The date
- Your destination and the business purpose
- The beginning odometer reading
- The ending odometer reading

Although you are not required to keep a daily log, you will usually have more deductions if you have good records. You will remember the smaller trips. If you use the "actual expenses" method, you also need to write down your gas, repairs, car washes, oil changes, and other expenses. Many people choose the 36.5¢ (34.5¢ in 2001) per mile method because the recordkeeping for expenses is easier.

When you use your actual expenses, you can depreciate your car. These rules differ depending on when you begin using your car for business and on how much you use your car for business. See the following chart.

	If you use your car 50% or less for business	If you use your car more than 50% for business
Depreciation method	You must use the straight-line depreciation method	You can use an accelerated depreciation method
If your business use drops to 50% or less in a future year	Not applicable	You must switch to the straight-line depreciation method AND you must pay tax on the extra deductions over the straight-line method that you took in previous years

If your car costs more than $15,300, you are subject to the luxury automobile rules. These rules limit the amount of depreciation you can deduct.

Use the amount from the following chart and multiply it by your business use to see the maximum amount you can deduct each year for depreciation.

	Car Purchased 2001 or 2002 *
First year	$3,060
Second year	4,900
Third year	2,950
Subsequent years	1,775

*2002 amount is an unofficial estimate

Choosing to deduct actual expenses rather than the cents per mile method often saves you money.

You buy a car for $18,000 in June 2001. You drive 3,900 miles for business purposes and 2,100 miles for personal purposes. You pay the following car expenses:

Gasoline	$ 400
Repairs	250
Insurance	400
Property tax	150
Total	$ 1,200

Your business-use percentage for 2001 is 65% (3,900 business miles divided by 6,000 total miles). Your depreciation for 2001 is $1,989 ($3,060 from chart x 65%).

If you use actual expenses, you can deduct $2,769 (($1,200 x 65%) + $1,989) of business car expenses. By comparison, if you use the mileage rate of 34.5¢ per mile, you can deduct $1,346 (3,900 miles x 34.5¢). Thus, by choosing to deduct your actual expenses for 2001, you can deduct $1,423 ($2,769 - 1,346) more than if you use the mileage rate.

When you choose to deduct actual expenses in the first year you use a car for business, you generally must use actual expenses for as long as you own the car. However, if you use the straight-line depreciation method to depreciate the car, you can use either actual expenses or the mileage rate, whichever is more, in future years. Also, when you get a different car, you can choose between deducting actual expenses or the mileage rate.

When you use a car phone for business, you can deduct the related expenses. Similar to cars, the rules for depreciating a car phone differ depending on how much you use it for business. (Refer to the chart which shows what happens if you use your car 50% or less for business.) In addition to depreciation, you can also deduct the business-use percentage of your monthly bills.

Deduct The Cost And Other Expenses Of Your Home Computer

When you use your home computer for business, you can deduct the related expenses, including paper, ink cartridges, and depreciation. The depreciation of your computer depends on how much you use it for business. See the following chart.

	If you use your home computer 50% or less for business	If you use your home computer more than 50% for business
Depreciation method	You must use the straight-line depreciation method	You can use an accelerated depreciation method
If your business use drops to 50% or less in a future year	Not applicable	You must switch to the straight-line depreciation method AND you must pay tax on the extra deductions over the straight-line method that you took in previous years

Unlike a car, there is no maximum amount of depreciation for equipment. Also, you can choose to expense the business portion in one year. See Tax Saving Idea #73.

Generally, computer software is deductible over three years. However, if the software has a useful life of less than one year, you can deduct it in the year you buy it.

To prove how much you use the computer for business, keep records of the times you use the computer and indicate the purpose.

Write Off 70% Of The Health Insurance Premiums For You And Your Family

For most people, health insurance premiums are medical expenses. Medical expenses are deductible as itemized deductions to the extent they exceed 7.5% of your adjusted gross income (AGI).

However, if you are self-employed, you have an advantage. You can deduct 70% (60% for 2001) of your health insurance premiums in arriving at your AGI. This includes health insurance premiums for you, your spouse, and your dependents. The remaining 30% (40% for 2001) of the premiums is a medical expense and is subject to the 7.5% of AGI limitation.*

There are two conditions you must meet to take this special deduction. First, you must have income from the business that provides the health insurance coverage.

Second, you must not be able to participate in a subsidized health plan maintained by any employer, including your spouse's employer. You can use a month-by-month check to see if you were able to participate in a subsidized health plan. If you are eligible to participate in a subsidized health plan for one month, you can still claim the 70% (60% for 2001) special deduction for the remaining eleven months.

NOTE: You might be able to get a full deduction for your family's health insurance premiums. If you employ your spouse, you can cover your spouse under your company's health insurance plan as an employee. Your spouse can elect full family coverage. The company gets the deduction and your spouse does not pay tax on the benefit. See Tax Saving Idea #65.

The write-off percentage increases to 100% for 2003 and later years.

*NOTE: Check your state tax rules. Some states allow a deduction for the remaining 30% (40% for 2001) of premiums if you are self-employed. This may save you even more in state taxes.

Deduct Your Tax Return Preparation Fees Against Your Business Income

Many people cannot deduct their tax return preparation fees because the fees are miscellaneous expenses. Miscellaneous expenses are deductible as itemized deductions to the extent they exceed 2% of your adjusted gross income (AGI). However, if you are in business for yourself, a major portion of your tax return preparation fees may be deductible against your business income. You can deduct the tax preparation fees for the following:

- Your business (Schedule C),
- Your rental properties (Schedule E), and
- Your farm (Schedule F).

You will need to ask your tax return preparer how much of the fee relates to these items. Deduct that amount on those specific forms. Allocating these fees saves you income taxes since it reduces your AGI which you use to compute several limitations on itemized deductions. This allocation also saves you self-employment tax if it relates to your business or farm.

You have $55,000 in business income, your spouse has $20,000 in wages, and you pay $750 for the preparation of your tax returns. Only your itemized deductions over $1,500 ($75,000 x 2%) are deductible. If your tax return preparation fee is your only miscellaneous itemized deduction, you get no tax deduction for the fees you pay. However, if your tax return preparer allocates 75% of the fee to your business, you can deduct $563 ($750 x 75%). This will save you about $238 in tax.

Savings of self-employment tax:		
Amount of deduction	$563	
Self-employment tax rate	x 15.3%	
Savings of self-employment tax		$ 86
Savings of income tax:		
Amount of deduction	$563	
Tax rate	x 27%	
Savings of income tax		152
Total savings		$ 238

Furthermore, if the Internal Revenue Service audits your tax return, and the main focus is your business, you can deduct your accountant's fees. Also, if you receive any governmental notices concerning your business, you can deduct the fees you pay your accountant to resolve the matter.

Hire Your Children In Your Business

If you have chores your children can do in your business, consider hiring them. Generally, your children will be in a lower tax rate bracket than you. Thus, you can shift the income from your higher tax rate bracket to their lower tax rate brackets.

Also, if your children are under 18, you as the employer do not need to withhold or pay either Social Security tax or Federal unemployment tax on the children's wages. The tax treatment under the different Federal employment taxes for family members is:

	Income Tax Withholding	Social Security & Medicare	Federal Unemployment
Son or daughter employed by parent	Taxable	Exempt until age 18	Exempt until age 21

There are four tests you must meet to deduct the pay to your children as a business expense. These are:

#1 Ordinary and necessary. You must show that the salary, like any other business expense, is an ordinary and necessary expense directly connected with your business.

#2 Reasonable. You must prove that the pay is reasonable at the time you contract for the services. Reasonable pay is the amount that you would normally pay for similar services under similar circumstances.

#3 Services provided. You must prove that services were actually provided. Also, you must reasonably expect your business to benefit from the services performed.

#4 Paid or incurred. You must pay the compensation or incur the expense during the tax year.

You are in the 27% tax rate bracket and you are subject to self-employment tax. If you have business filing, typing, cleaning, and other chores for which you hire your child, you can deduct your child's wages against your business income. The total you pay your 16 year old child in 2002 is $6,700. Your approximate savings would be:

Your tax savings since you can deduct the wages:		
Federal tax ($6,700 x 27%)	$ 1,809	
Self-employment tax ($6,700 x 15.3%)	1,025	
Your tax savings		$ 2,834
Your child's tax assuming no other income:		
Wages	$ 6,700	
Standard deduction	(4,700)	
Taxable income	$ 2,000	
Federal tax	$ 201	
Social Security tax	0	
Your child's total tax		(201)
Total Federal tax savings to the family		$ 2,633

Additionally, your child is eligible to contribute to an Individual Retirement Account (IRA). In the above example, if your child contributes $2,000 to a deductible IRA, your child pays no tax. The total tax savings to your family is $2,834 ($2,633 + 201). Thus, in 2002, your child can earn $6,700 ($4,700 amount of standard deduction plus $2,000 put into an IRA) without paying any Federal income tax.

Alternatively, your child could contribute to a Roth IRA. In this case, your child would pay $201 of Federal tax but all qualified distributions from the Roth IRA would be completely tax-free. See Tax Saving Idea #81.

Choose The Right Business Entity For You

You can operate your business as a sole proprietorship, partnership, corporation, or limited liability company. Many people begin as a sole proprietorship and then change to one of the other business entities. Others choose to start as a partnership, corporation, or limited liability company.

There are many factors — both tax and nontax — which influence your decision concerning which business entity to choose. The main nontax factors which affect your decision are:

- limited liability,
- ease of obtaining financing, and
- the availability of fringe benefits and retirement plans.

The main tax factors that affect your decision to choose a business entity are:

- the applicable tax rates,
- double taxation, and
- the pass through of losses to the owners.

Sole proprietorships

Sole proprietorships are the easiest form of business to operate. All you do is include Schedule C and Schedule SE with your individual tax return. Your income minus your business expenses are taxed at your individual tax rate bracket and are subject to self-employment tax. If you incur a loss, the loss offsets your other income, such as wages, interest, and dividends, if you have been active in the business.

There are many disadvantages, however, of operating as a sole proprietorship. First, you, as the sole proprietor, are at risk for liabilities arising from the business. The main risks are lawsuits initiated by creditors, vendors, customers, and employees. Not only might you lose the business, but you could lose personal assets, such as your home, car, or savings. Insurance provides some protection, but many people choose to incorporate their businesses or operate as limited liability companies to help avoid this risk.

Second, it is difficult to raise additional capital as a sole proprietorship. Borrowing money, using your personal assets and business assets as collateral, is about the only option available.

Third, the fringe benefit plans available to you as a sole proprietor are not nearly as extensive as the ones available to corporations.

Corporations

There are two types of corporations — the regular corporation, sometimes called a C corporation, and the S corporation. Both types of corporations are legal entities that are completely separate from their owners. The existence of both types of corporations is made possible by state law. These laws, which vary from state to state, govern the creation, operation, and dissolution of the corporations. Regular corporations can have one shareholder or many shareholders. A regular corporation, as a separate tax entity, must file its own tax form, either Form 1120 or the simpler Form 1120-A. S Corporations are limited to 75 shareholders and file Form 1120S.

The primary reason business owners choose to operate as a corporation is limited liability. Corporations, as separate legal entities, protect your assets from corporate liabilities. The reverse is also true: the corporate assets are protected from your personal liabilities. In other words, if you are a corporate shareholder and you comply with the numerous corporate formalities, such as keeping corporate minutes and holding shareholder meetings, you can generally only lose your investment in the corporation, not your personal assets.

Regular corporations: Currently, the income tax rates that apply to regular corporations are another advantage of operating as a corporation. Individual income tax rates on $50,000 of taxable income are at least 27%. Corporations with $50,000 of taxable income are taxed at a 15% rate. Individual income tax rates can be as high as 38.6%. The maximum corporate income tax rate is 35%. These differences mean that individuals can use corporations to shelter income from tax. This is often done by splitting income between a corporation and an individual to avoid paying tax at the highest income tax rates.

> You earn $110,000 in your retail business. Because of your other income, you are in the 35% tax rate bracket. You would pay $38,500 ($110,000 x 35%) of Federal income tax on your retail business income.

If your business was incorporated, it could pay you a $60,000 salary. You would pay $21,000 ($60,000 x 35%) of Federal income tax on your salary, and your corporation would pay $7,500 (($110,000 - 60,000) x 15%) of Federal income tax. Thus, you would decrease the Federal income tax $10,000 ($38,500 - ($21,000 + $7,500)).

Congress, in an effort to curb this income-splitting maneuver, eliminated the lower tax rate brackets for personal service corporations. In other words, corporations owned and operated by doctors, lawyers, accountants, and engineers are subject to a flat 35% tax rate. For other corporations, such as retailers and manufacturers, however, income splitting is possible.

A second reason you may choose to operate as a regular corporation is the availability of nontaxable fringe benefits, retirement plans, and incentive compensation plans. As an employee of the corporation, you can take advantage of nontaxable fringe benefits, such as life and health insurance and cafeteria plans. Corporations can also offer many types of retirement plans, including pension and profit sharing plans. To attract and retain quality people, many corporations also offer incentive compensation, such as restricted stock and stock options. Sole proprietorships, partnerships, and S corporations cannot offer the full range of compensation packages that are available through a regular corporation.

One of the biggest advantages of choosing the regular corporate form is the numerous options for raising money. Your corporation can borrow money by getting loans from people or banks or by issuing bonds. Your corporation can also raise money from the general public or people involved in the business by issuing different types of common and preferred stock, including voting and nonvoting stock.

Although there are many advantages of operating in the regular corporate form, there are two significant disadvantages. First, it is possible for corporate income to be taxed twice. Double taxation occurs when a corporation is taxed on its income and then pays you, the shareholder, a nondeductible dividend. You pay taxes a second time on the dividends. This negative aspect of corporate taxation is overemphasized because it is easy to avoid. Your corporation can make deductible payments to you and other shareholders in a variety of ways, including wages, interest payments, and rent payments. Although the Internal Revenue Service will scrutinize deductions that are unreasonable, making payments deductible in these ways leads to one level of taxation. This is similar to the taxation of a sole proprietorship or partnership.

The second disadvantage of operating in the corporate form is that you cannot deduct the losses of regular corporations on your individual tax return. The losses are trapped inside the corporation where they may be carried back or forward to other years when the corporation has income. The losses of active owners of sole proprietorships, partnerships, S corporations, and limited liability companies are deductible on the owner's individual tax returns. Because of the way losses are treated, the corporate form may not be the best alternative for start-up businesses.

S Corporations: For state law purposes, S corporations are not distinguished from regular corporations. However, the Federal tax laws treat S corporations differently. Although the S corporation may owe some taxes at the corporate level, generally the net income of an S corporation passes through to you, the shareholder. It is taxed on your individual income tax return. S corporations file Form 1120S and report your share of the income on Schedule K-1.

The tax advantages of S corporations are:

- the income is only taxed at the individual level; and
- the losses from an S corporation pass through to the individual owners.

The disadvantages are:

- S corporations cannot have more than 75 shareholders; and
- S corporations cannot provide the range of tax-free fringe benefits that a corporation can to its owners.

Partnerships

If you and another individual own and share the profits and losses of a business, you may be a partnership and not realize it. As a partnership, your relationships with your partners and with the public are governed by state law. In a general partnership, all partners have equal status and are at equal risk, although their shares of partnership profits and losses may be different. In a limited partnership, one or more partners run the business and assume a substantial portion of the risk. The other partners, by agreeing not to play an active role in the business, limit their risk to the amount they invest in the partnership. Although partnerships are merely reporting entities which do not pay taxes, both general and limited partnerships must report their income and expenses on Form 1065. You, as a partner, show your share of partnership income or loss on your individual tax return.

The main advantages of operating in the partnership form are:

- the possibility of losses passing through to you;
- lack of formality governing the business operations; and
- the taxation of partnership income at only the individual level.

Disadvantages of operating as a partnership include:

- the risk of loss because of the lack of limited liability; and
- the limitations on the fringe benefits that can be offered.

Limited Liability Companies

Limited liability companies (LLCs) and limited liability partnerships (LLPs) are the newest forms of business entities. LLCs and LLPs offer you liability protection similar to corporations and flow-through of losses similar to partnerships and S corporations. This is an almost perfect blend of the attributes of corporations and partnerships. LLCs and LLPs offer an advantage over S corporations because the number of owners is not restricted. However, similar to S corporations and partnerships, LLCs and LLPs cannot offer the tax-free fringe benefit packages available to corporate employees.

Although LLCs and LLPs are probably the entities of the future, at this time there are many unresolved issues. The rules governing LLCs and LLPs in the various states are not the same. In other words, LLC and LLP owners may not have personal liability protection in states where the rules are different from those in the LLC's or LLP's home state.

In summary, choosing the best business form for your situation can be extremely important in the formative years of your business. If you are considering forming a business entity, talk to a CPA or an attorney about the consequences of that business form in your state. Tax consequences vary from state to state, and there may be tax consequences when changing the form of ownership of your business.

Retirement
Plans

You Can Use IRAs To Save For Your Retirement And Let Your Money Grow Tax-Deferred

Retirement plans are the best tax shelter around. Usually, your money is not taxed or it is deductible when it goes into the plan. The money in the plan grows tax-free, and you are taxed only when the money comes out.

The most common retirement plan is an Individual Retirement Account (IRA). A frequently asked question is, "Can I do an IRA?" If you have earned income, such as wages, the answer is yes. Even if you cannot deduct your IRA contribution, you can put money into an IRA.

The annual maximum IRA contribution is $3,000 ($2,000 for 2001) unless your earnings from your job or business are less. If you are 50 or older, you can contribute an extra $500. See Tax Saving Idea #87. Many people can deduct their IRA contributions. If you are in the 27% tax rate bracket and you make a $3,000 deductible IRA contribution, your Federal tax savings is $810. You also reduce your state tax.

Beginning in 2002, you may be eligible for the "saver's credit" if you make a contribution of up to $2,000 to your IRA, 401(k) plan, or SIMPLE plan. You must be 18 or older, not a full-time student, and not someone else's dependent. Using the following chart, find your filing status and adjusted gross income to determine your credit rate:

Credit Rate Percent	Joint		Head of Household		All Others	
	Over	Not over	Over	Not over	Over	Not over
50%	$0	$30,000	$0	$22,500	$0	$15,000
20%	$30,000	$32,500	$22,500	$24,375	$15,000	$16,250
10%	$32,500	$50,000	$24,375	$37,500	$16,250	$25,000
0%	$50,000		$37,500		$25,000	

You are single, age 30, have adjusted gross income of $24,000, and are in the 15% tax rate bracket. You make a $3,000 IRA contribution. You can reduce your Federal tax by the saver's credit of $200 ($2,000 maximum x 10%). In addition, if your IRA is a deductible IRA, you save an additional $450 ($3,000 x 15%).

Use this chart to determine the tax consequences of the various IRAs:

Type of IRA	Deductible Contributions?	Earnings Taxable on Distribution?
Traditional Deductible	YES	YES
Traditional Nondeductible	NO	YES
Roth	NO	NO

Use the flow chart on page 224 to determine which type of IRA contributions you can make.

If either you or your spouse is an active participant in a retirement plan, and if you file separately, generally neither of you can make a deductible IRA contribution. However, if you are not an active participant in a retirement plan but your spouse is, a special rule applies. As long as you and your spouse have not lived together at any time during the year, you can deduct an IRA contribution up to the $3,000 ($3,500 if you are 50+; $2,000 for 2001) annual limit if you file separately.

To determine if you are an active participant in your company's retirement plan, look at your Form W-2. Your employer will check a box to show you are an active participant.

A major benefit of both traditional deductible and nondeductible IRAs is that the earnings, such as interest and dividends, are tax-free until you withdraw the money. This tax deferral allows you to save money for retirement without paying any current income taxes on the earnings. Your money grows more quickly. With a Roth IRA, generally all distributions are tax-free. See Tax Saving Idea #81 for information on Roth IRAs.

Penalties may apply if you take money out too early. Many people are reluctant to put money into retirement accounts because they do not want to pay penalties if they need the money early. However, even with the penalties, you generally come out ahead if your money is in a retirement plan as compared to a taxable account.

IRA CHOICES FOR 2001 AND LATER

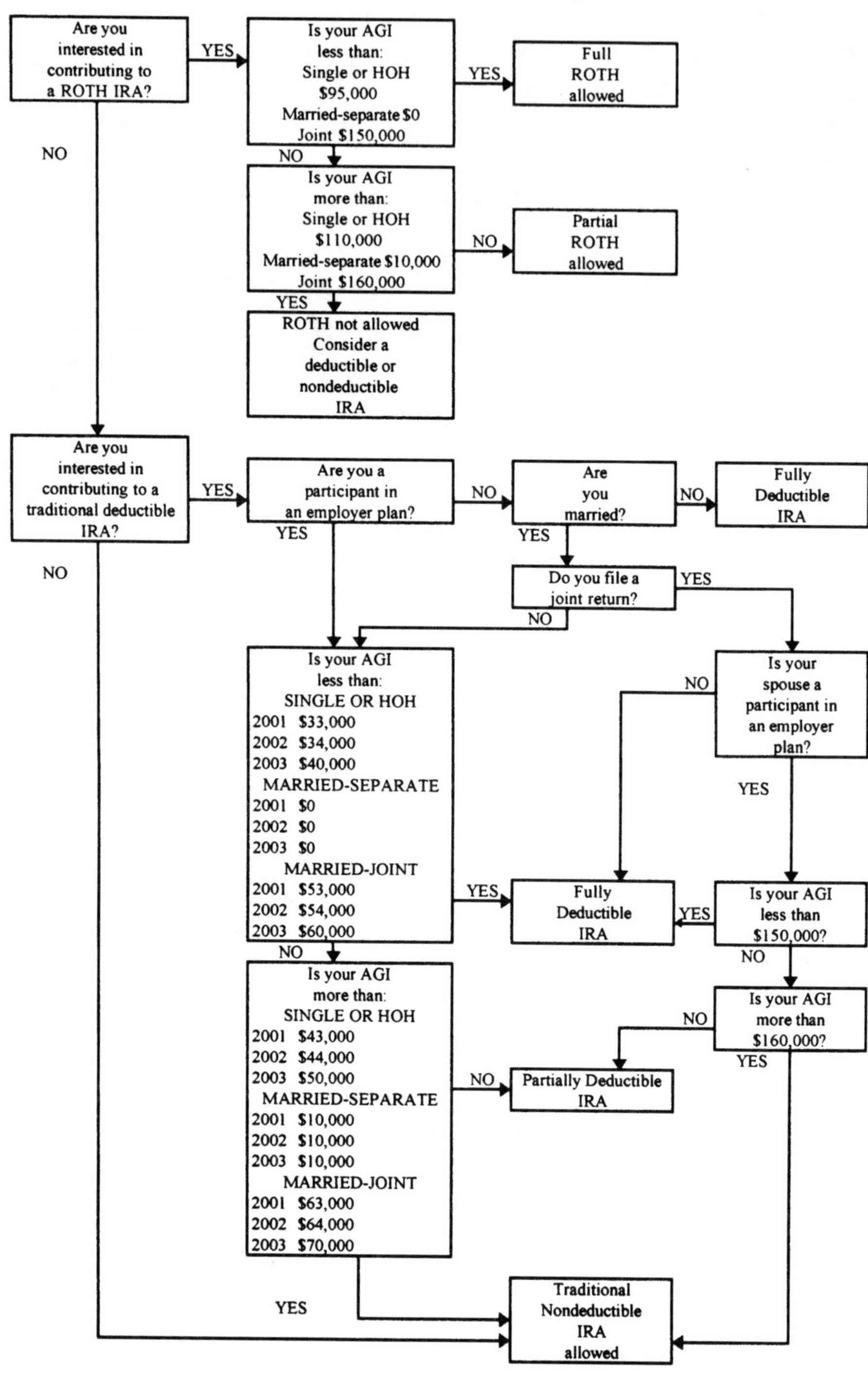

NOTE: You, and/or your spouse if you are married, must have earned income of at least the amount you contribute to your total IRAs

You have $3,000. You are in the 34% (27% Federal and 7% state) tax rate bracket. You earn 10% (6.6% after tax) (10% x (1-34%)) on your investments. You need the money in 11 years when your child will start college. Here is a comparison between putting your money in a taxable investment, putting your money into a Roth IRA, putting your money into a nondeductible IRA, and putting your money into a deductible IRA when you also invest the tax savings.

	Taxable Investment	Roth IRA	Nondeductible IRA	Deductible IRA
Contribution	$ 3,000	$ 3,000	$ 3,000	$ 3,000
Tax savings				
($3,000 x 34%)				1,020
Number of years				
until withdrawal	11	11	11	11
Account value-Year 11	6,060	8,559	8,559	8,559
Penalty on distribution	0			
(($8,559 - 3,000) x 10%)		(556)	(556)	
($8,559 x 10%)				(856)
Tax on distribution	0			
(($8,559 - 3,000) x 34%)		0	(1,890)	
($8,559 x 34%)				(2,910)
Net cash from tax savings including interest earned	0	0	0	2,060
Net cash	$ 6,060	$ 8,003	$ 6,113	$ 6,853

Thus, if you leave your money in a nondeductible IRA for at least 11 years (six years if you can deduct your IRA contributions and one year if you make a Roth IRA contribution), even after tax and the 10% penalty, you have more money than if you keep the money in a taxable savings account. The result varies depending on your tax rate and the rate of return on your money. The savings are even greater if you put money into your IRA each year and allow it to grow for a period longer than 11 years. So, you can use IRA accounts to save money not only for retirement but also for future goals, such as your child's education.

You have until April 15th to make an IRA contribution for the previous year. If you make your IRA contribution between January 1st and April 15th of the following year, you must indicate that you want your contribution to apply to the prior year or it will automatically be applied to the current year.

While you have until April 15th to make an IRA contribution for the previous year, the sooner you make the contribution, the sooner your money begins to grow tax-deferred.

Make Your IRA Contributions To A Roth IRA So All Future Withdrawals Are Tax-Free

The Roth IRA is a relatively new type of individual retirement account (IRA). Roth IRAs are similar to traditional IRAs in that the earnings in the account grow tax-free.

Roth IRAs are different from traditional IRAs in that generally any withdrawals you make will be completely tax-free. Also, unlike other IRAs, you can contribute to a Roth IRA after you are 70 1/2 as long as you have earned income, such as earnings from your job.

The maximum annual contribution you can make to all of your IRAs is $3,000 ($3,500 if you are 50+; $2,000 for 2001). Thus, depending on your income, you could split your annual contribution between a Roth IRA, a regular IRA, and a nondeductible IRA.

The maximum contribution to a Roth IRA phases out based on your adjusted gross income (AGI) as follows:

	Full Roth	Partial Roth	No Roth
Married filing jointly	<$150,000	$150,000-$160,000	$160,000+
Single and head of household	<$95,000	$95,000-$110,000	$110,000+
Married filing separately	$0	$0-$10,000	$10,000+

You and your spouse both work. You file jointly and have a combined AGI of $100,000. Each of you participates in your employers' retirement plans. You are eligible to make contributions to Roth IRAs of up to $3,000 each.

If your combined AGI is $155,000, you could make Roth IRA contributions of up to $1,500 each (since $155,000 is halfway through the phase-out range). You could also make nondeductible IRA contributions of up to $1,500 each.

You cannot deduct contributions you make to a Roth IRA. However, qualified withdrawals from a Roth IRA are both tax-free and penalty-free.

To be a qualified withdrawal, you must meet certain conditions. First, you must meet a five-year holding period. The five-year period begins on the first day of the year for which you make the contribution. For example, if you make a Roth IRA contribution on April 15, 2003, for the 2002 tax year, you would meet the five-year holding period beginning in 2007.

Second, your withdrawal must be for one of the following reasons:

- You are at least age 59 1/2
- You die and the distribution is made to your beneficiary
- You are disabled
- You are a first-time homebuyer (see Tax Saving Idea #89)

NOTE: Contributions to Education Savings Accounts do not count toward the annual maximum. See Tax Saving Idea #36 for more information about Education Savings Accounts.

You are in the 34% (27% Federal and 7% state) tax rate bracket. You earn 10% (6.6% after tax) (10% x (1 - 34%)) on your investments. You make $3,000 contributions at the beginning of the year for 20 years to the following accounts:

	Roth IRA	Traditional Deductible IRA	Traditional Nondeductible IRA	Taxable Account
Annual contribution	$ 3,000	$ 3,000	$ 3,000	$ 3,000
Tax savings				
($3,000 x 34%)		1,020		
Cumulative contributions	60,000	60,000	60,000	60,000
Account value – Year 20	189,007	189,007	189,007	125,517
Tax on distribution				
($189,007 x 34%)		(64,262)		
(($189,007 - 60,000) x 34%)			(43,862)	
Net cash from tax savings including interest earned		42,676		
Net cash	$189,007	$167,421	$ 145,145	$ 125,517

Thus, if your tax rate stays the same for all 20 years, and if you have a choice between the above accounts (based on your income level and your participation in a retirement plan), your first choice would be to make your contributions to a Roth IRA.

However, if your tax rate decreases after you retire, a traditional deductible IRA may be better. Assume your Federal tax rate drops to 15% (22% including the 7% state tax rate) in year 20 when you withdraw the money.

	Roth IRA	Traditional Deductible IRA	Traditional Nondeductible IRA	Taxable Account
Annual contribution	$ 3,000	$ 3,000	$ 3,000	$ 3,000
Tax savings				
($3,000 x 34%)		1,020		
Cumulative contributions	60,000	60,000	60,000	60,000
Account value – Year 20	189,007	189,007	189,007	125,517
Tax on distribution				
($189,007 x 22%)		(41,582)		
(($189,007-60,000) x 22%)			(28,382)	
Net cash from tax savings including interest earned		42,676		
Net cash	$189,007	$190,101	$160,625	$ 125,517

In this case, your first choice would be to make your contributions to a traditional deductible IRA.

Beginning in 2002, you may be eligible for the "saver's credit" if you make a contribution of up to $2,000 to your IRA. See Tax Saving Idea #80.

Convert Your IRA To A Roth IRA So All Future Distributions Are Tax-Free

You can convert your traditional individual retirement accounts (IRAs) to Roth IRAs. (See Tax Saving Idea #81.) Your cost to convert an IRA to a Roth IRA is the tax on the current value of the money. Your benefit is that qualified withdrawals from a Roth IRA are completely tax-free.

Your adjusted gross income (AGI) must be under $100,000 (before the income from the IRA conversion). This same income limit applies whether you are single or married. If you are married, you must file jointly to be able to convert your IRA to a Roth IRA.

You are married and file a joint tax return. You expect your AGI to be $75,000. You have an IRA valued at $50,000 for which you took deductions for all of your contributions. Your spouse has an IRA valued at $60,000, of which $16,000 was made on a nondeductible basis.

Since your AGI is less than $100,000, you can convert your existing IRAs to Roth IRAs. You will be taxed on the following amounts:

	You	Spouse
Total value	$50,000	$60,000
Basis (nondeductible contributions)	0	16,000
Taxable amount	$50,000	$44,000

NOTE: You are not required to convert the full value of your IRA to a Roth IRA. You can choose to convert a portion.

With traditional IRAs, you must begin taking distributions at about age 70 1/2. One potential estate planning benefit of a Roth IRA that is not available with traditional deductible and nondeductible IRAs is that there are no required minimum distributions. Thus, you can keep your money in the Roth IRA and continue to let it grow tax-free for a longer period of time.

You are in the 34% (27% Federal and 7% state) tax rate bracket. You expect to be in the same tax rate bracket when you make withdrawals from your IRA in 10 years when you are 60. The value of your IRA is $40,000, and all of your IRA contributions were deductible. You earn an 8% (5.28% after tax) return on your IRA. If you convert to a Roth IRA, you will pay $13,600 ($40,000 x 34%) out of your non-IRA savings account.

	IRA	Non-IRA Savings Account	Roth IRA
Value of IRA today	$40,000		$40,000
Tax cost to convert		$13,600	
Number of years until withdrawal	10	10	10
Account value – Year 10	86,357	22,751	86,357
Tax on distribution	(29,361)	0	0
Net cash after tax	$56,996	$22,751	$86,357
Add value in taxable account	22,751		
Total net cash after tax	$79,747		

In this case, you would choose to convert your IRA to a Roth IRA since you would have $6,610 ($86,357 - 79,747) more by converting to a Roth IRA.

Assume you will be in the 22% (15% Federal and 7% state) tax rate bracket when you make withdrawals from your IRA in 10 years when you are 60.

	IRA	Non-IRA Savings Account	Roth IRA
Value of IRA today	$40,000		$40,000
Tax cost to convert		$13,600	
Number of years until withdrawal	10	10	10
Account value – Year 10	86,357	22,751	86,357
Tax on distribution	(18,999)	0	0
Net cash after tax	$67,358	$22,751	$86,357
Add value in taxable account	22,751		
Total net cash after tax	$90,109		

In this case, you would choose to leave your IRA funds in your traditional IRA account since you would have $3,752 ($90,109 - 86,357) more in your IRA and non-IRA savings account.

Even A Nonworking Spouse Can Contribute $3,000 To An IRA

If you are married and either you or your spouse does not work, you may still be able to contribute to Individual Retirement Accounts (IRAs). The annual maximum IRA contribution per person is $3,000 ($3,500 if you are 50+; $2,000 for 2001). The total contribution for you and your spouse is the lesser of your combined earnings or $6,000. The maximum amount you can put into each of your separate accounts is $3,000 ($3,500 if you are 50+).

> You and your spouse file jointly and have adjusted gross income of $50,000: $500 from your wages, $45,000 from your spouse's wages and $4,500 from interest. Your spouse may contribute $3,000 to an IRA and you may contribute $3,000 to a spousal IRA.

With a Roth IRA, your contributions are not deductible, but generally all money you withdraw from your Roth IRA is tax-free. (See Tax Saving Idea #81 for limitations on making Roth IRA contributions.)

You may wish to contribute to a traditional IRA if you are ineligible to contribute to a Roth IRA due to the income limitations or if you want to deduct your IRA contribution. If you are in the 27% tax rate bracket and you make a $3,000 deductible IRA contribution, your Federal tax savings is $810. You also reduce your state tax. (See Tax Saving Idea #80 for limitations on deductible IRA contributions.)

If you are not eligible to make a Roth IRA contribution or a deductible IRA contribution, you can still make a nondeductible IRA contribution as long as you or your spouse has earned income. In some cases, depending on your current and estimated future tax rate brackets, you may choose to make nondeductible IRA contributions rather than Roth or deductible IRA contributions. Use the chart in Tax Saving Idea #80 to determine which type of IRA contributions you can make.

Encourage Your Employer To Set Up A Qualified Retirement Plan Or 401(k) And Take Advantage Of It

Qualified plans are deferred compensation plans set up by companies for employees. These plans are considered part of your total pay. Once the money is put into a plan, it is allocated to employees and cannot be returned to your employer. If an employee leaves and has not worked for the company for a set period of time, part or all of the money allocated to that employee is reallocated to the remaining employees.

Contributions to a qualified plan are generally deductible by your company in the current year. However, you are not taxed on the money until it is distributed, usually when you retire. At retirement, you can choose to have the money distributed over several years so it is not taxed to you all in one year.

The two types of qualified plans are defined contribution plans and defined benefit plans. Profit sharing plans are the most common defined contribution plan. With profit sharing plans, your employer specifies annually the amount that will be contributed on the employees' behalf. The benefits you later receive are determined by how much the contributions have grown over the years.

Pension plans are the most common defined benefit plan. With pension plans, your employer specifies the amount you will receive when you retire. This amount is usually based on the number of years you worked for the employer and the average pay you earned. Based on the projected payout from the pension plan, an actuary determines the amount your employer needs to contribute annually.

Typically a qualified plan has a vesting schedule. This schedule determines the amount you get when you terminate your employment prior to retirement. For example, if your account balance is $10,000 and you are only 40% vested, you will get $4,000 if you leave the company.

If you are thinking about leaving your company, you should check the vesting schedule to see how soon you will become another year vested.

Your company's retirement plan requires 1,000 hours of service during a year to entitle you to one more year of vesting. If you wait to leave the company until you meet that 1,000 hour requirement (which is about one half of a year for a full-time employee), you could gain an extra year of vesting.

If your employer has a qualified plan, certain opportunities are available to you. If you recently left another company where you participated in a qualified plan, you can usually roll over a distribution from the old company's retirement plan to the new company's retirement plan. Transferring the money from plan to plan avoids the 20% withholding that the IRS now imposes on distributions from retirement plans. Also, transferring your money from one plan to another keeps your money in a qualified plan where it can grow tax-free until you withdraw the money.

Some retirement plans allow distributions only upon reaching a certain retirement age. Be sure to read the information you receive from your company to determine when and how you can get money out of your retirement plan.

401(k) plans

A 401(k) plan is part of a profit sharing or stock bonus plan maintained by a company. Under a 401(k) plan, you can choose to defer a portion of your current salary and have it put into a qualified plan. Thus, anything you choose to defer receives the same tax advantages as contributions to a qualified plan, including no current income tax on the amount you defer and no current tax on the earnings.

Many employers will match a portion of the amount you choose to defer. For example, if your employer matches 50 cents for every dollar you defer up to 6% of your salary, you effectively earn an additional 50% on your money. For example, if you earn $30,000 and defer 6% of your salary ($1,800), your employer will contribute $900 on your behalf.

Any money which you defer is 100% yours if you leave the company. The matching amount paid by your employer is subject to the vesting schedule maintained by the plan. Thus, you may not be able to keep your employer's contributions.

The maximum percentage of salary you can choose to defer is 100%, although your company's plan may set a lower limit. The maximum amount of salary you can defer into a 401(k) for 2002 is $11,000 ($12,000 if you are 50+) and 2003 is $12,000 ($14,000 if you are 50+). This amount is adjusted annually for inflation. If you are a highly compensated employee, as defined by the Internal Revenue Code, sometimes you cannot defer the maximum

100% of your salary. This is a complex computation which your employer must make each year.

You earn $35,000. You elect to defer $5,250 annually (15% of your $35,000 salary). Although you must pay 7.65% FICA tax on your full $35,000 salary, you reduce your taxable income by $5,250. Thus, if you are in the 27% Federal tax rate bracket, you will save current income tax of $1,418 ($5,250 x 27%). You may also save state taxes.

Based on the terms of your company's plan, sometimes there are restrictions on the dates you can change the percentage you choose to defer. For example, some plans allow you to change your percentage on January 1st and July 1st, while other plans allow you to change your percentage any time you desire.

Many 401(k) plans are participant-directed. This means you choose how you want to invest your money in the 401(k) plan. Generally, the plan will provide you with several options for investments. This allows you to make the investment decisions for your retirement plan money.

Usually, you can contribute much more to a 401(k) plan than an Individual Retirement Account (IRA). Although there are more restrictions on getting your money out of a 401(k) plan, you can build a larger retirement account with a 401(k) plan than you can with an IRA.

Some 401(k) plans allow distributions only when you reach a certain retirement age. Be sure to read the information you receive from your company to determine when and how you can get money out of your 401(k).

SIMPLE plans

Small businesses with less than 100 employees and no other retirement plan can adopt a Savings Incentive Match Plan for Employees (SIMPLE) retirement plan. The SIMPLE plan can be either an IRA or a 401(k). Generally, your employer must match your contributions dollar-for-dollar up to 3% of your earnings. However, in certain cases a lower match can be elected or a 2% nonelective contribution can be made for all employees making at least $5,000. The maximum amount of salary you can defer into a SIMPLE plan is $7,000 ($7,500 if you are 50+; $6,500 for 2001). This amount is scheduled to increase annually. See Tax Saving Ideas #85 and #86.

NOTE: If your employer sets up a new retirement plan in 2002 or later, your employer may be eligible for a credit. The credit is 50% of the first $1,000 of administrative and retirement-education expenses for each of the first three years of the plan. This credit helps reduce the cost of establishing a new plan.

If You Are Self-Employed, You Can Set Up Your Own Retirement Plan

If you are self-employed, you can generally set up a retirement plan for yourself and make tax deductible contributions. Self-employed people can set up a Keogh plan or a Simplified Employee Pension Plan (SEP). A SEP is an individual retirement account (IRA).

A Keogh plan is a qualified plan. You can structure a Keogh plan like a profit sharing plan, which means what you put in the plan is discretionary. The amount you receive at retirement depends on how much you put in before you retire and how much the money grows. Alternatively, you can structure a Keogh plan like a pension plan, which means the amounts paid from the plan are predetermined, and you, as the employer, must put enough money in the retirement plan to pay the retirement benefits.

With SEPs and Keogh plans, you can contribute and deduct up to 25% (15% for 2001) of your net earnings annually. Due to the technical definition of "net earnings," this amount computes to somewhere between 18.5% and 20% (12% and 13.5% for 2001) of your earnings on Schedule C of your Federal tax return.

You make $35,000 after expenses from your business. Your self employment tax on this income is $4,945. With a 15% or 25% retirement plan, you can contribute and deduct $4,243 or $6,505, which you compute as follows:

Earnings after expenses	$ 35,000	$ 35,000
Less retirement plan contribution	4,243	6,505
Less 1/2 self-employment tax ($4,945 x .5)	2,473	2,473
Net earnings	28,284	26,022
Plan percentage	x 15%	x 25%
Retirement plan contribution	$ 4,243	$ 6,505

If you have employees, you may need to make contributions to the plan for them also. Generally, if you make a 25% (15% for 2001) contribution for yourself (even though this calculates to a lesser percentage due to the technical definition), you must make a 25% (15% for 2001) contribution for your employees. However, if you make certain elections when you set up your retirement plan, you will not need to make any contributions for employees who are under age 21 or for employees who have not worked for you during at least 3 of the last 5 years.

If you have 25 employees or less, and if 50% or more choose to make salary reduction contributions, you can fund a SEP with your employee's pre-tax earnings. This type of arrangement is called a Salary Reduction SEP (SARSEP). SARSEPs cannot be adopted after 1996. Generally, the maximum percentage an employee can defer is 100% (15% for 2001). The maximum salary any employee can defer into the SARSEP for 2002 is $11,000 ($12,000 if the employee is 50+; $10,500 for 2001). These plans are more complex than the straight SEP since each year you must make calculations to assure that the plan provides pre-tax elective deferrals that meet a deferral percentage test. There are similar provisions for salary reduction Keogh plans.

Small businesses can set up a Savings Incentive Match Plan for Employees (SIMPLE) retirement plan. The SIMPLE plan can be either an IRA or a 401(k). See Tax Saving Ideas #84 and #86.

A common question is: "If I start a retirement plan, do I have to make annual contributions?" Generally, the answer is no if you have a profit sharing plan where you elect to make discretionary contributions. However, if you have a pension plan, you may be required to make annual contributions to the pension plan.

If you have a money purchase Keogh plan, you may be able to contribute and deduct up to 25% of your net earnings for 2001 rather than 15%. Again, due to the technical definition of "net earnings," this amount computes to somewhere between 18.5% and 20% of your earnings. Many people choose to create two plans by setting up a Keogh profit sharing plan to which they contribute up to 15% of earnings and a Keogh money purchase pension plan to which they contribute an additional 10% of earnings.

The maximum amount you can contribute annually for each person in a defined contribution plan is $40,000 ($35,000 for 2001). Additionally, the maximum amount of earnings for each person you can use to calculate the deduction is $200,000 ($170,000 for 2001). The percentage you contribute to a money purchase pension plan is mandatory once you set up the plan, while the percentage you contribute to a profit sharing plan is voluntary and can change each year based on what you want to contribute.

The chart below compares Keogh, SEP and SIMPLE plans.

	KEOGH	SEP	SIMPLE
Date to set up new plan	By year-end (generally Dec. 31)	By due date of tax return	Generally before beginning of year
Date contribution due	Due date of tax return including extensions	Due date of tax return including extensions	Due date of tax return including extensions; elective deferrals due 30 days after last day of month for which contributions are made
Ability to customize plan	Yes	Minimal	Minimal
IRS annual filing requirements	Must file annually	None	IRA: None, but some employee notifications required 401(k): Must file annually
Participant loans available	Yes	No	IRA: No 401(k): Maybe
Participant withdrawals	Subject to plan restrictions	Can be made any time after contribution is made	Can be made any time after contribution is made, but 25% penalty if withdrawal is made during two-year period beginning on first day of participation

If it is after the end of the year and you are calculating your taxes, you may choose to set up a retirement plan for the previous year. You will need to use a SEP, because you must set up Keogh plans before the end of the year. Later, if you decide you want a more customized plan, you can stop making contributions to your SEP plan and set up a new Keogh plan.

Either you, as the employer, or the plan can pay the fees to set up your plan and to annually maintain it. Examples of fees are attorney's fees to draft the plan and broker's fees to administer the plan. The advantage to you, as the employer, of paying the fees is that you and your employees will have more money in the plan growing tax-deferred.

To set up a SEP, you can use IRS Form 5305-SEP, "Simplified Employee Pension-Individual Retirement Accounts Contribution Agreement," or IRS Form 5305A-SEP, "Salary Reduction and Other Simplified Employee Pension Elective-Individual Retirement Accounts Contribution Agreement." You keep this form and do not file it with the IRS.

While you must file annual returns for Keogh plans with the IRS, if your Keogh covers only you and your spouse, you can use the simplified Form 5500-EZ.

If you set up a new retirement plan in 2002 or later, you may be eligible for a credit. The credit is 50% of the first $1,000 of administrative and retirement-education expenses for each of the first three years of the plan. This credit helps reduce your cost of establishing a new plan.

Contribute The Maximum To A SIMPLE Plan

Savings Incentive Match Plan for Employees (SIMPLE plans) are relatively new types of retirement plans. They can be set up by small businesses with less than 100 employees that have no other retirement plan. The SIMPLE plan can be either an IRA or a 401(k), depending on which one you (if you are self-employed) or your employer set up.

Under a SIMPLE plan, you can choose to defer up to 100% of your current salary and have it put into a retirement plan. If you are self-employed, you can choose to defer a portion of your earnings from your business. Anything you choose to defer reduces your current income, and you will pay no tax on the earnings until you withdraw the money. However, the FICA tax, also known as the Social Security tax or self-employment tax, applies to the amounts you choose to defer.

The maximum amount of salary you can defer into a SIMPLE plan is $7,000 ($7,500 if you are 50+; $6,500 for 2001). This amount is scheduled to increase annually. See Tax Saving Idea #87. If you are self-employed and have employees, you must offer this plan to your employees, but you can contribute to your plan even if your employees choose not to contribute to theirs.

If you make contributions to your SIMPLE plan, you (if you are self-employed) or your employer must also make contributions. There is a choice that your employer makes. Generally, your employer must match your contributions to your SIMPLE plan up to 3% of your pay. Alternatively, your employer can choose to contribute 2% of your pay even if you choose to make no contributions, as long as your pay is at least $5,000. Only $200,000 ($170,000 for 2001) of your compensation can be taken into account for the calculation.

Unlike most pension and profit sharing plans, you immediately vest in any contributions that either you or your employer contribute to your SIMPLE plan. Thus, if your account balance is $12,000 and you terminate your employment, you will get the full $12,000.

Any distributions you make from your SIMPLE plan can be subject to a 10% penalty unless you are at least age 59 1/2 or meet another exception. See Tax Saving Idea #88 for the exceptions to the 10% penalty. Any distributions you make from your SIMPLE plan during the two-year period beginning on the first day you began participating in the SIMPLE plan are subject to a 25% penalty.

If you are self-employed or you are an employer, you can use either IRS Form 5304-SIMPLE or IRS Form 5305-SIMPLE to set up a SIMPLE plan. Use Form 5304-SIMPLE if you let each participant select where they set up their account. Use Form 5305-SIMPLE if you require all participants to use one financial institution for the accounts.

You make $24,000. Your employer has a SIMPLE plan and matches your contributions up to 3% of your pay. You choose to defer $4,000 into the SIMPLE plan.

Your contribution into the SIMPLE plan	$4,000
Your employer's contribution ($24,000 x 3%)	720
Total contributions into your SIMPLE plan	$4,720

Beginning in 2002, you may be eligible for the "saver's credit" if you make a contribution of up to $2,000 to your IRA, 401(k) plan, or SIMPLE plan. See Tax Saving Idea #80.

If You Are 50+, Contribute An Extra $500 To Your IRA And An Extra $1,000 To Your 401(k)

For 2002 and later, if you are age 50 or older, you may be able to contribute extra amounts to your retirement plan. While these are called "catch-up" contributions, you are eligible even if you have always contributed the maximum amount.

The extra amount you can contribute depends on the type of your retirement plan. Here is the regular amount, the extra amount, and the total amount you can contribute to your retirement plan if you are age 50 or older:

Year	Regular	Extra	Total	Year	Regular	Extra	Total
Individual Retirement Accounts (Traditional and Roth IRAs)							
2001	$2,000	$0	$2,000	2002-2004	$3,000	$500	$3,500
401(k)							
2001	$10,500	$0	$10,500	2003	$12,000	$2,000	$14,000
2002	$11,000	$1,000	$12,000	2004	$13,000	$3,000	$16,000
SIMPLE							
2001	$6,500	$0	$6,500	2003	$8,000	$1,000	$9,000
2002	$7,000	$500	$7,500	2004	$9,000	$1,500	$9,500

You must have at least as much earnings from your job or business as you contribute to your retirement plan. Also, you can make the extra contribution as long as you will be age 50 or older sometime during that year.

You are 55, earn $30,000 from your job, and are single. If your employer has a 401(k) plan, you can contribute up to $12,000 for 2002. Additionally, you can contribute up to $3,500 to your IRA, which could be either a traditional IRA or a Roth IRA.

Avoid 50% Penalties On Distributions From Your Retirement Plan

When it is time to withdraw money from your retirement plan, you should consider both nontax as well as tax considerations. Here are several of the nontax factors:

- Your need for the money
- Your life expectancy
- Your health
- Your future plans

The two main tax factors are:

- the penalties on withdrawing money from your retirement plan, and
- the tax you pay on withdrawing the money.

In previous Tax Saving Ideas, you learned about how to get money into a retirement plan (Tax Saving Ideas #80 and #81 for IRAs; Tax Saving Idea #84 for qualified plans; and Tax Saving Ideas #85 and #86 for self-employed retirement plans and SIMPLEs). Now we will focus on getting the money out without paying penalties.

There are many penalties that apply to both distributions and the failure to make distributions from retirement plans. The rules for avoiding the 50% penalty are:

- not too little, and
- not too late.

Not too little

Once you reach age 70 1/2, you must begin taking distributions from your retirement plans and non-Roth IRAs. The minimum distribution you must receive annually is the amount which will distribute the entire balance in your accounts over your distribution period. A 50% excise tax applies to distributions less than this amount. This 50% excise tax does not apply to distributions from retirement plans other than IRAs if you continue working after age 70 1/2 and you own less than 5% of the company.

You calculate your minimum distribution by dividing your account balance on December 31st of the prior year (or the plan year end in the case of a retirement plan) by your distribution period. You determine your distribution period using your age as of December 31st of the current year. The following table shows your distribution period. There are special rules if your spouse who is your beneficiary is more than 10 years younger than you.

Minimum Distribution Periods
Table for determining distribution period
Proposed Regulations 130477-00 issued in January 2001
Effective beginning January 1, 2002
(Can be used for distributions relating to calendar year 2001)

Age	Distribution Period	Age	Distribution Period	Age	Distribution Period	Age	Distribution Period
70	26.2	82	16.0	94	8.3	106	3.8
71	25.3	83	15.3	95	7.8	107	3.6
72	24.4	84	14.5	96	7.3	108	3.3
73	23.5	85	13.8	97	6.9	109	3.1
74	22.7	86	13.1	98	6.5	110	2.8
75	21.8	87	12.4	99	6.1	111	2.6
76	20.9	88	11.8	100	5.7	112	2.4
77	20.1	89	11.1	101	5.3	113	2.2
78	19.2	90	10.5	102	5.0	114	2.0
79	18.4	91	9.9	103	4.7	115+	1.8
80	17.6	92	9.4	104	4.4		
81	16.8	93	8.8	105	4.1		

Your traditional IRA had a $50,000 balance on December 31st. You are 71. Your spouse is age 68. Your distribution period is 25.3. Your minimum distribution is:

Account balance	$50,000
Divided by life expectancy	÷ 25.3
Minimum distribution	$ 1,976

Not too late

You must begin receiving distributions from your qualified plans and non-Roth IRAs no later than April 1st of the year following the calendar year in which you reach age 70 1/2 (your required beginning date). A 50% excise tax applies to distributions you receive too late. An exception to this 50% tax applies to distributions from retirement plans other than IRAs if you continue working after age 70 1/2 and you own less than 5% of the company.

The April 1st date is relevant only in the year following the year you reach age 70 1/2. After that, you must receive your annual distributions by December 31st. Many people make the mistake of bunching two distributions in the year after reaching age 70 1/2 — one on April 1st and the second on December 31st. As a result, they pay tax at a higher tax rate and subject more of their Social Security benefits to tax (see Tax Saving Idea #4) than if they had received only one payment. However, if your tax rate is lower now than it will be in the future, it may be good planning to bunch two payments into one year.

> Using the information in the prior example, if you were born November 15, 1936, you would be 70 1/2 on May 15, 2002. Thus, your first required distribution date is April 1, 2003.
>
> However, if you wait until 2003 to take your first required distribution, remember you must also take your next required distribution by December 31, 2003.

Distributions after you die

If your retirement plan or IRA has money in it when you die, this money is distributed to the beneficiary or beneficiaries you named for your retirement account. The beneficiary or beneficiaries as of the end of the year following the year you die may use the life expectancy tables to calculate the minimum amount to withdraw. However, if you have no beneficiary designated for your retirement account, generally the plan must distribute the money by December 31st of the fifth year following your death.

If your spouse is your beneficiary, your spouse may roll over your plan into an account in your spouse's name as owner. Thus, the new account will be your spouse's account.

Reporting

For information on how to report these penalties, see Federal Form 5329.

You May Be Able To Withdraw Money Penalty-Free From Your Retirement Plan Or IRA Before Age 59 1/2

Penalties generally apply if you withdraw money from your retirement plan before you reach age 59 1/2. The penalty is 10% of the taxable distribution. The penalty is 25% if you take a distribution from a SIMPLE retirement plan within two years of becoming a participant.

> You are 40 years old, receive $10,000 from your traditional IRA, are in the 27% Federal tax rate bracket, and do not meet any of the exceptions to the penalties. You owe the following tax and penalty:
>
> | | |
> |---|---|
> | Income tax at 27% tax rate | $ 2,700 |
> | Early distribution penalty | 1,000 |

You can avoid the penalty if:

- You receive a distribution from your retirement plan or IRA, and you are totally and permanently disabled.
- You are at least 55 years old and receive a distribution from a retirement plan upon terminating employment. This exception does not apply to distributions from IRAs.
- You receive a distribution as a beneficiary of an estate after the death of someone else.
- You receive a distribution from your IRA that you use to pay qualified first-time homebuyer expenses. This exception only applies to distributions from IRAs.
- You begin receiving annual distributions from your IRA that you will receive over your life expectancy or the joint life expectancy of you and your spouse. This exception applies only to distributions from traditional IRAs unless the distributions are from your company's retirement plan and start after you retire.
- You receive a distribution from your IRA that you use to pay medical expenses in excess of 7.5% of your adjusted gross income.
- You receive a distribution from your IRA that you use to pay qualified higher education expenses.

Qualified higher education expenses include expenditures:

- for tuition, fees, books, supplies, and equipment required for enrollment or attendance,
- at a postsecondary educational institution, including graduate-level courses,
- for you, your spouse, your child, or your grandchild.

Qualified first-time homebuyer expenses include expenditures:

- up to $10,000 during your lifetime,
- for amounts used within 120 days to buy, build, or rebuild a principal residence for a first-time homebuyer, including any usual or reasonable settlement, financing, or other closing costs,
- for you, your spouse, your child, your grandchild, or an ancestor of you or your spouse.

You can be a first-time homebuyer even if you have previously owned a home. To be considered a first-time homebuyer, you (and your spouse if you are married) may not have owned a home during the previous two years.

In 2001, you and your spouse sell your home and move into an apartment. In 2005, you buy a new principal residence. You withdraw $6,000 from your traditional IRA to use for financing costs and closing costs. You will not have to pay the 10% early distribution penalty on your IRA withdrawal.

Additionally, generally the income tax and early distribution penalty do not apply if you roll over your distribution to another qualified plan or IRA within 60 days.

If you take a nonqualified distribution from your Roth IRA that you funded with Roth IRA contributions, you may still avoid the 10% early distribution penalty if the distribution is not taxable to you. See Tax Saving Idea #81 for the definition of a qualified withdrawal. However, if you convert a traditional IRA to a Roth IRA, and within five years take a distribution, the 10% early distribution penalty could apply even if the distribution is tax-free to you.

You are 50 years old and made Roth IRA contributions of $2,000 per year for four years, giving you $8,000 ($2,000 x 4) of basis in your Roth IRA. You take a $5,000 distribution. Since you have at least $5,000 of basis from making Roth contributions, the $5,000 is tax-free to you. Additionally, since no amount is taxable to you and since the distribution was entirely attributable to annual contributions you made, the 10% early distribution penalty will not apply.

If instead you made a Roth IRA conversion of $8,000 two years ago, the full $8,000 was taxed to you at that time. If you made no other Roth IRA contributions, you would still have $8,000 of basis in your Roth IRA. A $5,000 distribution would be tax-free to you. However, since the conversion amount is distributed within the five-year period of when you made the conversion and the distribution is nonqualified, you will pay a $500 ($5,000 x 10%) early distribution penalty.

NOTE: Distributions from your traditional deductible or nondeductible IRA may be subject to income tax even though they are not subject to the early distribution penalty. Generally distributions from Roth IRAs will be totally tax-free.

NOTE: The rules for distributions from SIMPLE retirement plans are different. See Internal Revenue Service Publication 590, available by calling 1-800-TAX-FORM.

Consider The Ways To Get Money Out Of Your Retirement Plans

Periodic Payments

Many retirement plans allow you to take annuity payments. For example, you can withdraw amounts regularly over a period of time, such as $1,000 a month until you die. If your employer fully funded the plan (you did not put any money into the plan) or if you put in some money but it was pre-tax dollars (such as a 401(k) plan), the full amount you receive is taxable. If you made nondeductible contributions, only a portion of the amount you receive is taxable. The rules for calculating the taxable amount vary based on when your payments began.

For annuities beginning before November 20, 1996, you could choose between the general rule and the old simplified general rule. For additional information on these methods, get IRS Publications 575 and 939 by calling 1-800-TAX-FORM.

For annuities with starting dates after November 19, 1996, you use the modified simplified general rule. Under all methods, you calculate the amount you receive tax-free. The remainder is taxable to you.

You use the following formula to calculate the amount you receive tax-free.

Nondeductible contributions
you made
÷
Expected number of payments

Under the modified simplified general rule, you base your expected number of payments on your age when your distributions begin and one of the following charts.

Use this chart if your annuity starting date is after December 31, 1997, and your benefits are based on the life of more than one annuitant:

Combined Ages	Expected number of payments
110 and under	410
111-120	360
121-130	310
131-140	260
141 and over	210

Use this chart if your annuity is calculated on only your life:

Age	Expected number of payments for annuities starting after November 18, 1996	Expected number of payments for annuities starting before November 19, 1996
55 and under	360	300
56-60	310	260
61-65	260	240
66-70	210	170
71 and over	160	120

You are 62 and begin receiving $500 per month from your retirement plan based on your life expectancy. You made $26,000 of nondeductible contributions to the plan.

Using the modified simplified general rule, your monthly tax-free distribution is $100 ($26,000/260). Thus, you pay tax on only $400 ($500-100) per month.

If your distribution is based on your life and your spouse's (age 60) life, your monthly tax-free distribution is $83.87 (26,000/310). Thus, you pay tax on only $416.13 ($500 - 83.87) per month.

With the modified simplified general rule, you are spreading the income from your monthly payments, as well as the related income tax, over a period of time.

Lump-sum distributions if you were age 50 before 1986

When you receive a lump-sum distribution from a qualified pension or profit-sharing plan, you may be eligible for preferential income tax treatment. A lump-sum distribution is a payment of your full amount of benefits within one tax year. This amount represents one of the following:

- distribution made because of your separation from service if you are an employee,
- distribution made after you reach age 59 1/2,
- distribution made because of your death, or
- distribution made because of your disability if you are self-employed.

If you reached age 50 before 1986, you may be able to use the ten-year averaging treatment for your distribution. You can use this lump-sum method only once in your life. Alternatively, you can tax your distribution using your regular income tax rates. Compare your tax using the two available methods. Select the one that gives you the lowest result. You use Form 4972 to make these choices.

You are age 67 and receive a lump-sum distribution of $100,000. You have not previously used your lump-sum distribution election. You are in the 35% tax rate bracket. Your tax on the distribution under the two alternatives (using 2001 tax rates) is:

Ordinary income	$35,000
Ten-year averaging	14,471

Thus, if you do not anticipate a future lump-sum distribution, you could elect to use ten-year averaging to achieve the lowest tax on the distribution.

Borrowing money from a qualified retirement plan

You may be able to borrow money from a qualified retirement plan. You must meet the plan requirements for repayment of the principal amount with interest. If you borrow the money to buy your house and you use the house to secure the loan, you can generally deduct the interest. Thus, you pay deductible interest to your retirement plan. The interest is tax-free in your retirement plan until you withdraw the money.

The maximum amounts you can borrow are:

Your vested amount in the plan	Maximum borrowing
$20,000 or less	lesser of $10,000 or your vested balance
$20,000 - $100,000	50% of your vested balance
Over $100,000	$50,000

Your plan may set lower amounts or not allow borrowing.

Generally, you must repay a loan from your retirement plan within five years. However, if you borrow the money to buy your principal residence, the five-year limit does not apply.

Borrow Money From Your IRA For Less Than 60 Days Without Paying Tax Or Penalties

If you need money for a short time, consider making a withdrawal from your Individual Retirement Account (IRA). As long as you put the money back into an IRA within 60 days, you are not taxed on the withdrawal.

You may be able to roll over a distribution you receive from a qualified plan. Qualified plans eligible for the rollover treatment include IRAs, individual retirement annuities, qualified trusts, and annuity plans. The maximum amount you can roll over is the amount that would be taxable to you if you did not roll over the amount. If you roll over a qualified plan distribution into an IRA, it is important that you do not mix the qualified plan distribution with other IRA money. If you do, you cannot use the special averaging tax treatment for lump-sum distributions at a later time.

You must roll over a distribution within 60 days after you receive it to qualify for rollover treatment. The IRS is very strict on the 60-day requirement.

Any amount you do not roll over is taxable to you. If there was Federal income tax withholding taken from your distribution, you can still qualify for the rollover treatment. In this case, you need to redeposit the full amount of the distribution, including the amount of the Federal withholding, into your IRA.

There is a limitation on how often you can roll over money from one IRA to another IRA. If you withdrew the funds and used the rollover treatment during the previous 365 days, you cannot use it again for that IRA. For example, assume you withdraw $2,500 from your IRA on November 1st and roll over the money into another IRA within 60 days. Then four months later you withdraw another $3,000 from your first IRA. This second distribution is not eligible for rollover treatment and is taxable to you.

You can transfer money directly from one IRA to another at any time. Direct transfers are not subject to the once-a-year rule. Thus, if you are just moving money between IRAs, use a direct transfer so you avoid any problems with the 60-day rollover period and the once-a-year limitation.

Divorce

Work With Your Spouse To Reclassify Child Support As Alimony

Divorce

Approximately half the marriages entered in the United States end in divorce. When a couple gets divorced, tax matters are usually the farthest thing from their minds. The couple is much more concerned about who is going to get the antique table, who is going to have the children for Christmas, and who is going to pay the legal fees. It is a very emotional time.

Primarily because emotions are running so high, it is important for you to get expert advice. Experts, such as an attorney and an accountant, besides having experience with the legal, financial, and personal aspects of divorce, are objective. They can help you with:

- drafting of documents,
- valuation of property, such as businesses and retirement plans,
- analysis of the tables used by most states to determine alimony and child support, and
- communication with your spouse.

Most importantly, experts help you look past the short-term pain of divorce.

State divorce law has evolved in response to the number of divorces and because of the emergence of the two-earner society. The days when the mother received the house, alimony, primary custody of the children, and child support are disappearing. The house is just one asset in the property division. Often the division of property is equal, with one spouse writing a check for a small difference.

Alimony, if it is awarded at all, is usually temporary, allowing the recipient spouse time to complete school or otherwise adjust. Determining alimony in many states is as easy as looking up an amount based on relative salaries on a table.

Most states require joint custody of children unless there is risk to the children from an abusive or addictive parent. Child support is usually determined from a table that considers relative incomes, relative custody, child care costs, medical insurance costs, and travel costs.

Virtually every issue in divorce has tax significance. Like the state laws, the Federal tax laws pertaining to divorce have evolved. The tax law that applies to you depends on when your divorce was final and whether you have modified your divorce decree. Under present law, the general rules are:

- Gains and losses from the exchange of property in a property settlement are nontaxable;
- The spouses are not single until the divorce is final;
- Alimony is includable in the income of the recipient and deductible by the payer;
- Child support is not includable in the income of the recipient and not deductible by the payer;
- The dependency exemptions for children are under the control of the custodial parent; and
- The legal expenses arising from a divorce are not deductible.

There are many tax planning opportunities when you get divorced. Although it may seem difficult to cooperate with your spouse at the time, working together will help both of you.

One common example of a planning opportunity that requires cooperation involves reclassifying child support as alimony. Child support is not taxable to the recipient and not deductible by the payer. Alimony is taxable to the recipient and deductible by the payer. Consequently, by treating child support payments as alimony, you can shift income from a high tax rate spouse to a low tax rate spouse.

> You are in the 30% tax rate bracket and are willing to pay $9,000 of child support. Your spouse is in the 15% tax rate bracket and wants $11,000. Both of you can stay close to your goals and perhaps reach a compromise by treating the payments as alimony. Because you can deduct alimony payments but not child support, you should be indifferent between paying $9,000 in child support and $12,857 ($9,000 /(1 - .30)) in alimony. If your spouse receives $12,857 in alimony, your spouse will have $10,928 ($12,857 x (1 - .15)) cash after paying taxes. Reclassifying the payments from child support to alimony accomplishes both of your goals.

If the payer is in the lower tax rate bracket, it is usually better to treat the payments as child support rather than alimony.

If you decide to treat child support payments as alimony, it is important that the payments not decrease because of an event in your child's life, such as a birthday, graduating from high school or college, or leaving home. You must treat the future decrease as child support from the start if the decrease is based on an event in your child's life. It does not matter that the divorce decree calls the payments alimony. You can avoid this reclassification by saying in your divorce decree that you are paying alimony for the length of time you were married, for ten years to help your spouse start a new career, or for another reason not related to an event in your child's life.

To avoid reclassification of alimony as a property settlement, it is also important that your payments not be "front loaded" during the first three years. Alimony recapture rules apply if alimony payments decrease too much or terminate during the first three years.

In summary, when you get divorced,

- consult experts,
- think about the tax consequences of your decisions, and
- work with your spouse toward a compromise you can both live with.

When Dividing Property In A Divorce, Look At The After-Tax Values Of The Property

When couples divorce, they divide the property they own, including stock, real estate, and furniture. This property division may have been prearranged by a prenuptial agreement or may be controlled by state law. Most states require the equal division of your property, although the state laws usually allow you to keep property you brought into the marriage, received as gifts, and inherited.

The general rule for divorces after 1984 is that the property division is tax-free. In other words, if you transfer the property to your spouse, you will not recognize a gain. If you receive the property, the basis of the property will stay the same as it was when you were married.

Pursuant to your divorce decree, you transfer stock you own to your spouse. The stock has a basis of $60,000 and a fair market value of $100,000. You recognize no gain as a result of the transfer, and your spouse takes your $60,000 basis in the property. If your spouse sells the stock shortly after the divorce for $101,000, your spouse will have $41,000 ($101,000 - 60,000) of taxable gain.

Thus, when you are dividing property, be sure to consider the after-tax value of the property. It is better to keep properties that have little gain potential and transfer properties that have large gains.

If you have the choice of transferring Property A that has a value of $100,000 and a basis of $60,000 or Property B that has a value of $100,000 and a basis of $90,000, you should transfer Property A, the one with the $60,000 basis. You avoid paying tax on the $40,000 gain.

If you are in the 20% tax rate bracket for capital gains, Property A's after-tax value is $92,000 ($100,000 - ((100,000 - 60,000) x 20%)). Property B's after-tax value is $98,000 ($100,000 - ((100,000 - 90,000) x 20%)). Even though the two properties have the same fair market value, Property B's after-tax value is higher. This strategy assumes that both properties have equal appreciation potential and equal sentimental value.

If you and your spouse work together, you can shift income by transferring property with large gains to the spouse with the lower tax rate.

Before 1985, the person who gave property often recognized gain equal to the difference between the fair market value of the property and the property's basis. The recipient's basis in the property was equal to the fair market value. Thus, if you are selling stock or real estate you received from a pre-1985 divorce, remember that your spouse probably recognized gain. Your basis in the property is the fair market value at the time of your divorce, not the original purchase price.

When you divorced in 1983, you received land with a fair market value of $75,000. Your spouse's basis in the land was $20,000. Your spouse recognized a gain of $55,000. If you sell the land for $90,000, your taxable gain is $15,000 ($90,000 - 75,000), not $70,000 ($90,000 - 20,000) as it would be under the current rules.

Homes

The home is often the major asset transferred in a property division. You can handle the future ownership of the home in one of several ways.

Usually one spouse "moves out" and the spouse who continues to occupy the house "buys" the other spouse's interest in the house. This sale is not really a sale. The transfer is part of the property division and is tax-free. If you are the spouse who moves out, you do not need to buy a new home to avoid recognizing gain. If you are the spouse who keeps the house, you will keep the cost basis you had as a couple in the house. You may recognize gain when you sell the house, but any gain will probably be tax-free because of the $250,000 ($500,000 if you are married filing a joint return) exclusion for sales of principal residences. See Tax Saving Idea #59.

Sometimes the home is sold because neither spouse wants the house or neither can afford it alone. If you and your spouse sell the house, the sale is not tax-free. You will recognize gain unless you qualify for the $250,000 ($500,000 if you and your spouse quality) exclusion.

A third possibility is that you and your spouse will live apart, but continue to jointly own the home until some future time, perhaps when the children leave home. This arrangement may lead to a portion of the mortgage payments being treated as alimony. The $250,000 exclusion of gain is available to each spouse as long as one owner-spouse or the other continues to occupy the house as a principal residence. Thus, if the house is sold eight years after the divorce for a $300,000 ($150,000 each) gain, both former spouses can use their $250,000 exclusion to avoid recognizing the gain as long as each spouse otherwise qualifies.

Retirement plans

When dividing their property, many divorcing couples overlook their retirement plans. These plans include pension and profit sharing plans, Keogh plans of a self-employed individual, 401(k) plans, SIMPLE plans, and tax-deferred annuities. The money in these plans is as much a part of the marital property as the house.

Many spouses think that retirement plan assets are out of reach in a divorce, but that is not so. You can use a qualified domestic relations order (QDRO) to get to the money in a retirement account. QDROs permit qualified retirement plan benefits to be used to meet alimony, property division, or child support obligations. A QDRO is a court order that clearly specifies the amount of the participant's benefits that the plan administrator must pay to the alternate payee, usually the former spouse or child. Generally, the alternate payee can treat the payments the same as the participant could treat them. Thus, if you receive a distribution from your spouse's retirement plan, you can elect ten-year averaging on a lump-sum distribution if your spouse was age 50 or older before 1986 and otherwise qualifies for such treatment. See Tax Saving Idea #90.

You can avoid the tax on the retirement plan distributions by transferring the benefits to an IRA within 60 days. See Tax Saving Idea #91. Payments that are not rolled over into an IRA are taxable, but they are not subject to the 10% early withdrawal penalty even if the participant and the recipient are under age 59 1/2.

Amounts paid to a child as the alternate payee are taxed to the participant, not the child. These payments also are not subject to the 10% early withdrawal penalty.

In short, if you get divorced, consider the after-tax values of your property as well as the fair market value of your property. Also, for retirement plans, QDROs are an important planning tool.

Before You Are Divorced, You May Be Able To Use The Abandoned Spouse Rule To Claim Head Of Household Filing Status

Filing status affects filing requirements, income determination, deductions, the standard deduction, credits, and tax rates. When you are getting divorced, you need to consider your filing status before the divorce and after the divorce.

You are not single until you are officially divorced. If you are separated under a written separation agreement or temporary court order, you are not yet divorced.

If you and your spouse have no children, you must file either married filing jointly (MFJ) or married filing separately (MFS) until you are divorced. You will probably pay less tax by filing jointly. However, you are jointly and individually responsible for any tax, interest, and penalties due on a joint tax return even if your divorce decree states otherwise. You can avoid this exposure by filing separately or if you can prove you are an innocent spouse. Recent changes make it easier for you to avoid paying your former spouse's tax, but you still must show you were not aware of the mistake in the return.

In rare instances, you may pay less tax by filing separately. Generally, filing separately is not desirable because both spouses must itemize if one itemizes, credits such as the dependent care credit are lost, and one spouse is usually pushed into higher tax rates. See Tax Saving Idea #26.

After you are divorced, you and your spouse will use single filing status. You may pay less tax. Because of the marriage penalty, many two-earner married couples pay more tax than they would if they could file as single taxpayers. This situation occurs partly because the breaks into the higher tax rate brackets for joint filers are not twice the amounts for single individuals. By divorcing, you may avoid the marriage penalty. See Tax Saving Idea #23.

If you have children, some planning opportunities are available to you. Generally, similar to the couple without children, you must choose between filing MFJ and MFS until your divorce is final. However, you may be able to file as a head of household (HOH) under the abandoned spouse rule.

Filing as a HOH offers several advantages. First, you avoid the joint exposure that accompanies a joint return. Second, you avoid the drawbacks of filing a separate return. In other words, you can claim the standard deduction even if your spouse itemizes on a separate return. Your standard deduction is higher than the amount you can claim if you file MFS. Your exposure to the various marginal tax rates occurs at higher income levels than if you file MFS. Filing HOH allows you to claim credits that you cannot claim if you file MFS.

To qualify as an abandoned spouse, you must:

- file a separate return;
- pay more than half the cost of keeping up your home for the tax year; and
- live apart from your spouse for the last six months of the tax year.

Your primary home must be the home of a child, stepchild, adopted child, or foster child that you claim as a dependent, or could have claimed as a dependent if the exemption was not allowed to your spouse.

If you file as a HOH under the abandoned spouse rule, your spouse must file MFS until you are divorced unless he or she also qualifies as an abandoned spouse. If you have two children, you probably can plan it so you both qualify as abandoned spouses.

You and your spouse are getting divorced. In 2002, you earn $70,000 and your spouse earns $50,000. You have two children. You both claim the standard deduction.

	TAX*		
	You	Spouse	Combined
Married filing jointly			$20,837
Married filing separately (MFS)	$13,228	$7,718	20,946
Both head of household (HOH)	10,430	5,069	15,499
You, HOH; Spouse, MFS	9,620	8,528	18,148
You, MFS; Spouse, HOH	14,128	4,619	18,747

As you can see from the chart above, you and your spouse are best off if you can both file HOH. You save $5,338 ($20,837 - 15,499) compared to MFJ and $5,447 ($20,946 - 15,499) compared to MFS.

*Amounts were calculated using the Tax Tables before credits.

Head of household is also the best filing status after the divorce, but you generally must have custody of a child to qualify.

By Getting Custody Of Your Children In A Divorce, You Can Claim The Exemption Deduction, File As Head Of Household, And Take The Child Care Credit

Child custody is the most volatile issue in divorce. Emotional, nontax factors often control who keeps the children. Although tax factors are insignificant in the determination of who has custody of the children, the tax benefits of having custody of the children are significant. The custodial parent can claim head of household filing status, the exemption deduction, and the child care credit. The custodial parent is usually the parent who has custody for the greater portion of the year, but it is possible to identify the custodial parent in the divorce decree.

To qualify for head of household (HOH) status, you must have custody of your child for over half the year and pay more than half the cost of keeping up your home. In other words, you can file HOH even if the noncustodial parent claims the exemption deduction for the child.

Filing as a HOH rather than single significantly reduces your tax. Consider the chart below which compares the tax liability of single and HOH filers with earnings of $50,000 and two exemptions in 2002.

Filing status	Tax
Single	$6,964
Head of household	5,069

If you file HOH, you save $1,895 ($6,964 - 5,069) because of the larger standard deduction and more favorable tax rates.

Generally, the custodial parent also claims the exemption deduction for the child. By claiming the exemption deduction, the custodial parent can also claim the $600 child tax credit, the HOPE Scholarship credit, and the Lifetime Learning credit. The custodial parent can give the exemption to the noncustodial spouse in the divorce decree or by signing a Form 8332, Release of Claim to Exemption for Child of Divorced or Separated Parents. Giving the exemption to the noncustodial spouse is a good idea if the custodial spouse does not receive as much tax benefit from the exemption deduction or the credits.

If you have $75,000 of income and your spouse has $25,000 of income, you will receive $900 ($3,000 x 30%) of tax benefit from the deduction and a child tax credit of $600 for one child. If your spouse claims the exemption deduction, your spouse would receive the $600 child tax credit, but only $450 ($3,000 x 15%) of benefit from the deduction. You should arrange with your spouse to claim the exemption deduction even if your spouse is the custodial spouse. However, the tax benefits from the exemption deduction and the child and education credits are phased out (reduced) above certain income levels. If your deduction or credits are subject to phase-out, the spouse with the lower income may receive more benefit from claiming the exemption deduction.

Only the custodial parent can claim the credit for child and dependent care expenses. If the noncustodial parent pays the expenses, then neither parent can claim the credit.

Divorcing couples work through these rules in a variety of ways. If there are two or more children, many couples specify in the divorce decree that one parent has custody of one child and the other parent has custody of the other. This approach makes it possible for both parents to claim head of household filing status, both to claim an exemption, and both to claim credits which relate to the children. If you establish custody in this way, having custody of the youngest child will usually give you deductions for a longer time.

If there is only one child, it generally makes sense to name the higher income spouse the custodial parent. However, because of the nontax factors involved, only the exemption deduction, not child custody, is usually given to the higher income spouse.

You Can Deduct Payments For Tax-Related Legal Advice

Generally, the legal expenses arising from a divorce are nondeductible, personal expenses. An exception to this rule allows you to deduct the portion of the legal fees that relates to tax advice or the production of income. To take this deduction, however, you must get documentation from your attorney showing the portion of the legal fees that relates to tax advice or the production of income. Tax-related issues encountered during divorce include gain from the property division, the taxability of alimony and child support, and distributions from retirement plans. Production of income issues include attempts to obtain alimony or distributions from a qualified retirement plan.

> You are getting divorced. Your legal fees total $5,000. The attorney indicates on his invoice that $2,000 of the legal fees relates to tax advice. You may be able to deduct $2,000 of the legal fees on Schedule A of your tax return. The expenses are a miscellaneous itemized deduction and are deductible to the extent that all of your miscellaneous itemized deductions exceed 2% of your adjusted gross income.

You cannot claim legal fees arising from a divorce as business expenses. The legal fees are considered personal even if you feel you are protecting your business from division or poor management.

If you pay your spouse's legal fees, you cannot deduct the payment unless it is classified as alimony. Alimony payments are deductible by the payer, but they are also income to the recipient. For this reason, many recipients do not like the idea of treating the payment of the legal fees as alimony. Nonetheless, treating the payment of legal fees as alimony is a good idea if the recipient is in a lower tax rate bracket than the payer and the recipient's legal fees are deductible as tax advice.

Family
Tax
Planning

You Can Avoid The Kiddie Tax By Choosing Investments That Do Not Increase Your Child's Taxable Income

Before 1986, parents shifted investments to children so that interest and dividend income from the investments would be reported on the children's returns. Often, children paid little or no tax because they sheltered the investment income with their standard deduction and exemption deduction and paid tax at their low tax rates.

In 1986, Congress attacked this tax strategy in three ways. First, only one exemption deduction per person is allowed. If you claim your child as a dependent on your return, your child loses his or her personal exemption deduction.

Second, if you claim your child as a dependent on your return, your child's standard deduction decreases to the greater of $750 or the compensation income of the child plus $250. Thus, if your child's compensation income is $400, your child's standard deduction is $750. If your child's compensation income is $1,800, your child's standard deduction is $2,050. This increased standard deduction is one advantage of hiring your children to work for you. See Tax Saving Idea #78.

Third, if your child is under age 14, your child's investment income over $1,500 may be taxed at your tax rate.

You file jointly with your spouse and report $120,000 of taxable income on your 2002 return. Your tax rate is 30%. Your 10-year old son receives $4,800 of interest income from certificates of deposit (CDs) given to him by you and your spouse. Your child's tax computation is shown below.

Interest income	$4,800	
Standard deduction	(750)	
Exemption deduction	(0)	
Taxable income	$4,050	
Taxed at your rate:		
($4,800 - 1,500)	$3,300	
Tax rate and tax	x 30%	
		$990
Taxed at your child's rate:		
($4,050 - 3,300)	$ 750	
Tax from Table		76
Child's tax on $4,800 in interest income		$1,066

Your child reports this tax on his or her own tax return. Your tax does not change.

Including your child's income on your return

If you have children under 14 who must pay tax, you can choose to include this income on your return by completing Form 8814. To do so, you must meet the following requirements:

- The income must be only from interest and dividends. None of the income can be from wages or capital gains other than mutual fund capital gain distributions,
- Your child's interest and dividends must be more than $750 and less than $7,500, and
- Your child must not pay separate estimated tax payments.

Including your child's income in your return on a Form 8814 may be a bad idea. By including your children's income in your own return, you increase your adjusted gross income (AGI). As a result, your deductions could decrease. First, your deductions for medical expenses, casualty losses, and miscellaneous deductions are limited based on your AGI. To illustrate, your miscellaneous deductions are limited to amounts over 2% of your AGI.

If you increase your AGI by including $4,800 of your child's interest income in your income, you reduce your miscellaneous itemized deductions by $96 ($4,800 x 2%).

Second, if your employer's retirement plan covers you, you must reduce the amount of the individual retirement account (IRA) contribution you can deduct if you are single and your AGI is over $34,000 ($33,000 for 2001) or if you are married and your AGI is over $54,000 ($53,000 for 2001). If you include your child's investment income in your return, you may decrease your IRA deduction.

Third, you are eligible to make a full Roth IRA contribution if your AGI is under $95,000 if you are single and under $150,000 if you are married filing a joint return. Including your child's investment income may cause you to exceed these amounts.

Fourth, your itemized deductions and exemption deductions could be phased out (reduced) starting at $103,000 ($99,725 for 2001) of AGI. By adding your child's investment income to your own, you may pay more tax because your deductions are phased out.

Many parents include their children's income in their returns to avoid the hassle or cost of filing Federal and state returns for their children. Although this reasoning is understandable, you may pay more tax if you include your children's income in your return.

Strategies to avoid the Kiddie Tax

You can use several strategies to avoid paying tax on your child's investment income at your tax rates. First, you do not even need to file a return for your child if your child's income is under $750.

Second, your child who is under age 14 can receive $1,500 of investment income in addition to compensation income before paying tax at your rate. For 2002, your dependent child's standard deduction is the greater of $750 or your child's compensation income plus $250 up to $4,700.

If your child has $1,250 of investment income and no compensation income, then your child's taxable income is $500 ($1,250 - 750). The income is taxed at your child's tax rate.

If your child has $1,700 of investment income and $4,850 of compensation income, then your child's taxable income is $1,850 ($1,700 + 4,850 - 4,700). Of the $1,850, $200 ($1,700 - 1,500) is taxed at your tax rate and $1,650 ($1,850 - 200) is taxed at your child's 10% tax rate.

In other words, compensation income can increase your child's standard deduction and it does not change the amount of investment income your child can receive before your tax rate applies to his or her income.

Third, when your child's investment income reaches $1,500, consider investments that do not increase your child's taxable income. Examples include:

- Tax-exempt municipal bonds,
- Growth stocks which pay no current dividends,
- Real property which appreciates in value, and
- Tax-deferred U.S. Savings bonds.

Fourth, split your child's income with a trust. A trust is a separate tax entity. Trusts pay tax on income that is kept in the trust and not paid to your child. The first $1,850 ($1,800 for 2001) of trust taxable income is taxed at a 15% tax rate. Thus, for 2002, up to $3,350 ($1,850 in the trust and $1,500 distributed to your child) of income is taxed at a 10% or 15% tax rate. Although this strategy is worth considering, few parents use it because of the initial cost of setting up a trust and the annual cost of filing trust returns.

Many parents shift income to their children so they can save money for the child's college costs at a lower tax rate. However, until the child turns 14, the child may pay tax at the parent's tax rate. You can avoid this higher rate of tax by knowing how much income your child can receive before your tax rate applies and choosing investments that do not increase your child's taxable income.

NOTE: If you are investing money in a child's name to save money for college, you should consider qualified tuition plans. They are generally better vehicles for such savings, particularly when the child is under age 14. See Tax Saving Idea #34.

You Can Reduce Your Tax By Making Gifts To Others

Whenever you are considering gifts to others, you must consider the income tax, gift tax, and estate tax consequences. Making gifts to others while you are alive offers many income and estate tax advantages.

First, the income from the property, such as interest and dividends, is transferred to the other person. Thus, you will no longer pay income tax on it.

Second, the property you give to others is no longer included in your estate. In other words, you avoid the estate tax on the value of that property when you die.

> You own stock which has a value of $11,000. You bought the stock three years ago for $1,000. You are in the 30% income tax rate bracket. If you sell the stock, you will pay $2,000 (($11,000 - 1,000) x 20%) of income tax on the gain, since the maximum tax rate on long-term capital gains is 20%. If you give the stock to your daughter, who is in the 15% income tax rate bracket, and your daughter sells the stock, she will only pay $1,000 (($11,000 - 1,000) x 10%) of income tax on the gain, since her maximum tax rate on long-term capital gains is 10%. Your family saves $1,000 ($2,000 - 1,000) of income tax. Furthermore, you have reduced your estate by $11,000, since the stock will not be included in your estate.
>
> Giving the stock to your daughter may be a good idea even if she does not sell the stock. If the stock pays dividends of $1,000 per year, you pay $300 ($1,000 x 30%) of income tax per year. If you give the stock to your daughter, she will only pay $150 ($1,000 x 15%) of income tax per year on the dividends if she is 14 or older. Giving the stock to your daughter saves your family $150 ($300 - 150) of income tax per year. These tax savings over a 5, 10, or 15 year period can significantly increase the amount of money you save for college.
>
> Furthermore, if you are in the 50% estate tax rate bracket and the value of the stock increases to $50,000 by the time you die, you avoid $25,000 ($50,000 x 50%) of estate tax by transferring the property to your daughter.

What about the gift tax?

Gifts you make during your lifetime can trigger a gift tax. The gift tax is the counterpart of the estate tax. It applies to transfers while you are alive. The estate tax applies to transfers at your death. The gift tax and the estate tax rates are the same. Rates start at 18% and increase to 50% (55% in 2001) on transfers over $2,500,000.

The gift tax is cumulative, which means that gifts you make this year are added to gifts you made in prior years to determine which tax rates apply. However, you can give away up to $1,000,000 in 2002 and 2003 ($675,000 in 2001) of cash or property during your lifetime or at death without paying gift or estate tax. To the extent you give property away during your life, you decrease the amount you can give away tax-free at death.

It is possible that gifts you make will not be subject to gift tax. First, when you spend money for someone you are legally obligated to support, such as a child, you have not made a gift. This includes education and medical expenses, as well as everyday living expenses.

Second, you can give $11,000 ($10,000 in 2001) of cash or property to as many people as you want each year without owing gift tax. Thus, if you have five children, you can give up to $55,000 ($11,000 x 5 children) per year without making a taxable gift.

Third, if you are married, you can "split gifts" with your spouse. By splitting gifts, you double the $11,000 annual limit to $22,000 per person per year. With proper planning, you can also double your $1,000,000 lifetime limit to $2,000,000.

If you are single and give $12,000 to your daughter, only $1,000 ($12,000 - $11,000) is subject to the gift tax. If you have not given away more than $999,000 ($1,000,000 - 1,000) of property during your life, you will not owe gift tax.

However, if you are married and split gifts with your spouse, the $12,000 transfer will not even count as a taxable gift. You could have given up to $22,000 to your daughter without making a taxable gift. Not only do you not pay gift tax, you do not use any of your $1,000,000 lifetime limit.

Keeping Property Until You Die Can Reduce The Income Tax Your Heirs Pay

When you die, your heirs inherit your property. Inherited property offers a couple of tax advantages. First, inheriting property does not cause income tax. In other words, your heirs can receive the property without having to pay income tax on the value of the property they receive.

Second, the cost basis of inherited property generally changes to the value of the property at your death. This change of basis means that you should keep property that has gone up in value until you die.

> If you own a rental house that you bought for $50,000 and is now worth $200,000, you will recognize $150,000 of gain if you sell the house. If you still own the house when you die, the full $200,000 value of the house may be subject to estate tax rates up to 50%. However, your estate will not pay income tax on the $150,000 gain in the house. If your heirs sell the house for $200,000, they will not recognize gain either because their cost basis in the house is $200,000.

Congress allows this change in basis (also called a step-up in basis) because the property may be subject to estate tax and it is difficult for your heirs to find out how much you paid for property after you die. It is also difficult for your heirs to find out when you bought the property. Consequently, Congress also treats all gains from property your heirs inherit as long-term capital gains.

This rule does not always operate to your advantage. If the property has gone down in value since you bought it, the basis of the property steps down at death. Thus, with depreciated property, you should sell the property before you die and recognize the loss from the sale on your income tax return.

Which do you choose?

On the one hand, it seems like a good idea to give property away while you are alive. By doing so, you can avoid having the property included in your estate and possibly being subject to a 50% estate tax rate. You also avoid paying tax on the income from the property while you own it and paying tax on any gain if you sell it.

On the other hand, if you give the property away, the donee will take your cost basis in the property. Thus, the donee misses the chance to have the property's basis stepped up to its fair market value when you die. The controlling factors in this dilemma are:

- when the property will be sold,
- whether or not you will owe an estate tax, and
- whether or not the property is going up in value.

If you are planning to sell the property in the near future and your income tax rate is higher than your donee's income tax rate, then you should give the property to the donee. By making the gift before you sell the property, you shift the gain from the sale to the person with the lower income tax rate.

If it is likely that you will owe an estate tax and the property is increasing in value, then it is generally a good idea to give the property away. Any future appreciation is not subject to tax in your estate. Although the donee will take your cost basis in the property and owe income tax on the gain when the property is sold, you avoid estate tax on the full value of the property. The estate tax rates are generally higher than the income tax rates.

There are situations when you should consider keeping the property until you die. Examples include:

- when the property's value is not increasing or decreasing;
- when you will not owe an estate tax because your estate value (net worth) is less than $1,000,000 in 2002 and 2003;
- when you are planning to give the property to your surviving spouse;
- when you will owe a gift tax unless Congress reinstates the estate tax, and
- when you want to keep the property for any other nontax reason.

In these situations, you should keep the property so your heirs will get a higher cost basis when you die.

NOTE: The 2001 tax law repeals the step-up in basis rule for estates over $1,300,000 starting in 2010 and replaces it with a modified carry-over basis rule.

Working
With Your
Tax Adviser

Do Not Throw Your Tax Returns Away

"How long should I keep my tax returns and supporting documentation?" is a frequently asked question. The safe, quick answer is keep your old tax returns, W-2's, and information with tax planning relevance permanently. Keep less important supporting documentation for seven years.

Generally, the IRS has three years from the due date of your return to audit and adjust your return. Similarly, you have three years following the due date to amend your return.

> The due date for your 2002 tax return is April 15, 2003. Even if you file your return on March 1, 2003, the IRS has until April 15, 2006 to audit your return. You have until April 15, 2006 to amend your return. If you extend the due date of your return, the period of time the IRS has to audit your return and the period of time you have to amend your return are also extended.

Sometimes the IRS has longer than three years to audit your return. For example, the IRS has six years to audit your return if you fail to report over 25% of your gross income. If you do not file a return, or you file a fraudulent return, the IRS can audit your records for that tax year at any time.

You should keep all supporting documentation, including summaries, cancelled checks, receipts, and 1099's for at least the three years following the due date of your tax return. To be safe, many advisers recommend that you keep these records for seven years.

You should keep your tax returns and W-2's permanently. Keeping a tax return permanently provides you with support if the IRS contends you did not file a return or filed a fraudulent return. Furthermore, you may need to refer to an old return to obtain information about:

- home purchases and sales;
- depreciation of a home office, rental property, or business equipment;
- Individual Retirement Account (IRA) contributions;

- the purchase price of stocks, bonds, and mutual funds; and
- the taxability of pensions and annuities.

Keep W-2's permanently because they include important information about Social Security wages and withholdings and income tax withholdings. If you ever need to prove your earnings or your Social Security and Medicare contributions, you will have the records if you keep your W-2's.

Supporting documentation

Generally, you can destroy most records after seven years. For tax planning support, however, there are countless situations when it is desirable to have your records from earlier years. For example, when you sell a home, it is necessary to calculate your gain. To calculate the gain, you need records of the cost of the home, improvements to the home, and depreciation of the home. For some people, this information may go back forty years or more. Furthermore, if you rolled over the gain on the pre-1998 sale of your prior home, it is necessary to have records for the prior home.

Another example of when earlier records are helpful is when you sell mutual funds. There are several planning strategies that you can use to reduce your gain in this situation. To use them, however, it is necessary to have information about purchases, distributions, and sales from earlier years.

In summary, you should never throw out your tax returns, W-2's, and records that might have future tax relevance. In particular, you should keep all home records, brokers' statements for securities you still own, and retirement plan information. You should keep other tax-related records for seven years.

NOTE: The Social Security Administration now sends Earnings and Benefit Statements to all participants every three years. You can also request a current Earnings and Benefit Statement on the internet at www.ssa.gov or get Form SSA-7704-SM from your local Social Security office. You should verify your earnings record when you receive this report. Errors discovered after three years have passed are difficult to correct. As an added bonus, the Social Security Administration will project your estimated future Social Security benefits.

Use The 5 Cs When Selecting Your Tax Adviser

When selecting a tax adviser, you should think about the five Cs:

- competent;
- current;
- comfort;
- cost; and
- care.

Choose an adviser who is competent. The tax law at the international, Federal, state, and local levels is complicated. It is important that you select a person who is familiar with the provisions of the law that will affect you. If you are a professional, find someone who has experience with professionals. If you are self-employed, find someone who has experience working with self-employed people. If you are a construction worker, find someone who has experience with the construction industry. In addition, choose someone who is detail-oriented and conscious of deadlines. Part of being competent is being accurate and punctual.

Choose an adviser who follows current developments. The tax law changes daily. It is important to have an adviser who monitors these developments, understands how they apply to you, and notifies you when a significant change occurs or is about to occur. Your adviser should help you plan with the past, in the present, and for the future.

Choose an adviser you are comfortable with. Some advisers take unnecessary risks and worry their clients. If you are not comfortable taking risks, your adviser should be sensitive to that and not encourage you to sign a return which will cause you to lose sleep. At the same time, you should expect a competent adviser to take positions on your return which have support in the law.

Choose your adviser on the basis of cost. You will not work well with an adviser you cannot afford. At the same time, you want an adviser who meets the other Cs. Talk with your adviser about billing rates and the services you can expect. Your adviser can estimate the cost of preparing your return and talking with you midyear about year-end planning. Expect to pay extra for research your adviser does even if the research conclusions are not what you want.

Choose an adviser who cares about you. You will see your tax adviser more often than you will see your attorney or doctor. It is important for you to want to communicate with your adviser about your goals and finances. Your adviser should be a good listener and be able to answer your questions in language you understand. Your adviser should be patient and spend the necessary amount of time with you. Most importantly, you should trust your adviser.

Here are some suggestions for finding an adviser:

- Usually the best way to start is to ask your friends and coworkers whom they recommend.
- You can also call your state's CPA society.
- Interview several advisers before choosing one.
- Compare the advisers by asking them questions about their backgrounds, research sources, attitudes toward planning, and charges.

The five Cs are helpful criteria for choosing an adviser. Your adviser may be a CPA, attorney, enrolled agent, or someone who works for a volume tax service. Your adviser's credentials and place of employment are not as important as your ability to work effectively with the person.

Highlights of Recent Tax Law Changes

Recent legislative changes

Highlights of "Economic Growth and Tax Relief Reconciliation Act of 2001"

NOTE: All provisions and amendments made by this bill sunset (expire) after December 31, 2010.

Marginal Tax Rate Reduction

- Individual income tax rate structure revised beginning in 2001.
- Rebate checks issued fall 2001 — $300 single; $500 head of household; $600 joint.
- Overall limitation on itemized deductions phased out beginning 2006; fully phased out by 2010.
- Restrictions on personal exemptions phased out beginning 2006; fully phased out by 2010.

Tax Benefits Relating to Children

- Child tax credit increased and phased in over 10 years beginning in 2001 ($600 for 2001).
- Adoption tax benefits expanded and extended permanently.
- Dependent care tax credit increased beginning in 2003.
- Employer-provided child care facilities credit enacted beginning in 2002.

Marriage Penalty Relief

- Standard deductions for joint couples increased to twice the amount of singles phased in over 5 years beginning in 2005.

- 15% tax rate bracket for joint couples expanded to twice the size of singles over 4 years beginning in 2005.
- Earned income credit simplified and expanded for joint couples.

Education Incentives

- Education IRAs expanded — annual limit increased to $2,000, contributions allowed through April 15 for prior year, phase-out range for joint couples increased, contributions allowed to Education IRA and Qualified Tuition Program in same year, and education credits allowed in same year as exclusion from income — beginning 2002.
- Qualified Tuition Programs expanded — distributions excluded from income if used to pay qualified expenses, and rollovers allowed for same beneficiary once every 12 months — generally effective in 2002.
- Exclusion for employer-provided educational assistance expanded to include graduate education and extended permanently — for courses beginning in 2002.
- Student loan interest deduction modified to increase phase-out ranges and repeal limit on number of months during which interest paid is deductible beginning in 2002.
- Deduction for qualified higher education expenses enacted effective for 2002 through 2005.

Estate, Gift, and Generation-Skipping Transfer Tax

- Rates phased down gradually between 2002 and 2009.
- Estate and generation-skipping transfer tax repealed in 2010 (sunsets on December 31, 2010).
- Estate tax transfer exemption increased gradually to $3,500,000 ($1,000,000 in 2002).
- Gift tax transfer exemption increased to $1,000,000 in 2002.
- Modified carryover basis added for property acquired from decedent beginning in 2010.

Pensions and Individual Retirement Arrangements

- Annual contribution limit of IRAs increased gradually to $5,000 ($3,000 for 2002).

- Employers permitted to accept Roth 401(k) contributions beginning in 2006.
- Individuals age 50+ allowed additional IRA contributions and 401(k) contributions beginning in 2002.
- 401(k) elective deferral amounts increased gradually to $15,000 ($11,000 in 2002).
- Credit enacted for making elective deferrals or IRA contributions beginning in 2002 for certain individuals.

Alternative Minimum Tax, Other, and Sunset

- Individual AMT exemption increased $4,000 for joint couples ($2,000 for singles) in 2001-2004.
- Corporate estimated tax payments due September 17, 2001, deferred until October 1, 2001.
- All provisions in this bill sunset December 31, 2010.

Recent court cases and government rulings

Income

- A back pay award to baseball players under a settlement agreement between the player's association and the baseball club was subject to employment taxes in the year the award was paid, not the year the disputed wages should have been paid (*U.S. v. Cleveland Indians Baseball Co*).
- A taxpayer cannot adjust his basis in his retirement annuity to account for inflation between the date of his contributions to the plan and the annuity starting date (*Kenneth L. Nordtvedt*).
- Employees who pay long-term disability premiums on an after-tax basis can exclude benefits received from income. Employer plan must allow for after-tax payments and employee must make election prior to beginning of plan year (PLR 200119005).
- Statutory attorney's fees awarded directly to taxpayer's attorney under fee-shifting provision of Age Discrimination in Employment Act were taxable to the taxpayer as income. The fee was then allowable as a miscellaneous itemized deduction, which is subject to 2% of adjusted gross income and not deductible for alternative minimum tax (*Sinyard v. Commissioner*).

- Excluded income from discharge of indebtedness increases the basis in the shareholder's S Corporation stock (*Gitlitz v. Commissioner*). NOTE: There is pending legislation that would reverse this Tax Court opinion.
- Payments received from insurance company on policy that paid certain credit card debt in case of death, disability, or unemployment was taxable (*Khen T. Huynh*).

Investment/Rental income

- A dermatologist who invested in a jojoba farm tax shelter was liable for both negligence and substantial understatement penalties (*D.A. Lopez*).

Business expenses

- The payment of officer/shareholder's trips was constructive dividends. The corporation was formed to develop a time-share resort in Virginia and incurred travel and entertainment expenses (which totaled over $1.3 million). The trips were taken around holidays (Thanksgiving, Christmas, and New Year's), the shareholders made no written report of their "research," and the shareholders offered no convincing explanation of why or how the corporation benefited from their "research at resorts thousands of miles away" (*Gow v. Commissioner*).
- Raised flooring built over existing floor to facilitate the installation of computer systems is a structural component of the building, not 5-year life property as previously indicated in FSA 200033002 (FSA 200110001).
- The cost of tires and tubes must be capitalized assuming a useful life of more than one year. The taxpayer purchased numerous vehicles without tires, purchased tires in bulk, and had the tires placed on the vehicles (FSA 200122002).
- While maintenance visits costs for aircraft airframe are generally deductible, the costs must be capitalized to the extent they materially add to the value of or substantially prolong the useful life of the airframe, or adapt the airframe to a new or different use. Also, costs as part of a plan of rehabilitation, modernization, or improvement must be capitalized (Revenue Ruling 2001-4).
- A self-employed welder was not allowed to modify his Section 179 election to include three assets recharacterized as depreciable business property as a result of an IRS audit. (The taxpayer failed to report $135,638 of welding income, and rather than having a loss for the year, the

taxpayer instead had a gain.) In holding for the IRS, the Tax Court stated, "We are cognizant of the fact that [taxpayer's] circumstances are of his own making. His need to revoke (modify) his section 179 election only arose after [the IRS] uncovered [his] failure to report all of his income and his misclassification of the very assets for which section 179 treatment is sought" (*Sam Patton*).

Itemized and other deductions

- Costs of medical diagnosis tests qualify for deductions as medical expenses, and thus these costs could be reimbursed by a medical flexible spending account. However, the IRS did not rule on costs for DNA collection and storage since the facts did not indicate whether the DNA would be used for medical diagnosis (PLR 200140017).
- Contributions to a university that used a sweepstakes drawing to solicit funds were deductible. Prospective participants were not required to make a contribution to participate in the sweepstakes program, and a voluntary contribution did not increase the chances of winning a prize (PLR 200012061).

Individual Retirement Accounts

- Although a taxpayer divorced his spouse and Washington state law automatically revokes designation of a spouse as beneficiary of certain assets (including life insurance policies and employee benefit plans) upon divorce, the state statute was pre-empted by ERISA. Thus, upon the taxpayer's death, his ex-spouse was the beneficiary of a life insurance policy and pension plan provided by his employer (*Egelhoff v. Egelhoff*).

Method of accounting

- More "small" taxpayers are allowed to use the cash method of accounting. Small taxpayers are now those with average annual gross receipts of $10,000,000 or less (Notice 2001-76).

Filing status

- An unmarried taxpayer with same-sex partner was not entitled to use the filing status of married couple filing a joint return (*R. Mueller, Dec. 54,517 (M)*).

Credits

- A prison inmate's earnings did not qualify for the earned income credit (*Harold Wilson*).
- An intra-oral camera system purchased by a dentist, which was generally useful in his practice, is not eligible for the disabled access tax credit (*Fan v. Commissioner*).

Other

- The IRS has launched a small business Web site which will provide:

  1. Answers to many basic tax questions
  2. A calendar of important deadlines
  3. Online access to IRS forms, and
  4. Links to court opinions, rulings, regulations, state tax information, and other small business resources

  www.irs.gov/smallbiz/index.html (IR 2001-26).
- The IRS provided guidance for retirement plans adopting provisions of the Economic Growth and Tax Relief Reconciliation Act of 2001 for the 2002 plan year (Notice 2001-56).
- The IRS provided sample plan amendments for changes to the retirement plan qualification requirements as a result of the Economic Growth and Tax Relief Reconciliation Act of 2001 (Notice 2001-57).
- The IRS plans to levy for unpaid taxes by deducting 15% of amounts paid to Social Security recipients (IR-2001-89).
- No deduction is allowed for a fee charged by a credit card company for using a credit card to pay the individual's personal income taxes. The fee is considered to be a nondeductible personal expense since it is unrelated to determining the extent of the taxpayer's tax liability (SCA 200115032).
- Expedited review and approval process for new organizations seeking tax-exempt status to provide relief to victims of terrorist attacks (IR-2001-82).

Looking To The Future: Proposed Tax Legislation

Changes proposed in the past that might become law in the future

INCOME

- A payroll tax holiday would apply, allowing one month of a worker's income to be exempt from payroll taxes.
- Up to $400 ($200 for single filers) of investment income could be excluded from income.
- The use-it-or-lose-it rule on cafeteria plans could be modified to allow amounts not used in one year to be used in a subsequent year.
- The deduction for health insurance premiums for self-employed taxpayers could be increased to 100% immediately, rather than in 2003 as currently scheduled.
- Losses from the sale of a principal residence could be allowed to reduce subsequent gains on the sale of principal residences.
- Taxpayers who rent out their homes may be taxed on all of the rents received, reduced by expenses up to the amount of rents received (thus repealing the rule that allows 14 days of home rental income to go untaxed).
- Health insurance premiums paid by your employer may no longer be tax-free.
- Foreign currency exchange gains of up to $200 in personal transactions may become nontaxable to individuals.
- The way capital gains are taxed could change. The basis of stocks, bonds, and other property would be adjusted (indexed) for inflation, and 50% of gains would be excluded from taxation. The basis adjustment would reduce the amount of gain and possibly lead to more capital losses. The exclusion would provide an incentive for individuals in all tax rate brackets to own investment property.

- The 85% tax rate imposed in 1994 on Social Security benefits could be repealed. The maximum tax rate on Social Security benefits would revert to 50%, the old law rate.

DEDUCTIONS

- The amount of capital losses an individual may deduct could be increased from $3,000 to $5,000.
- People who take the standard deduction could be allowed to deduct half of their charitable contributions in excess of $2,000 ($1,000 for single taxpayers).
- Businesses could deduct 30% of the cost of new equipment and furniture in the year of acquisition.
- The election to expense up to $24,000 of business equipment and furniture could be increased to $35,000.
- Leasehold improvements would be treated as 15-year property for calculating depreciation.
- Net operating losses could be carried back 5 years.
- Deductions for individual retirement account (IRA) contributions could be reinstated for everyone. Currently, single individuals who are covered under qualified retirement plans cannot take IRA deductions if their adjusted gross income is over $44,000 ($64,000 if married filing jointly).
- Businesses could be able to depreciate more than the original cost of new equipment over the life of the asset.
- Independent oil and gas producers could be given additional tax breaks to encourage exploration, research, and development.

CREDITS

- Child tax credit could be doubled to $1,000 per child.
- $500 tax credit could be allowed for parents who stay at home with newborn children.
- $1,000 credit could be allowed to families providing long-term care to disabled relatives.
- $4,000 credit could be allowed to those who purchase high-mileage hybrid cars.

- 10% of training costs up to $525 credit per employee could be allowed for businesses.

OTHER TAXES

- The capital gains tax structure could be simplified by eliminating the 5-year holding period. Thus, the maximum tax on long-term capital gains would be 18% (8% for taxpayers in the 15% or lower tax rate bracket).
- Out-of-state mail-order companies could be required to collect state and local sales taxes.
- Distributions to S corporation shareholders would be subject to self-employment tax.
- A consumption or value-added tax could be enacted to either supplement or replace the current Federal income tax.
- The marriage penalty could be reduced by allowing a 10% deduction for the earnings of the lower-paid spouse.
- The marriage penalty could be reduced by allowing married couples the option to file separately as singles.
- Alternative minimum tax relief could be enacted for taxpayers claiming the child tax credit or education credits.
- The corporate alternative minimum tax could be repealed.

OTHER

- Workers could voluntarily set up private accounts with a portion of their Social Security taxes and make investment decisions on those funds.

Appendix A

2001 TAX RATE SCHEDULES FOR INDIVIDUALS

Single Individuals

If Taxable Income Is:	*The Tax Is:*
Not over $27,050	15% of taxable income
Over $27,050 but not over $65,550	$4,057.50 plus 27.5% of the excess over $27,050
Over $65,550 but not over $136,750	$14,645.00 plus 30.5% of the excess over $65,550
Over $136,750, but not over $297,350	$36,361.00 plus 35.5% of the excess over $136,750
Over $297,350	$93,374.00 plus 39.1% of the excess over $297,350

Married Filing Jointly or Qualifying Widow(er)

If Taxable Income Is:	*The Tax Is:*
Not Over $45,200	15% of taxable income
Over $45,200, but not over $109,250	$6,780.00 plus 27.5% of the excess over $45,200
Over $109,250, but not over $166,500	$24,393.75 plus 30.5% of the excess over $109,250
Over $166,500, but not over $297,350	$41,855.00 plus 35.5% of the excess over $166,500
Over $297,350	$88,306.75 plus 39.1% of the excess over $297,350

Married Filing Separately

If Taxable Income Is:	*The Tax Is:*
Not Over $22,600	15% of taxable income
Over $22,600, but not over $54,625	$3,390.00 plus 27.5% of the excess over $22,600
Over $54,625, but not over $83,250	$12,196.88 plus 30.5% of the excess over $54,625
Over $83,250, but not over $148,675	$20,927.50 plus 35.5% of the excess over $83,250
Over $148,675	$44,153.38 plus 39.1% of the excess over $148,675

Head of Household

If Taxable Income Is:	*The Tax Is:*
Not Over $36,250	15% of taxable income
Over $36,250, but not over $93,650	$5,437.50 plus 27.5% of the excess over $36,250
Over $93,650, but not over $151,650	$21,222.50 plus 30.5% of the excess over $93,650
Over $151,650, but not over $288,350	$38,912.50 plus 35.5% of the excess over $151,650
Over $297,350	$90,636.00 plus 39.1% of the excess over $297,350

Appendix B

Research Sources for Tax Saving Ideas

1. Section 61 defines gross income. Nontaxable income, exclusions from income, are discussed in Sections 71 through 135. The qualified retirement planning services exclusion was added by the Economic Growth and Tax Relief Reconciliation Act of 2001.

2. The tax benefit rule is described in Section 111.

3. The deduction for gambling losses is allowed by Section 165(d). Losses from the trade or business of gambling are discussed in *Groetzinger*, 480 U.S. 23 (USSC, 1987) and *Valenti*, T.C. Memo 1994-483 (1994).

4. Social Security payments are subject to tax under Section 86.

5. The rules for the standard deduction and itemized deductions are in Section 63.

6. Medical expenses are described in Section 213 and Regulation Section 1.213-1. The rules concerning nursing home expenses are in Regulation Section 1.213-1(e)(1)(v). The rules concerning medical savings accounts are in Section 220. The rules concerning smoking cessation programs are in Revenue Ruling 99-28, 1999-25 C.B. 6.

7. Long-term care medical expenses and premiums are described in Section 213. The treatment of long-term care insurance benefits is described in Section 7702B. The provisions for long-term medical expenses were added to the law by the Health Insurance Portability and Accountability Act of 1996.

8. Medical expenses are described in Section 213 and Regulation Section 1.213-1. The definition of dependents for medical deduction purposes is in Section 152(e). For relatives you cannot claim as dependents, see Regulation Section 1.213-1(a)(3).

9. State and local taxes are described in Section 164.

10. State and local taxes are described in Section 164. Revenue Ruling 82-208, 1982-2 C.B. 58, discusses intentional overpayments of state estimated tax payments.

11. Property taxes are described in Section 164. The deduction for business and rental real estate property taxes is supported by Section 62.

12. Mortgage interest is described in Section 163(h). Home equity loan interest is described in Section 163(h).

13. The rules for points and prepaid interest are in Section 461(g). Seller-paid points are discussed in Revenue Procedure 94-27. The rules for points and prepaid interest are in Section 461(g). Also see Revenue Ruling 86-67, 1986-1 C.B. 238, and Revenue Ruling 87-22, 1987-2 C.B. 466.

14. Investment interest is described in Section 163(d). Also see Form 4952, Investment Interest Expense Deduction. The election to include long-term capital gains in net investment income is described in Sections 1(h) and 163(d)(4)(B).

15. Charitable contributions are described in Section 170. The documentation provisions are in Section 170(f)(8).

16. Charitable contributions are described in Section 170. The definition of fair market value is in Regulation Section 1.170A-1(c)(2). Also see Form 8283, Noncash Charitable Contributions.

17. Charitable contributions are described in Section 170.

18. The treatment of casualty losses is described in Sections 165(h) and (i). The rules for the deferral of gains from involuntary conversions are described in Section 1033. See Section 123 for the rules on reimbursement of living expenses. Also see IRS Publication 584, Nonbusiness Disaster, Casualty, and Theft Loss Workbook, and IRS Publication 547, Nonbusiness Disasters, Casualties, and Thefts.

19. The 2% floor for miscellaneous expenses is described in Section 67. Also see IRS Publication 529, Miscellaneous Deductions.

20. The deduction for moving expenses is allowed by Section 217. Moving expenses are deductible for AGI according to Section 62(a)(15). Also see Form 3903, Moving Expenses. Reimbursements for moving expenses are discussed in Sections 82 and 132(a)(6). Also see Form 4782, Employee Moving Expense Information.

21. The rules for exemptions are described in Section 151 and 152. The rules for multiple support agreements are described in Section 152(c). Also see Form 2120, Multiple Support Declaration.

22. The tax rate schedules for the different filing statuses are in Section 1. Determination of marital status is described in Section 7703. Married filing joint returns are allowed by Section 6013. The rules for Head of Household and Qualifying Widows are described in Section 2.

23. The tax rate schedules for the different filing statuses are in Section 1. Determination of marital status is described in Section 7703. Married filing joint returns are allowed by Section 6013.

24. The tax rate schedules for the different filing statuses are in Section 1. Determination of marital status is described in Section 7703. The rules for Head of Household are described in Section 2.

25. The child tax credit is described in Section 24.

26. The rules for the dependent care credit are described in Section 21. See also Form 2441, Child and Dependent Care Expenses. The medical care expense versus dependent care credit rules are described in Regulation Section 1.44A-4(b).

27. The rules for the earned income credit are in Section 32. The rules for advance payments of the earned income credit are in Section 3507.

28. The AMT formula, adjustments, preferences, exemptions, and rates are described in Sections 55 to 59. Also see Form 6251, Alternative Minimum Tax — Individuals. Calculation of the AMT credit is described in Section 53. Also see Form 8801, Credit for Prior Year Minimum Tax — Individuals and Fiduciaries.

29. The rules for the adoption credit are described in Section 23. The rules for adoption assistance programs are described in Section 137.

30. See IRS Publication 926, Employment Taxes for Household Employees, and IRS Employer's Tax Guide. The statutory references are Sections 3121 and 3401.

31. See Section 3402(f) and IRS Publication 919, Is My Withholding Correct?

32. The underpayment penalty and exceptions are discussed in Section 6654. Also see Publication 505, Tax Withholding and Estimated Tax, and the *American Institute of Certified Public Accountants Estimated Tax Practice Guide.*

33. Agreements for installment payments with the IRS are described in Section 6159. Rules for extensions of time for paying tax are described in Section 6161. Undue hardship is described in Regulations Section 1.6161-1(b).

34. The rules for qualified state tuition plans are in Section 529.

35. The rules for scholarships are in Section 117.

36. Coverdell Education Savings Accounts are described in Section 530. The definition of an educational organization is in Section 170(b)(1)(A)(ii).

37. The deduction for interest paid on student loans is described in Section 163.

38. The Lifetime Learning credit is described in Section 25A.

39. The HOPE Scholarship credit is summarized in Section 25A.

40. The HOPE Scholarship and Lifetime Learning credits are described in Section 25A. The rules for exemptions are described in Sections 151 and 152.

41. The education deduction is described in Section 222.

42. The statutory authority for capital gain and loss treatment is found in Sections 1(h), 1211(b), 1212(b), 1221, 1222, and 1223. Also see Schedule D, Capital Gains and Losses.

43. The authority for the 20%, 10%, and 8% rates of taxation on long-term capital gains is Section 1(h). The ordinary income rates are discussed in the rest of Section 1. The $948 is calculated using time value of money principles.

44. The rules for determining gain and loss are found in Sections 1001, 1011, 1012, and 1016.

45. The capital gain election is described in The Taxpayer Relief Act of 1997, Section 311(e).

46. The taxability of dividends is discussed generally in Sections 61 and 316. Stock dividends are discussed in Sections 305 and 307; capital gain distributions in Section 852(b); insurance policy dividends in Section 72(a); and patronage dividends in Section 1385(b). Also see Schedule B, Interest and Dividend Income.

47. Mutual fund distributions are discussed in Section 852(b). The rules for calculating basis are discussed in Regulation Sections 1.1012 -1(c) and (e).

48. Accrued interest from bonds is discussed in Regulation Section 1.61-7(d). Original issue discount is addressed in Sections 1272 and 1273. Market discount is discussed in Sections 1276 and 1278. The taxation of premiums is described in Section 171.

49. The election to include U.S. Savings Bond interest income is in Section 454(a). The exchange provision with Series HH bonds is in Section

1037. The higher education exclusion is in Section 135. Also see Form 8815, Exclusion of Interest From Series EE U.S. Savings Bonds Issued After 1989.

50. The exclusion for interest on state and local bonds is discussed in Section 103. Private activity bonds are discussed in Sections 103(b) and 146.

51. The taxation of options is described in Section 1234 and Regulation Section 1.1234-1(a)(1).

52. Losses from worthless securities are described in Section 165(g)(1). The extended statute of limitations period is described in Section 6511(d).

53. Section 1244 allows ordinary loss treatment on the sale of small business stock. The 50% exclusion is described in Section 1202; the rollover to other small business stock is described in Section 1045; and ordinary loss treatment is described in Section 1242.

54. Business and nonbusiness bad debts are discussed in Section 166.

55. The taxation of passive losses is described in Section 469. The real estate exception is included at Section 469(i). Also see Form 8582, Passive Activity Loss Limitations.

56. Property exchanges are described in Section 1031.

57. Installment sales are discussed in Section 453. Also see Form 6252, Installment Sale Income.

58. The deductibility of interest is discussed at Section 163(h). The deduction for real estate taxes is allowed by Section 164. The $250,000 ($500,000 if you are married filing a joint return) exclusion is described in Section 121.

59. Section 121 describes the exclusion of gain rules.

60. The rules concerning basis for loss and depreciation when you convert your home to business or rental use are in Regulation Sections 1.165-9(b)(2) and 1.167(g)(1).

61. When considering whether to take a home office deduction, consider Section 280A(c), the Supreme Court decision in *Soliman*, 93-1 USTC P50,014 (USSC, 1993), and Form 8829, Expenses for Business Use of Your Home. The authority for not prorating gain in the year of sale when you do not use the home office in the year of sale is Revenue Ruling 82-26, 1982-1 C.B. 114.

62. The rules for vacation homes are in Sections 280A(d) and (g). The Court Method is described in *Bolton*, 82-2 USTC P9699 (CA-9, 1982). The IRS Method is described in Proposed Regulation Section 1.280A-3(d)(4).

63. See your state tax instructions for the definitions of resident and nonresident taxpayers and your state's tax rates.

64. Fringe benefits are excluded from income tax withholding and employment taxes by Sections 3401 and 3121. The exclusion for group-term life insurance is found in Section 79. The Table showing premium amounts is in Regulation Section 1.79-3(d)(2) and Temporary Regulation Section 1.79-3T.

65. The exclusion for health insurance benefits is found in Section 105. The rules for medical savings accounts are in Section 220.

66. Dependent care assistance plans are discussed in Section 129.

67. The rules for job-related educational deductions are discussed in Regulation Section 1.162-5. Working condition fringe benefit treatment for job-related education expenses is allowed by Section 132(j)(8). Educational assistance plans are described in Section 127.

68. The rules for no-additional-cost services, qualified employee discounts, working condition fringe benefits, and de minimis fringe benefits are described in Section 132.

69. Cafeteria plans are described in Section 125.

70. The authority for taking business deductions is Section 162. The 2% limitation for employee business expenses is in Section 67. Also see Schedule C, Profit or Loss From Business, and Form 2106, Employee Business Expenses. The calculation of self-employment tax is described in Section 1402. Also see Schedule SE, Self-Employment Tax. Retirement plans are discussed in Section 401. Keoghs are discussed in Section 401(c). Simplified employee pension plans are discussed in Sections 408(j) and 408(k). SIMPLE plans are discussed in Section 408(p). The alternative minimum tax adjustment for miscellaneous itemized deductions is found in Section 56(b).

71. These factors are described in Revenue Ruling 87-41, 1987-1 C.B. 296. Worker classification is also discussed in an Internal Revenue Service Training Guide.

72. The hobby loss rules are found in Section 183. The nine factors are found in Regulation Section 1.183-2.

73. Depreciation deductions are allowed by Section 168. The $24,000/$25,000 immediate expensing election is found in Section 179. Also see Form 4562, Depreciation and Amortization.

74. Depreciation deductions are allowed by Section 168. The $24,000/$25,000 immediate expensing election is found in Section 179. Depreciation expenses for cars are limited by Section 280F. Also see Form 4562, Depreciation and Amortization.

75. Depreciation deductions are allowed by Section 168. The $24,000/$25,000 immediate expensing election is found in Section 179. The listed property rules, limiting depreciation deductions, are found in Section 280F. Also see Form 4562, Depreciation and Amortization. The rules concerning software are in Section 167(f).

76. The deduction of 60%-100% of the health insurance premiums of self-employed individuals is allowed by Section 162(l).

77. The authority for deducting fees for tax advice as a miscellaneous deduction is Section 212. The deductibility for deducting fees for tax advice on Schedule C, Profit or Loss From Business, and Schedule E, Supplemental Income and Loss, is supported by Sections 162 and 212 and Revenue Ruling 92-29, 1992-1 C.B. 20.

78. The employment tax rules are discussed in Section 3121(b) and the *IRS Employer's Tax Guide*. Individual retirement accounts are discussed in Sections 219 and 408.

79. For more information on these entity choices, see the following IRS publications: Publication 334, Tax Guide for Small Business; Publication 541, Tax Information on Partnerships; Publication 542, Tax Information on Corporations; and Publication 589, Tax Information on S Corporations.

80. Retirement plans are discussed generally starting at Section 401. The deduction for individual retirement accounts (IRAs) is allowed by Section 219. IRAs are discussed in Section 408. The early distribution penalty is found in Section 72(t). Also see IRS Notice 87-16, 1987-1 C.B. 446, Form 5329, Return for Additional Taxes Attributable to Qualified Retirement Plans (Including IRAs), Annuities, and Modified Endowment Contracts, and Form 8606, Nondeductible IRA Contributions, IRA Basis, and Nontaxable IRA Distributions.

81. Roth IRAs are described in Section 408A.

82. Conversions to Roth IRAs are described in Section 408A.

83. IRAs for nonworking spouses are described in Section 219(g)(7).

84. Retirement plans are discussed generally starting in Section 401. Section 401(k) describes the rules for 401(k) plans. SIMPLE plans are discussed in Section 408(p).

85. Retirement plans are discussed generally starting in Section 401. Keoghs are discussed in Section 401(c). The calculation of self-employment earnings is described in Section 1402. Simplified employee pension plans are discussed in Section 408(j). SIMPLE plans are discussed in Section 408(p). NOTE: The Code was not properly changed to reflect Congress' intent to change SEP contributions to 25%. A technical correction to the Code is anticipated.

86. SIMPLE plans are discussed in Section 408(p).

87. Catch-up retirement contributions are discussed in Section 414 (v).

88. The 15% excess distribution penalty is described in Section 4980A. The 50% excise tax on minimum distributions is found in Sections 401(a)(9) and 4974. The 10% early distribution penalty is described in Section 72(t). Also see Form 5329, Return for Additional Taxes Attributable to Qualified Retirement Plans (Including IRAs), Annuities, and Modified Endowment Contracts. The three-year suspension of the 15% excess distribution tax is discussed in Section 4980A(g). The table for determining the distribution period is in Prop. Reg. 130477-00 issued in January 2001.

89. Distributions from retirement plans before the age of 59 1/2 are described in Section 72(t).

90. The rules for distributions from retirement plans are described in Section 402. The annuity rules are described in Section 72(a) - (c). The rules for lump-sum distributions are found in Section 402(e). Also see Form 4972, Tax on Lump-sum Distributions. The rules for qualified plan loans are found in Section 72(p).

91. The rollover rules for individual retirement accounts (IRAs) are in Section 408(d)(3).

92. The rules for property divisions are found in Section 1041; filing status in Section 7703; alimony in Sections 71 and 215; child support in Section 71(c); exemptions in Section 152; and legal expenses in Sections 212 and 262.

93. The rules for property divisions are found in Section 1041. Qualified domestic relations orders (QDROs) are discussed in Section 414(p). The 10% early distribution penalty is found in Section 72(t). The rules for property divisions are found in Section 1041. Section 121 describes the rules for excluding gain from the sale of a home.

94. The tax rates for the various filing statuses are found in Section 1. The abandoned spouse rule is found in Section 7703(b). Head of household filing status is discussed in Section 2(b). The rules for filing jointly and separately are found in Sections 6013 and 7703.

95. The rules for filing status are found in Section 7703; exemptions in Section 152; the dependent care credit in Section 21; the child tax credit in Section 24; and the HOPE Scholarship and Lifetime Learning credits in Section 25A.

96. Legal expenses for divorce are not deductible because they are personal in nature, Section 262. Also see *Gilmore*, 372 U.S. 39 (USSC, 1963) which dealt with a taxpayer trying to deduct legal fees from a divorce as business expenses. The exception for tax advice and production of income is found in Section 212 and Revenue Ruling 72-545, 1972-2 C.B. 179. The rules for property divisions are found in Section 1041; alimony in Sections 71 and 215; and child support in Section 71(c).

97. The rules for a dependent child's exemption are found in Section 151(d); for the reduced standard deduction in Section 63(c); and taxation of a child under age 14 at the parent's rate in Section 1(i). Also see Form 8615, Tax for Children Under Age 14 Who Have Investment Income of More Than $1,400, and Form 8814, Parent's Election to Report Child's Interest and Dividends.

98. Gifts can be received tax-free under Section 102. The basis of property received as a gift is determined under Section 1015. The gift tax is generally described in Sections 2501 to 2524.

99. Inheritances can be received tax-free under Section 102. The basis of inherited property is determined under Section 1014. The estate tax is generally described in Sections 2001 to 2057.

100. The statute of limitations for assessments and amended returns is described in Sections 6501 and 6511.

Appendix C

Learn to Look Up Answers for Yourself

Although the tax law is very complex, there are many places where you can find answers to your questions. There are two types of authorities in the tax law — primary authorities and secondary authorities. The top primary authority is the Internal Revenue Code. It is law enacted by Congress and signed by the President.

Other primary authorities interpret this law. They include:

- Legislative History recording the ideas of the legislators as they pass the law;
- Regulations prepared by the Treasury Department; and
- Court cases resulting from disputes between the government and taxpayers.

Less important primary authorities include pronouncements of the IRS such as:

- Private Letter Rulings responding to taxpayers' questions;
- Revenue Rulings and Revenue Procedures published to guide IRS agents and tax advisers;
- IRS Publications;
- IRS Tax Forms and Instructions; and
- A host of other IRS announcements.

One of the cardinal rules of tax advising is that you only rely on primary authorities. You cannot rely on opinions stated in secondary authorities, such as newspaper and magazine articles. The risk of relying on an opinion in a secondary authority is that you could be subject to penalties if you are audited. Thus, before you take any deduction, make sure you are basing your decision on a primary authority.

Nonetheless, secondary authorities are an invaluable source of information. They provide planning ideas, help in the search for current developments, and explain what the primary authorities mean. Secondary authorities include:

- newspaper articles;
- magazine articles;
- opinions of tax consultants; and
- books about tax, including this book.

The opinions expressed in secondary authorities are usually based on an interpretation of primary authorities. However, that does not mean you can rely on the secondary authority without checking the primary authority yourself to be sure that you agree with the opinion and that is applies to you.

Tax services are books used by many tax advisers to do tax research. They offer a blend of primary and secondary authorities. The tax services found at many libraries are Commerce Clearing House's Standard Federal Tax Reporter and Research Institute of America's U.S. Tax Reporter.

Both services are organized similarly. Each topic, such as medical expenses, starts with the applicable Internal Revenue Code Section. The Code Section is followed by the Legislative History, Regulations, summaries of court cases and IRS pronouncements, and explanations of what it all means. Thus, for each topic you have the related primary and secondary authorities.

You find the topic by using the extensive index contained in the Index volume of the service. You can also find your topic if you know a case name or Revenue Ruling number. The index will give you a paragraph number that you can use to find the topic in the remaining volumes of the service. After you find a tentative answer, you need to check the Current Developments volume for recent changes. These services are generally updated weekly. If you need more current information, you can use a computer service, such as Lexis or Westlaw. These computer services are updated daily.

With this background, you can do some tax research yourself. If you see a tax planning idea in the newspaper or hear a tip from a friend, you can check its accuracy by going to your local library and doing research on the internet. The links available at www.taxsites.com are particularly helpful. If you want more assurance, you can take the information you find to your tax adviser. By doing your own research, you may avoid IRS penalties, decrease your adviser fees, and reduce your taxes.

Appendix B lists primary authorities for the Tax Saving Ideas in this book. If you want to research an idea further, use these authorities as a starting point. If you are working with a tax adviser, show your adviser the Tax Saving Idea and the supporting authority.

Appendix D lists helpful, related Web sites.

Appendix D

Useful Web Sites

www.meara.com	Meara, King & Co. Certified Public Accountants
www.irs.gov	Federal tax forms and publications
www.irs.gov/smallbiz/index.html	IRS small business site
www.savingsbonds.com	Information on U.S. savings bonds
www.taxsites.com	Links to major tax sites
www.mocpa.org/outside_links.html	State revenue or tax departments
www.aicpa.org	American Institute of Certified Public Accountants
www.fpanet.org	Financial Planning Association
www.rothira.com	Roth IRA analyzer
www.isquare.com	The Small Business Advisor
www.ssa.gov	Social Security Administration
www.savingforcollege.com	Information on Section 529 plans

Appendix E

Education Incentives

(Prepared by Randy Gardner, LLM, CPA, CFP,™ and Julie Welch, CPA, CFP,™ authors of *101 Tax Saving Ideas*)

INCENTIVE	TAX BENEFIT	HIGHER EDUCATION EXPENSES COVERED	PHASE-OUTS
Qualified Tuition Plans	Up to $100,000 or more can be contributed to a tax-deferred account per beneficiary. If not used for education, then earnings subject to 10% penalty. Can be rolled over to other beneficiaries.	Tuition, fees, books, supplies, equipment, room, and board.	Not applicable.
HOPE Scholarship Credit	Credit of $1,500 per student for each of the first two years of postsecondary education. Credit is 100% of first $1,000 of expenses and 50% of second $1,000 of expenses. These amounts could be indexed for inflation in 2003.	Tuition and related expenses of taxpayer, taxpayer's spouse, or taxpayer's dependent. Not room, board, books, student activity fees, athletic fees, insurance expenses, or transportation expenses.	Phased out for single taxpayers from $40,000 to $50,000 ($80,000 to $100,000 for joint filers).
Lifetime Learning Credit	Credit of 20% of up to $5,000 ($10,000 after 2003) of higher education expenses paid by the taxpayer. Cannot be used in year HOPE credit is claimed.	Same as HOPE credit.	Same as HOPE credit.
Education Savings Account	Up to $2,000 per year can be contributed to a tax-free account. Limited to $2,000 per beneficiary (child). Not taxable when used for beneficiary's education expenses. If not, then subject to additional 10% penalty. Can be rolled over to other beneficiaries.	Tuition, fees, books, supplies, equipment, room, and board. Also, qualified elementary and secondary education expenses, such as tuition, fees, academic tutoring, and special needs services, and computers or Internet access fees during any school years of the beneficiary.	Phased out for single taxpayers from $95,000 to $110,000 of AGI and for joint filers from $190,000 to $220,000 of AGI.
Interest on Education Loans	Above the line deduction for interest on student loans. $2,500.	Tuition, fees, books, supplies, equipment, room, and board.	Phased out for single taxpayers from $50,000 to $65,000 of AGI and for joint filers from $100,000 to $130,000 of AGI.
Educational Savings Bonds	Interest earnings can be withdrawn tax-free if used for education.	Same as HOPE credit, but taxpayer must be at least age 24.	Phased out for single taxpayers from $57,600 to $72,600 of AGI and for joint filers from $86,400 to $116,400 of AGI.

Appendix F

Retirement Plan Alternatives for 2002

(Prepared by Randy Gardner, LLM, CPA, CFP,™ and Julie Welch, CPA, CFP,™ authors of *101 Tax Saving Ideas*)

PLAN TYPE	CONTRIBUTIONS	DISTRIBUTIONS	PHASE-OUTS
Individual Retirement Accounts (IRA)	Limited to $3,000 ($3,500 if age 50+) per person or rollover amount. Deductible if not active participant in qualified plan or if under phase-out levels.	Taxable unless contributions were not deductible. May be subject to 10% penalty tax unless taxpayer is 59 1/2, dead, disabled, first-time homebuyer, receiving over life expectancy, using for higher education expenses, or using for deductible medical expenses.	If active participant, $34,000 of AGI if single ($54,000 if married). Rising to $50,000 for single and $80,000 for married by 2007. If spouse only is active participant, $150,000 to $160,000 of AGI.
Roth IRA	Limited to $3,000 ($3,500 if age 50+) for IRAs and Roth IRAs, or rollover. Not deductible. May be made after age 70 1/2. Conversion opportunity.	Not taxable. May be subject to 10% penalty if made early.	Phased out for single taxpayers from $95,000 to $110,000 of AGI and for joint filers from $150,000 to $160,000 of AGI.
Simplified Employee Pension Plan (SEP)	Deductible up to the lesser of $40,000 or about 20% of compensation. Discrimination rules apply.	Taxable. May be subject to 10% penalty if made early.	Not applicable.
Keogh Plans	Deductible. Depending on the plans, about 20% of earnings. Discrimination rules apply.	Taxable. May be subject to 10% penalty if made early.	Not applicable.
401(k) Plans	Exclusion from wages up to lesser of 100% of wages or $11,000 ($12,000 if age 50+).	Taxable. May be subject to 10% penalty if made early.	Not applicable, but special rules apply for highly compensated employees.
SIMPLE Plans	Deductible up to $7,000 ($7,500 if age 50+). Requires employer match for most employees.	Taxable. May be subject to 10% penalty if made early.	Not applicable.

Appendix G

CAPITAL GAINS FOR NONCORPORATE TAXPAYERS

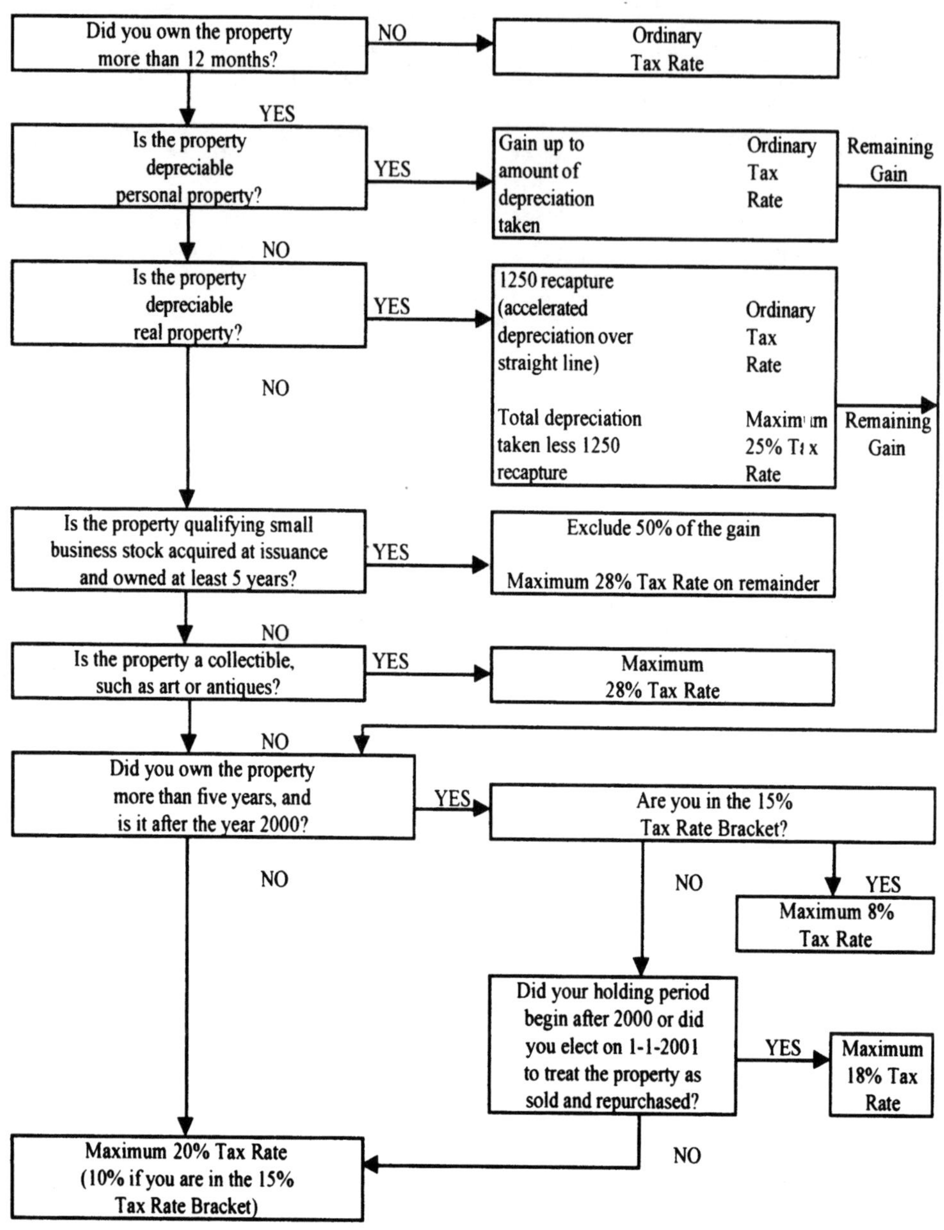

Index

References are to Tax Saving Idea numbers. TP refers to Tax Planning chapter. TF refers to Tax Formula chapter.

References are to Tax Saving Idea numbers. TP refers to Tax Planning chapter. TF refers to Tax Formula chapter.

References are to Tax Saving Idea numbers. TP refers to Tax Planning chapter. TF refers to Tax Formula chapter.

References are to Tax Saving Idea numbers. TP refers to Tax Planning chapter. TF refers to Tax Formula chapter.

References are to Tax Saving Idea numbers. TP refers to Tax Planning chapter. TF refers to Tax Formula chapter.

References are to Tax Saving Idea numbers. TP refers to Tax Planning chapter. TF refers to Tax Formula chapter.

ORDER FORM

101 TAX SAVING IDEAS

SIXTH EDITION

by Randy Gardner, LLM, CPA, CFP,™ and Julie Welch, CPA, CFP™

Price per copy	$19.95
Quantity ordered	___________
Subtotal	$___________
Sales tax*	$___________
Shipping and handling**	$___________
Total	$___________

*Please add Missouri sales tax of 6.85% for books shipped to Missouri addresses.
**Please add $3 per book for shipping and handling. Allow 30 days for delivery.

Name: ____

Company: ____

Address: ____

City, State, ZIP: ____

Phone Number: ____

PAYMENT:

☐ Check – Payable to Wealth Builders Press, LLC

Quantity Orders Invited

Please write for bulk account prices

SEND TO:

WEALTH BUILDERS PRESS, LLC

800 West 47th Street, Suite 430
Kansas City, MO 64112

Or Fax To: (816) 561-6296

Full payment must accompany your order. Prices subject to change without notice.

About the Authors

Randy Gardner, LLM, CPA, CFP,™ is a Professor of Taxation and Director of the Personal Financial Planning Program at the University of Missouri - Kansas City. He earned a Master of Law in Taxation from the University of Missouri - Kansas City, his Juris Doctorate and Masters of Business Administration from the University of Kansas, and a Bachelor of Arts degree in Philosophy from Harvard University.

Mr. Gardner is also a tax consultant. He has written and taught continuing education seminars throughout the country. The author of numerous articles on tax planning, he has been interviewed by national print and broadcast media on many tax issues.

Mr. Gardner serves on the Board of Directors of Consumer Credit Counseling Service, Inc. He lives in a suburb of Kansas City with his wife and four children.

Julie Welch (Runtz), CPA, CFP,™ is a shareholder and the Director of Tax Services for Meara, King & Co., a Kansas City based CPA firm. She graduated from William Jewell College with a Bachelor of Science in Accounting and Business Administration and obtained a Masters in Taxation degree from the University of Missouri - Kansas City.

Ms. Welch consults with hundreds of individuals and small businesses annually about tax planning. She has written numerous articles and presented tax planning seminars to various groups. She serves as a discussion leader for the American Institute of Certified Public Accountants' National Tax Education Program. She also serves on the Taxation Committee of the Missouri Society of CPAs and as the Treasurer of the Greater Kansas City Chapter of the Financial Planning Association.

Ms. Welch serves on the Board of Directors of several community and professional organizations. She grew up in St. Louis, Missouri, and now lives in Kansas City with her husband.